Destiny by Choice

Destiny by Choice

The Inaugural Addresses
of the
Governors of Texas

Edited by Marvin E. De Boer

Foreword by Governor Ann W. Richards

THE UNIVERSITY OF ARKANSAS PRESS
FAYETTEVILLE 1992

96 95 94 93 92   5 4 3 2 1

This book was designed by John Coghlan using the typeface Sabon.

The paper used in this publication meets the minimum requirements of
the American National Standard for Permanence of Paper for Printed
Library Materials Z39.48-1984. ∞

Library of Congress Cataloging-in-Publication Data

Destiny by choice : the inaugural addresses of the governors of Texas /
edited by Marvin E. De Boer; foreword by Ann W. Richards.
     p.   cm.
  Includes bibliographical references.
  ISBN 1-55728-232-3 (cloth)
    1. Governors—Texas—Inaugural addresses. 2. Texas—Politics and
government—Sources.   I. De Boer, Marvin E., 1925–   .
  J87 . T415   1992   91-15794
  353 . 976403'54—dc20   CIP

This volume is dedicated to Sandra Anne De Boer,
whose sense of responsible independence and adventure
has been a source of pride and inspiration to her parents.

Contents

Preface

In our democratic society the election of a chief executive officer of the nation or of a state culminates in a ceremony of inauguration. On this occasion the oath of office is administered and the newly installed officer is expected to deliver an address to those assembled for the occasion. Some may perceive these inaugural addresses as innocuous ceremonial rhetorical fluff; however, on closer examination, these addresses reflect prevailing public concerns and provide insights into current ideas, values, philosophy, and attitudes. The study of such speeches can help us to understand our emerging collective selves.

In 1807 former United States President John Adams observed that a complete history of the American Revolution could not be written until the history of each state was known. This is so, argued Adams, because the democratic principles were interpreted differently in every one of them.

Therefore, to help "write" this history, to understand our collective national diversity, we are drawn to the evidence that best exemplifies the interpretation of democratic principles. Focusing on the office of governor provides significant insights. The governor of a state is the central personality and key spokesperson on political matters within the state. The pronouncements emanating from that political position best symbolize the attitudes, values, and beliefs of the majority of the voters. While a governor is constitutionally required to submit a legislative program to the legislature and to give an accounting of his term at its conclusion, these messages frequently deal with specific problems, proposals, and accomplishments. The inaugural address, on the other hand, reflects a kind of crystallized set of assumptions, perceptions, and philosophy on which his legislative proposals may rest, and that helps us to better understand the interpretation of democratic principles.

This volume contains the sixty-seven inaugural addresses of the thirty-eight persons who have been elected governor of our twenty-eighth state, Texas, since 1846. Texas brought to the union of states a unique heritage that continues to influence and to permeate the consciousness of Texans and the rest of the nation as well.

Originally, along with Mexico, Texas was Spanish territory. In 1821 Mexico won its independence from Spain, and the territory of Texas was deeded to Mexico. When Santa Anna rose to power as Mexican dictator, Texans sought independence. Although defeated at the Alamo by Mexican forces, Texans gained revenge at San Jacinto in April 1836. The Independent Republic of Texas was proclaimed, and Sam Houston was elected president.

The ten years as an Independent Republic were not easy ones, and it soon became apparent that the state's future would best be served by annexation to the Union. The legislature of the Republic formally adopted that position on July 4, 1845; the following December, the United States Congress admitted Texas to the Union. This Texas heritage, as well as the significance of its admission to the Union, was well captured in the closing remarks of the Republic's last president, Anson Jones, on February 19, 1846:

> The lone Star of Texas, which ten years since arose amid clouds, over fields of carnage, and obscurely shown for a while, has culminated, and following an inscrutable destiny, has passed on and become fixed forever in that glorious constellation which all freemen and lovers of freedom in the world, must reverence and adore—the American Union. . . . The final act in this great drama is now performed: The Republic of Texas is no more.

Following President Jones's remarks, the first governor of Texas, James Pinckney Henderson, was sworn into office and delivered his inaugural address.

While President Jones characterized the period of independence as an inscrutable destiny, certainly, since statehood, the destiny of Texas reveals that it has been and continues to be a *Destiny by Choice*. Throughout its nearly 150 years as a state, Texans, in pursuit of their destiny, have made choices, the most important one has been the choice of a governor who would be most responsive to their collective needs and aspirations.

This collection of inaugural addresses of the elected governors of Texas provides a rather human and personalized documentary history of the state. In addition to their obvious value to the state historian and political scientist, these speeches also hold value for scholars in other disciplines. The addresses speak to a wide range of social issues that are the responsibility of government and for which the citizenry seeks resolution.

This volume, containing the inaugural addresses of the elected governors of Texas, is unique. Of all the other states, only the inaugural addresses of the governors of Arkansas have been searched out and presented in a single volume. In 1917 the Texas State Library published a volume entitled *Governors' Messages: Richard Coke to Lawrence Sullivan Ross, 1874–1891.* In 1979 the Library published Archie P. McDonald's *On This Day of New Beginnings: Selected Inaugural Addresses of Texas Governors.* This volume contains sixteen selected inaugural addresses. Writing in the foreword to that publication, former Governor Price Daniel expressed surprise to learn that not all the messages of the chief executives of Texas had been compiled and published.

The inaugural addresses were usually printed in either the Texas *Journal of the House of Representatives* or the *Journal of the Senate.* However, in a few instances they were omitted in both journals, in which case the text was located in a newspaper. The source for each speech is noted.

All who worked on this volume made a diligent effort to assure the accuracy and integrity of the texts of the speeches. Except for the correction of obvious typesetting errors, the spelling and punctuation were reproduced. The reader should be reminded that these were oral presentations and that the punctuation may not follow the contemporary rules of English composition. The sometimes unusual punctuation may reflect then current practice. Furthermore, in a speech, punctuation facilitates the speaker's delivery.

Accompanying each speech is a brief biographical essay that focuses on such salient factors as educational background and experiences of these people prior to their winning the governorship. This information was selected from standard biographical directories.

While the editor takes full and final responsibility for this volume, it could not have been completed without the generous assistance of several others. The editor expresses appreciation to the Research Council and administration of the University of Central Arkansas for underwriting the expenses of the project. Mr. Michael Green, reference archivist of the Texas State Library's State Archives Division, and his able assistant, Mr. David Richards, went beyond duty in accommodating my requests, both when I visited the Archives and when I corresponded with the archivists. Professionally and personally, they epitomized the Texas state motto, "Friendship." Dr. Willie Hardin, director of Torreyson Library at the University of Central Arkansas, and his staff, especially Mary Coleman of the inter-library loan department, were generous and efficient in responding to my research needs.

Finally, a special expression of gratitude is due Mr. Ralph Elder, head of Public Services of the Eugene C. Barker Texas History Center of the University of Texas, who provided biographical material and a copy of Governor Ann Richards' inaugural address, both of which enabled me to meet a publication deadline.

The transcription of speech texts from sometimes dim but always diminutive journal and newspaper copy to computer disk and ultimately producing a final draft of the manuscript was ably and efficiently accomplished by Shari Smith.

The significant responsibility of proofreading the text to assure accuracy was under the direction of my wife, Connie, with the editor serving as her assistant. For her invaluable assistance, which utilized unusual perceptive talents and language skills, as well as forbearance and patience, I am especially grateful.

Foreword

As the thirty-eighth governor of Texas, I live in a house where Sam Houston agonized over the tragic issue of Texas secession. My office is in the Capitol, a majestic domed building across the street from the Governor's Mansion. For more than a century, the Capitol's pink-granite walls have echoed to the sounds of the people's representatives crafting the laws that govern this state. A Texas governor readily understands what the poet Wallace Stevens meant when he observed that "all history is modern history."

Reading the sixty-six inaugural addresses that preceded mine evokes a similar awareness. It is to realize anew that we are part of an ongoing experiment—an experiment we call democracy. The addresses, unique expressions of their time and place, give voice to the experiment. They convey the personalities involved. They speak to issues that shaped, and continue to shape, a people.

Collectively, the inaugural addresses provide a fascinating record of a state's evolution. Listen to Houston, for example, as he takes the oath of office the year before war breaks out and speaks poignantly to a people about to embark on a tragic undertaking:

> It is in the diversity of opinion that Democracy may rest securely. The right to think adversely, to us is a guarantee of American Republicanism, and though this privilege may often be carried to extremes, and to our detriment, yet the very safety of our institutions depends upon our maintaining it as a republican principle. When thought becomes treason, the traitor is as much the enemy of one section as of the other.

Despite his eloquence, Houston's fellow Texans were not amenable to his wise counsel. When his beloved state severed its ties to the Union and joined the Confederacy, the Texas Secession Convention declared the office of governor vacant. Houston went home to Huntsville; his forced retirement was, in fact, a lonely exile for a hero whose time had passed. He did not live out the war.

To read the words of one of Houston's successors, Governor James Webb Throckmorton, it is a miracle to me that Texas itself survived. In his address, delivered in 1866, Throckmorton painted a most distressing picture of Reconstruction-era Texas:

> At a time like the present, when we have just emerged from the most terrible conflict known to modern times, with homes made dreary and desolate by the heavy hand of war; the people impoverished, and groaning under public and private debts; the great industrial energies of the country sadly depressed; occupying in some respects the position of a State of the Federal Union, and in others, the condition of a conquered province, exercising only such privileges as the conqueror in his wisdom and mercy may allow; the loyalty of the people to their General Government doubted; their integrity questioned; their holiest aspirations for peace and restoration disbelieved, maligned and traduced, with a constant misapprehension of their most innocent actions and intentions; with a frontier many hundred miles in extent, being desolated by a murderous and powerful enemy, our devoted frontiersmen filling bloody graves, their property given to the flames, or carried off as booty, their little ones murdered, and their wives and daughters carried into a captivity more terrible than death, and reserved for tortures such as savage cruelty and lust can alone inflict; unprotected by the government we support, with troops quartered in the interior, where there is peace and quiet; unwilling to send armed citizens to defend the suffering border, for fear of arousing unjust suspicions as to the motive . . ."

Throckmorton's incredible litany of woe continues. He speaks of "a heavy debt created before the late war, . . . an empty treasury, . . . embarrassments in every part of our internal affairs . . ." He feels "sadly oppressed," he says, "with the difficulties which lie before me."

Is there any wonder? Governor Throckmorton's lamentations are depressing—not least because they were true—but I find them useful in one respect. Our own problems may be burdensome, but there is some consolation in knowing that things have been worse, much worse. It is worthwhile to know that Texas, despite the difficulties, survived and prospered.

The years pass. Every two years and then every four years (the term of office was changed in 1974), a governor stands on the Capitol steps at noon on a January day, takes the oath of office and seeks to articulate the needs and aspirations of a people. One governor urges economic development. Another calls for good roads. One governor seeks to comfort Texans whose lives have been ravaged by the Depression. Another promises a government that gives the people of Texas "a dollar's worth of goods and services for every tax dollar spent."

When my turn came, on a sunny winter day in 1991, I was keenly aware that a new century is dawning. I offered brush strokes for a New Texas, and I urged my fellow Texans to help me turn dreams into reality. It was a glorious day, a day of celebration.

These days, inaugural addresses are not as long as they used to be, the rhetoric not as grandiloquent, but the aim over the years has remained basically the same. Whether outlining specific programs or resorting to airy eloquence, each governor seeks to inform, to inspire, to encourage. Taken together, we trace the Texas story.

"This is who I am," we are saying. "This is who *we* are as citizens of this state. This is who we can be. This is our destiny by choice."

Ann W. Richards
Governor of Texas

I

James Pinckney

HENDERSON

1846–1847

Courtesy of Archives Division, Texas State Library

JAMES PINCKNEY HENDERSON (*March 31, 1809–June 4, 1858*), the son of an attorney, was born in Lincolnton, North Carolina. Henderson attended Lincoln Academy and the University of North Carolina, but left the university to read law. He was admitted to the bar at the age of twenty and practiced law in North Carolina and Mississippi.

In 1836 he led a company of militia to Texas to fight in the revolution and was commissioned brigadier general by Texas President David G. Burnet. Later that year, he was appointed attorney general of the Republic of Texas. After the death of Stephen F. Austin in 1836, Henderson was appointed to succeed Austin as secretary of state. Between 1837 and 1844 he served as the Republic's envoy to Great Britain, France, and the United States.

An advocate of annexation, Henderson was elected to the Convention of 1845, which approved the annexation of the Republic to the United States. In December 1845 he was elected the first governor of Texas by a commanding margin. Henderson took office and delivered his inaugural address to a joint meeting of the house and senate of the first legislature on February 19, 1846.

When the war with Mexico broke out later that year, he took leave from office to lead four regiments of Texans as a United States Army major general. He successfully negotiated the surrender of Monterey. He returned to his gubernatorial duties in 1847, but declined to stand for reelection.

Inaugural Address *

February 19, 1846

GENTLEMEN OF THE SENATE, AND HOUSE OF REPRESENTATIVES:

This day, and within this very hour, has been consummated the great work of annexation. This consummation, it seems to me, should be a full compensation to our citizens for all their toils and sufferings, endured for ten long years—Our hearts should be full of gratitude to the giver of all good, for the many favors he has bestowed upon us at all times, and under all circumstances. In the beginning of our revolution, when the frowns of the world were upon us, his protecting arm shielded us from danger, and now, at its close, when we have so happily completed our labors and attracted the attention of the principal nations of the earth, he is still with us. Who can look back upon our history, and not be fully and deeply impressed with the consideration that the arm of deity has shielded our nation, and his justice and wisdom guided us in our path? It is therefore our duty, in deep humility, to make our acknowledgements for his many favors. It is with a deep sense of the responsibility which I have incurred that I now enter upon the duties of the station which my fellow-citizens have called me to fill. This station, and this responsibility, my own disposition did not lead me to seek, and I can only hope to be able to discharge the duties which have thus devolved upon me in a manner satisfactory to the country, by the aid of the Representatives of the people, who will I feel assured, act with wisdom and harmony. If there has heretofore existed any cause of dispute, or difference between the different sections of our country, in regard to the policy, most proper to be pursued, surely there is now no cause for disunion, since we have the protecting arm of the United States, thrown around us, and can repose quietly under her broad banner. Let us then, I beseech you, commence our existence as a state of

*Journal of the House of Representatives of the First Legislature of the State of Texas (1846), pp. 18–20.

this great union in the spirit of harmony and forbearance, and act our parts throughout as becomes the agents of a free enlightened christian people.

By our Constitution which has been freely and fully approved by the almost unanimous voice of the people, more power and patronage are given to the Executive than is given by most of the other States of the Union to their Executives; and the merits of the system which we have adopted will greatly depend upon the prudence, impartiality, and wisdom with which the Executive exercises, those powers conferred upon him by our Constitution. As far as my actions are concerned, I can only promise that I will endeavor to act cautiously, and impartially, guided by whatever judgment I may be able to command, having in view only the public good. Regarding a good Judiciary as one of the main stays of our Constitutional Liberties, it is my anxious wish to see that Department of our Government placed upon the best possible footing. Judges who are possessed of violent political party prejudices, are dangerous in any State. In exercising the veto power conferred upon me by the Constitution, I shall feel constrained as a general rule to confine it to arresting the passage of unconstitutional laws, and such laws as are calculated, in my opinion, to impair public confidence, and embarrass the revenue of the State.

This is not a proper time for me to advert, to measures which it may seem to me should be acted upon by the Legislature—that I will do in a short time, in making to you the communication required of me by the Constitution.

We have this day fully entered the Union of the North American States—let us give our friends who so boldly and nobly advocated our cause, and the friends of American Liberty, no reason to regret their efforts in our behalf. Hence forth, the prosperity of our Sister States will be our prosperity—their happiness our happiness—their quarrels will be our quarrels, and in their wars we will freely participate.

II

George Thomas

WOOD

1847–1849

Courtesy of Archives Division, Texas State Library

GEORGE THOMAS WOOD (*March 12, 1795–September 3, 1858*) is believed to have been born in Cuthbert, Georgia. Little is known about his education. At the age of nineteen he participated in the Creek War at Horseshoe Bend, after which he returned to Cuthbert and became a merchant. In 1837 and 1838 he was a member of the Georgia state legislature.

Wood moved his family to San Jacinto County, Texas, in 1839 and established a cotton plantation. He served as a member of the sixth Texas Congress and was a member of the State Constitutional Convention in 1845. The following year he served in the state senate.

During the Mexican War, he commanded the Second Texas Regiment of Volunteers. Wood, a Democrat, was elected second governor of Texas in 1847 and was inaugurated on December 21. He sought a second term in 1849 but was defeated.

Inaugural Address *

December 21, 1847

GENTLEMEN OF THE LEGISLATURE, AND FELLOW CITIZENS:

The present occasion inspires me with pleasing and greatful emotions. I am deeply affected by the recent manifestation of the partiality of the people of Texas, in conferring upon me the distinguished office of Governor of the State; and I avail myself of this opportunity to return to them, through their honorable representatives, my most sincere and hearty thanks, with the solemn assurance, that, in the discharge of the high trust so generously confided to me, my highest aim shall be, to merit their continued and abiding esteem.

I will regard the solemn injunctions of the oath, which the Constitution requires me to take, but not more sacredly than I will the moral obligations imposed upon me by a brave and generous people.

Upon this occasion, a full exposition of my views of State policy cannot be expected. At an early day I will recommend to the consideration of the Legislature, as the Constitution requires me to do, such measures as the public interests may seem to require.

To such measures as the Legislature in its wisdom may adopt, to promote the public welfare, I can promise an honest and cordial co operation.

Gentlemen, I am apprized of the arduousness and responsibility of the duties which will soon devolve upon me; nor am I insensible of my own inexperience and inability. I therefore, feel less hesitancy in requesting of you, in the outset, your aid and reciprocal co-operation. Your patriotism and intelligence, together with your uniform courtesy and kindness, is a sufficient guarantee to me, that in the constitutional discharge of my duties, your valuable assistance will be accorded readily and cordially.

Journals of the House of Representatives of the State of Texas, Second Legislature (1848), pp. 90–92.

Senators and Representatives! You are already, actively engaged in the discharge of your important duties. Your constituents, while they have honored you with their preference, have entrusted you with their most sacred interests. I will not reflect upon your integrity, by urging upon you the importance of a zealous advocacy of, and adherence to such measures and principles as will promote their present and future prosperity. I will only indulge the hope, that the present session commenced under such auspicious circumstances, may result in abundant good to our common constituents.

During the administration of my predecessor, the rights of Texas to her territorial limits, as uniformly asserted, have been recognized by the Executive of the United States. The invasion of our soil has been repelled, and hurled back upon our *vain glorious* foe; and the sword—that alternative long delayed, until forced upon us by Mexico, has successfully done its work of retributive justice upon our obstinate, but *now defeated* enemy.

During the progress of the war, in which the patriotism and valor of the nation, have been most signally displayed; the conduct of Texians, has sustained their high reputation for chivalry, already won on many a hard fought field. They have proved themselves among the *foremost* to march at their country's call.—They have fought in the *front ranks of battle;* and, by their *valor* and numbers, have added *strength to the armies of the Union,* and *fresh laurels* to the martial character of their State!

As the Executive officer of the State, it will be my effort to aid and assist the present administration of the national Government, in its general policy; and, especially in a continued *vigorous prosecution of the war* against our common enemy, as the only proper means of securing a lasting and honorable peace: and, relying upon the support of your honorable bodies, I shall endeavor to sustain, to the utmost, our territorial limits; and guard, with vigilance, the rights of our State, guaranteed by the compact of annexation, and the original compromises of the Federal Constitution.

In conclusion, gentlemen, I would recommend to you, harmony of action. It is an essential element in Legislation. *Guard against local and sectional prejudices.* Let us cultivate friendly and social intercourse with each other; and may one impulse prompt, and one spirit animate us—*a disinterested desire to prove ourselves worthy servants of a deserving people*—so that when our labors are ended and we retire to the peaceful quietude of our homes, we will bear with us the grateful conscious-

ness of having acted well our parts, and the welcome thanks of a generous constituency will attend us.

But, gentlemen, as it is human nature to err, we should not omit, in
our councils, to invoke the aid of the Supreme Being, who, while he is
the Fountain of Wisdom, is the Gracious Dispenser of National, as well
as individual blessings.

III

Peter Hansborough

BELL

1849–1853

Courtesy of Archives Division, Texas State Library

PETER HANSBOROUGH BELL (*May 12, 1812–March 8, 1898*) was born in Culpepper County, Virginia. He attended the Culpepper public schools. From 1831 to 1836 he was a merchant in Petersburg, Virginia. In 1836, at the age of twenty-four, he migrated to Texas to fight in the Texas Revolution.

From 1837 to 1839 he was assistant inspector general of the Texas Army and became inspector general in 1839. Between 1840 and 1846 he served as captain of the Texas Rangers. During the Mexican War he served as lieutenant colonel in the command of Zachary Taylor.

In the 1849 gubernatorial election, Bell defeated incumbent Governor Wood and assumed office on December 21.

In the election of 1851 he was successful in winning a second term by defeating four other candidates. He took office on December 22. He resigned the governorship in 1853, having accepted appointment to the U.S. House of Representatives to fill the unexpired term of the incumbent who had died in office.

Inaugural Address *

December 21, 1849

GENTLEMEN OF THE LEGISLATURE, AND FELLOW CITIZENS:

The present occasion, interesting as it is to every patriot citizen, comes to me with an accumulated weight of hopes and fears, producing an active struggle of varied emotions. Against this I am sustained only by the firm and unshaken reliance, that its origin is derived from a knowledge on my part, that heavy and important duties, involving a common interest, are about to be assumed, and in a pure desire to meet them with manly firmness and a proper intelligence in the discharge of every obligation.

Called by the unbiassed will of the people of Texas, in the exercise of the exalted privilege of the elective franchise, to preside as their Chief Magistrate, I appear before you to take the solemn and sacred oath, "that I will perform the duties incumbent upon me, according to the best of my skill and ability, and agreeably to the constitution and laws of this State, and of the United States." This solemn asseveration, to be made in the presence of GOD and my fellow-countrymen, brings into lively requisition every moral, every ennobling sentiment, and excites every slumbering patriotic sensibility. My heart would be obdurate and insensible, indeed, if it did not swell with unusual emotions on an event fraught with so many consequences to myself, either for good or evil, and involving considerations of vital importance to you. The distinguished mark of confidence and respect, from a great and growing State, implying as it does, high regard for my integrity and ability, demands from me the deepest expression of gratitude.

A custom, established by precedent and honored by time, makes it appropriate before assuming the usual constitutional qualification, that, in making a suitable expression of thanks to my fellow-citizens at large,

---

Journals of the House of Representatives of the State of Texas, Third Session (1849), pp. 320–27.

for the honor they have conferred, I should, also, advert concisely to some of the principles and sentiments which will govern me in conducting the civil administration of the State.

I now offer to you, fellow-citizens, in the sincerity of my heart, the humble tribute of my thanks for the sacred trust confided to me; and desire to join you in hearty congratulations, that the Great Author of all good has vouchsafed to our beloved State peace, health, and prosperity; and all the elements, physical, moral, and religious, necessary to constitute us a truly great and glorious people.

In coming to the position assigned me, it is not unfit that I should advert to days that are past, in order that we may be directed with more certain aim to those which are advancing. The experience of the past affords lessons of wisdom and instruction for the future; and a retrospect of days gone by in our history, as a people, whilst it affords ample cause of exultation and cheering hopes, comes, also, mingled with melancholy emotions. It is never unprofitable, when alluding to our country, to recur to our early history—the days of thirty-five and six; and to the brilliant and soul-stirring scenes to which the events of those days gave rise.

In doing this, the mind performs a holy, religious pilgrimage, in visiting the graves of our departed friends and heroes who have fallen by the desolation of war—cherishing their memories and recounting their virtues. It is food for the mind and greatly improves the heart—placing us higher in the scale as social beings, and making us better citizens. The great aim and end of our institutions are, to afford the jewel of comfort and solid happiness; and whatever current of thought tends to moral culture, becomes a great auxiliary to this object. Fellow citizens ! the price of liberty in Texas was dearly paid in the blood of her patriot sons. Let that be held in grateful remembrance, and to us, and to those who are to succeed us, it should be the highest incentive to virtue, patriotism and honor. The best vindication of their motives and the principles for which they contended, is to be found in a determined, successful effort on our part to secure to those who are to come after us, the multiplied advantages which their sacrifices have brought to us.

With an object so high and holy, it is not for us to slumber in the pathway of duty. With an awakened sense of our just claims, and a true appreciation of our peculiar position, it behoves us to move forward to the performance of such measures for the promotion of intelligence, and her hand-maid, virtue, as wisdom and experience may dictate. Let us, then, not forget or undervalue our superior advantages; but with a broad, elevated, and ardent patriotism, unite heart and hand in advancing Texas to the proud destiny that awaits her. With a country great in extent, and beautiful as she is great—fertile in soil—salubrious in climate—established in her institutions and general laws, and progressive in the moral improvement of her people, she cannot fail soon to realize the fondest hopes of the patriot, and succesfully vindicate her claims to an elevated rank among the States of the Union.

The most pleasing evidences of gradual and permanent improvements are to be seen at many points. And we cannot behold so glorious and gratifying a prospect for our infant State, and not be animated with the most profound and grateful acknowledgements to the Great Author of our being, for these manifold and inestimable blessings. Our vigilance and unceasing care for the benefits we enjoy should be proportionably increased for their perpetuation.

Our hopes, interests, and affections, are centred here; and every true lover of his country should sacrifice every selfish, every ambitious, motive on the hallowed altar of patriotism; and in the same spirit of generous compromise which gave to our Union a constitution, and to our State a name, *unite* to harmonize all conflicting interests, and lend aid in such measures as will be conducive to the public good.

Texas has, perhaps, as much substantial cause for a high appreciation of her present political position and advantages as any country, claiming sovereignty, on earth. The circumstances and incidents of her birth are strange and interesting, if not illustrious. Springing into political existence, as by magic, at a point so obscure as to be almost entirely unknown on the map of the world; astonishing her friends by the unexpected declaration that she resolved to be "free, sovereign, and independent;" confounding her enemies by a practical enforcement of that declaration, with no extrinsic advantages to draw to her aid, and with no friend but her genius and valor, she moved steadily onward, almost without men and means, conquering and to conquer, with an energy that defied all misfortune, and an indomitable courage almost supernatural, until her one starred banner waved in triumph at every point where her enemies dared present themselves.

What an anomaly in the progress of human freedom does it present, that this "forlorn hope" should in a few years assert, and actually establish, a right over a territory of such magnitude and importance, as to attract the attention, and excite the cupidity of monarchical Europe. Our father-land, too, an inactive spectator of the struggle, with something of sympathy, and more of interest, witnessing Texas dash from her lips the poisoned chalice which haughty Mexico presented, aroused by a feeling slightly imbued with jealousy towards a power not American, opened at last the door of alliance. In this auspicious hour, (I hope it was auspicious) Texas, with as much diplomatic adroitness in the cabinet as she had displayed valor in the field, moved gracefully, and by a sudden transit, within the folds of the star-spangled banner; and there, fellow-citizens, we have the happiness to find her. The picture, though poorly drawn, is true to the life; and affords consolation to those, at least, who found her in her weakness tottering to the fall, and who now behold her in beauty and strength. Her brightness may be dimmed, for a time, by the superior constellation which surrounds her, but it needs not the aid of prescience to determine that, in a few years, we shall behold our State, with the rich bounties nature has bestowed with a prodigal hand, shielded by a good constitution and laws, as a beacon light and a hope, attracting to her bosom the oppressed of every land. That God, in his mercies, may grant this consummation, is the wish of every true patriot.

Fellow-citizens, when contemplating the position we occupy, and so lately assumed, every consideration of self-respect and national duty requires that we should be deliberative and cautious in the measures we adopt, or the laws we enact, local or general, for the purposes of justice. The youngest member of the Union, and, I may add, the "fairest and the freest," we shall be daily and hourly subject to the animadversions and criticisms of the jealous and malignant. There is no defence against such attacks, except such as is to be found under the panoply of justice and truth; with this we shall be thrice armed, and can march forward with confidence to the goal of our destiny. The character which our State will hereafter bear, is now to be formed; and from the aggregate acts of her Government, and general bearing of her citizens, her reputation amongst her sister States will be proportionably elevated or depressed. From this consideration, then, how strong is the appeal to those of her public servants to whom the most responsible agencies are intrusted, to look with a clear perspective to those measures which are most likely to subserve her present interests and future advancement; and to her citizens for their prompt acquiescence in all that contributes to the establishment of law and order.

That our Government is well adapted to perform all its functions harmoniously, and to answer the end originally intended by its framers, is clearly demonstrable in the increase of population, the manifest improvement in morals and social bearing, and the universal disposition to respect the laws. Time and observation will suggest many alterations and improvements; and, from experience in our past legislation, they will, no doubt, be readily adopted. Did the occasion allow, I could with pleasure run the parallel between what Texas was, what she is, and what, with the favor of Heaven, she is destined to become.

In her contest for freedom, she conducted her war upon the most liberal and humane principles known to civilized nations—always meeting her enemy upon honorable ground, and beating them only by superior valor; alleviating by kindness the miseries of the unfortunate, she took from the battle its crime, and imposed no chains by her conquests; "Liberty unsheathed her sword—necessity stained it—victory returned it to its scabbard." Having been a participator in her struggles, from the dawn of her revolution, I can lay my hand upon my heart and say, I never yet felt dishonored by the association. A people, whose conduct has been thus marked by all the characteristics which would do honor to the oldest and most enlightened nations, has claims to the admiration of mankind, for having extended the area of human rights. And we find the same people who, in war, could exert the most exalted clemency, on the restoration of peace, maintaining her national character and consistency, by pursuing the admonitions of virtue, wisdom, and moderation, in the conduct of her civil affairs. What a field is here presented for the philanthropic mind to dwell upon? We behold a nation, which had declared and maintained its independence through innumerable disadvantages, suddenly merging her nationality—not through the usual agencies, the heat and bustle of revolution, but making a dignified and peaceable transfer of power, by the more potent influences to enlightened minds, of reason and virtue.—Here, then, is a beautiful political horizon before us, after having triumphantly solved the problem, whether or not we were capable of governing ourselves. Nor is the prospect marred by ignorance or superstition; and we have no rankling, established prejudices to lead us into the mists of error. All is plain and auspicious; and our country is as a blank, prepared to receive good impressions or bad.

Here, too, is an ample field for the highest aspirations of genius and enterprise, and Providence, in having bestowed so rich a boon, has imposed on those who enjoy it, the responsibility of watching, with jealous care, the benefits it confers. It is an inheritance confided to us, to be transferred with interest to posterity. The new and delicate relation to the American confederacy, voluntarily assumed by Texas, was the result of a policy on the part of that power, to enlarge the scope of free principles, and to strengthen the bond of Union. In this we will go with her hand in hand, and so long as her counsels are administered with justice and equality, and with due deference to the rights reserved by our common charter, we will hail with pleasure and pride the day of our alliance.

There is no want of patriotic feeling and devoted kindness amongst us for the Union, as it is. Support of our State Constitution, and the Constitution of the United States, becomes our highest duty. It is the surest basis for the security of peace and the safety of our institutions. But, fellow-citizens, whilst inculcating with zeal this wholesome doctrine, it is necessary, in our internal organization, that we should throw the proper guards around our own peculiar rights. The day of her declaration was for Texas the unequivocal assertion of her maturity, and nobly has she given the proof. The day of annexation was her wedding day. She will yield all to the Union which bridal modesty doth warrant, but can never forget her reserved rights.—We will always endeavor to do our duty to the Union. This is an obligation, and implies reciprocity. "Too just to invade the rights of other," we will be too "proud to surrender our own."

In relation to our own State, fellow-citizens, to maintain our national faith and standing by a rigid compliance with all our obligations—to ascertain and relieve our public resources by an honorable estimation and prompt adjustment of our liabilities—to protect all personal and private rights, by enacting and strictly enforcing salutary laws, are principles which should be at an early day engrafted upon our statute books. In the legislative halls or our country, a spirit of concession and compromise should be invoked—preferring amicable discussion and a just accommodation of all difficulties, to any other mode. All sectional and local prejudices, as far as possible, should be banished from the public councils. The distinction of Texas, East and West, should not be known, except geographically. Patriotic sacrifices were common to both, "in times that tried men's souls," and in the days of her prosperity, kindness, friendship, and a common interest should bind all Texians. Remember! that the blood of patriots, from East and West, consecrated the land we this day enjoy.

Fellow-citizens ! it would be no difficult task for me to detain you with an extended enumeration, of what I deem to be the great and essential principles which should guide us in our civil policy. It would, however, I know full well, be considered a work of supererogation in one so humble in pretensions to wisdom as myself. Fortunately for our country, those who entrust power, are in the aggregate as watchful of the country's interest, and as enlightened too, as their agents. The channels of intelligence are open to all and closed to none, except those of the number, "who, having eyes, see not; and having ears, hear not the things which most concern them."

I shall enter upon the duties assigned me by my fellow-citizens, trusting to a just and enlightened verdict at their hands, after an honest and faithful effort to discharge those duties, rather than attempt to elicit good opinions in advance, by an imposing declaration of principles.

With the Constitution and laws as my guide, backed by an honest determination to do what is right, I shall, I trust, be able to accomplish the duties which may devolve upon me.

To recommend such measures as may seem necessary and proper, and to see that the laws are faithfully executed, will be my constitutional duty. From this I shall never shrink.

But, fellow citizens, with a firm determination to do my duty, I know full well the many embarrassments I must encounter.—Unpracticed in the duties of civil life, and conscious of my great deficiencies, my position is well calculated to awaken distrust and presentiments, naturally inspired by a disproportion of ability to the magnitude of my duties.

The intelligence of my countrymen, and a charitable construction of my acts, together with the counsels of those whom the Constitution has designated as my auxiliaries in the civil administration, will, I am confident, greatly supply my defects. With these, and aided by the honorable representatives of the people, amongst whom I shall look for examples of wisdom and ripened experience, I may hope for success. And to you, gentlemen of the Legislature, coming as you do from every part of our growing State—bringing with you sentiments and intelligence of a local character—and possessing, as a body, a broad and comprehensive view of national concerns—to you I shall anxiously look, to give such an impress and direction to our public affairs, as will place upon your acts the seal of wisdom and the approbation of our common constituents.

Beyond this, I shall look with humble supplication for aid from that beneficent and superintending Providence through whose abundant kindness and mercies our beloved country was safely conducted amidst the trials of revolution to the haven of peace, tranquillity, and happiness.

Second Inaugural Address *
December 22, 1851

GENTLEMEN OF THE LEGISLATURE, AND FELLOW-CITIZENS:

By the generous confidence of the people of Texas, I am called upon to renew, to-day, in the presence of this enlightened assembly, the constitutional oath which two years ago was administered to me within this capitol. The exalted compliment which that confidence conveys, and the flattering manner in which it has been indicated, very naturally excites in me feelings of pride and satisfaction; which, to indulge, is both grateful and consolatory. The honor conferred has created a debt of gratitude which, I fear, neither services nor sacrifices on my part will ever enable me to repay; and there is no language which will adequately express to my fellow-citizens at large, the high appreciation I have placed upon their approval of my public acts, during the eventful period that I have had the honor to preside at the head of the State Government.

In again assuming the position of Chief Magistrate of the State, I am sensible of the weight of responsibility resting upon me, and of the elevated character of the duties it devolves. My notice is first directed to that Supreme Being whose aid and comfort I have ever sought, in every vicissitude and trial; and who has so often vouchsafed his guardian care to our beloved country, by relieving her through his providential assistance from the perils and snares with which she has been encompassed, in her efforts to achieve and preserve social, political, and religious freedom. I now invoke His blessings upon our young State, and His aid in the consecration of the glorious institutions of our common country to Liberty and Independence forever.

Since my connection with the civil department, it has been impressively realized to me, that if there is one thing more than any other

Journal of the House of Representatives of the State of Texas, Fourth Legislature (1852), pp. 364–69.

calculated to sustain the public servant, in his efforts faithfully to discharge his duties, it is the well-defined approbation of those whose agent he is. To the mind directed by honest impulses, it comes as a balm and a healing, to soothe and bind up the wounds which envy, malice, or ambition, sometimes seeks to inflict. Although as exempt, perhaps, as many others more meritorious than myself, occupying a similar position, from the poisoned arrows of vituperation, yet, I have not been entirely free from the noxious mists which error and misrepresentation have attempted to throw around the humble, ardent and honest exertions which I have devoted to the relief of our promising young State, in her comparatively new experiment of State organization. Of this, I do not complain; for it is a distinguishing characteristic of this glorious country of ours, guarantied by the constitutional charter under which our social and political rights are maintained, that individuals, measures, and parties, are equally the legitimate subjects of comment and criticism. It reflects much honor upon our citizens that the "liberty of speech and of the press" seldom, if ever, are so far abused as to require an appeal to the statutory provisions of the land; the cause being traceable to that high-toned moral sentiment pervading our community, which sooner or later applies a much more potent and salutary check, than is to be found in the restraining penalties of the law; and if, as is declared in the political axiom, that "error ceases to be dangerous when truth is left free to combat it," it is far better to leave the privilege referred to unrestrained, in order to reveal useful and important facts, than attempt to close up the channels of intelligence; which, if left open and unimpeded, will often prove the medium of throwing off disguises, and of exposing to general view, the motives and acts of public agents, should they at any time manifest a desire to sacrifice the public weal to purposes of self-aggrandizement.

The events of the past two years associated with the operations of our State Government have been marked by more than ordinary interest. Many of the questions to be met and decided, contained from their very nature the elements of high excitement and disagreement, if not of discord. The people, the Legislature and the Executive, respectively, have had their own parts assigned them to act, in full view of these new and most important measures prior to their consummation; subjecting the country thereby to the severe ordeal of conflicting opinions, through which it could not safely pass but by a patriotic surrender of all sectional and selfish views to the one great and common object— that of preserving the interest of our State free from injury, and her integrity without a blemish. Amidst these conflicts of opinion, there has really been no diversity of interests, and it will now, as all passion has subsided, and reason is again permitted to resume her just prerogatives, be allowed that all desired the attainment of the same end, but by very different channels, and with antagonistic views in reference to its accomplishment.

Differing, as I have done as your Executive, with another important branch of the Government, and many of my fellow-citizens, in reference to several measures of vital importance, I can find no occasion more appropriate than the present to declare in great sincerity, that whatever diversity of opinion may exist in the legislative counsels, or amongst my fellow-citizens generally in relation to my official acts, or how various soever may be the estimates placed upon them, I have on all occasions been governed only by a strong, uncompromising conviction of what I considered to be my duty, coupled with a firm determination to perform it no matter what the inconvenience or hazard to myself; repudiating at all times, as far as it was in the power of weak humanity, that prejudice and passion so naturally springing from the speculations and conflicting theories touching the operations of Government so freely indulged, and which if not resisted, remain a stumbling block to the attainment of public justice, and are utterly subversive of good order, good feeling, and that harmony which should always distinguish public agents entrusted with important and sacred duties.

I have been careful freely to accord to others the same honesty of purpose and devotion to the best interests of the country that I claim for myself; I embrace this occasion further to remark, that to those of my fellow-citizens who have sustained me with a generous confidence and noble advocacy in the measures I have recommended, and the views which I have thought it my duty to promulgate, I now return my sincere thanks, the best tribute of a grateful heart. For those whose opinions have been adverse to my own, with an opposition characterized by manly independence, I entertain no feelings but those of respect and kindness. For others, who opposed my public course (with too much acrimony perhaps,) I have no censure, and nothing to urge, but respectfully request that they will carefully revise, and if consistent with a liberal and ingenuous consideration of the error which inseparably attaches to us all, reverse the decision, originating no doubt in the purest intentions, but amidst excitement too strong for sound conclusions.

With these remarks, fellow-citizens, explanatory of the motives and feelings that have actuated me during my official term just expired, I throw myself upon the magnanimity and justice of a constituency, who, by their liberal sanction and distinguished support, have imparted to me increased incentives to fidelity in re-commencing my labors.

Discarding, then, the recollection of past dissensions, and looking forward only to the best measures of conducting our public affairs to a successful termination, I enter upon the new administration with a determination to meet, as far as I can, the just expectations of a people who have done me signal honor, and whom I can best repay by exerting whatever of qualification I may be able to command in the promotion of their best interests. This qualification I shall endeavor to seek in a proper intelligence to discern, discretion to execute, and industry to fulfill every duty intrusted.

Having already, in my late message to the Legislature and in other previous communications, given my views in relation to what I conceived to be the most important subjects connected with the general policy of the State, and having made such suggestions touching the same as my judgement approved, it is therefore unnecessary, and would perhaps be deemed out of place for me again to advert to them on this occasion.

Let it be sufficient for me to repeat that, with the constitution and laws as my guide, it will be my constant aim to preserve, as far as my agency will allow, all the great fundamental principles which the framers of our State charter intended to secure and perpetuate. Entertaining a profound reverence for the constitution of the United States, constituting—as it was intended to do by those who framed it—the foundation of our national peace and strength, I shall consider it my duty, as it will be my pleasure, to support it, "as well in its limitations as in its authorities," and at the same time to respect the rights and authorities reserved to the States and to the people "as essential to the success of the general system."

I cannot conclude this address without expressing to you who are now present, and to my fellow-citizens generally, my heartfelt congratulations upon the prosperous condition of our young State. To me, the contrast between what Texas now is and what she was in 1836, is indeed most striking: it is difficult to realize the great and happy change which has taken place.—Sixteen years ago, with a soul filled with the wild ardor and aspirations of boyhood, I left my well remembered and much-loved native hills to make my home in this distant land, to aid her people in their patriotic struggle for freedom. I landed with no exile's feelings on the shores that were henceforward, and for weal or woe, to be my abiding place, for I dwelt with delight upon the kind recollections of the home I left behind me and all the endearments of family associations.

A dark cloud then hung lowering over this fair land. The Lone Star shone fitful through the gloom—now beaming with the light of peace and hope—now almost quenched in blood, yet ever with a halo of glory encircling it. We have lived to see that lost Pleiad restored to its proper place among its sisters, no longer obscured by doubt or difficulty, but shining far abroad to the nations of the earth, a beacon, which every day grows brighter and more glorious. Hers was no meteor light springing from the mists of Ignorance and Superstition, such as faintly shines at intervals over the benighted lands of Mexico and Cuba, which gleam but for a moment only to lead the unwary to disappointment and destruction, but steady and pure like the north star, a guide to every wanderer who seeks an asylum from oppression or inexorable misfortune. Honor, eternal honor to the brave dead who offered up their lives to make Texas what she now is. Let us never forget that to them we are mainly indebted for the proud inheritance we this day enjoy.

Though the days of the Republic were "the days of our glory," that deeds of devoted patriotism and daring chivalry were then performed which would have graced the heroic pages of Greece and Rome, it cannot be denied that she held an unenviable place amongst the nations of the world. With a sparse population, exhausted by war, it could not be otherwise.

I cannot better convey to you my feelings than by adopting the sentiment so beautifully expressed by that distinguished and highly talented patriot, the last President of the Republic, upon the solemn occasion when he pronounced, "the Republic of Texas is no more!"

"The Lone Star of Texas, which, ten years since, arose amidst clouds and fields of carnage, and obscurely shone for awile, has culminated, and, following an inscrutable destiny, has passed on and become fixed forever in that glorious constellation which all freemen and lovers of Freedom in the world must love and adore—the American Union. Blending its rays with its sister States, long may it continue to shine: and may a gracious Heaven smile upon this consummation of the wishes of the two Republics, now joined together in one! May the union be perpetual! And may it be the means of conferring benefits and blessings upon the people of all the States!"

It was not until Texas took her place as one of the States of the great

American Union that she occupied the position which nature designed for her. From that period to the present, her onward march to power and improvement has been unexampled. Nations behold the fruition of our hopes. From every land emigrants are flocking, in welcome crowds, to partake of our prosperity. From the vine-clad hills of France and Germany, from Ireland's green shores and England's smiling fields, and from our own sister States, they swell the living tide—until the solitary plains have been made to rejoice and the wilderness to blossom as the rose. A land more fair and happy never sun viewed in his wide career; salubrious, mild, its hills are green, its woods and prospects fair, prairies fertile; and, to crown the whole, it is our home—the land of Liberty and all its sweets!

IV

Elisha Marshall

PEASE

1853–1857

Courtesy of Archives Division, Texas State Library

ELISHA MARSHALL PEASE (*January 3, 1812–August 26, 1883*) was born in Enfield, Connecticut. He attended Westfield Academy. At the age of fourteen, he left the Academy to work as a clerk in a country store in Hartford.

In 1835 Pease migrated to Bastrop, Texas, and read law. He attended the 1836 Texas Independence Convention. He served as chief clerk of the Texas Navy in 1836 and 1837. From 1837 until 1846 he practiced law in Brazoria, Texas. He was a member of the Texas legislature from 1846 until 1850.

Running in the 1853 gubernatorial race as a Democrat, Pease defeated his Whig opponent and was sworn in as the fourth governor of Texas. In 1855 he won a second term.

A Unionist, Pease retired from public life during the Civil War. In 1866 he was nominated for governor by the Radical Republicans, but lost the election to J. W. Throckmorton, a Conservative Democrat.

Throckmorton was removed from office in 1867 by the United States military commander, and Pease was appointed Provisional Governor. He resigned on September 30, 1869, but continued to serve until January 8, 1870, when Edmund Davis was sworn in.

*Inaugural Address**
December 21, 1853

In appearing before you to assume the duties of the office to which I have been called by the partiality of my fellow-citizens, I feel sensibly the magnitude and importance of the trust that has been confided to my charge, and a sincere diffidence of my ability to acquit myself of it in a manner that will meet their just expectations.

In discharging the varied functions of the government over which I have been selected to preside, I shall rely with confidence on the cordial support and co-operation of the legislature, without which my efforts can be productive of but little benefit.

Our past history is of peculiar interest; ours is the only State that has come into the Union by voluntary annexation; our introduction led the way to an extension of its limits over New Mexico, Utah and California, embracing a territory nearly equal to the entire area of the Union at its formation. Although some fears were for a time entertained of the effect that such a large and sudden acquisition might have upon the peace and perpetuity of the Union, yet experience has demonstrated the fact that no danger is to be apprehended from its expansion so long as the exercise of its powers is confined to those objects contemplated by the constitution.

Our present attitude before the world is not less interesting; with a territory containing more square miles than many of the governments of Europe; possessing by nature nearly every element necessary to constitute a great and powerful State, with a large public domain unequalled for diversity and fertility of soil, and a climate adapted to the production of all the necessaries and most of the luxuries of life, with a vast mineral wealth and great capabilities for manufacturing purposes, we have it in our power by a proper use of all these advantages, and a judicious application of our means, to lay the foundation for those public improvements

---

Journal of the House of Representatives of the State of Texas, Fifth Legislature (1853), pp. 3–4.

and institutions which will hereafter rank Texas as the first State in the American Union.

While we have so many causes for congratulation in the contemplation of our past and present situation, it becomes us as a people to remember with reverence that Being who has hitherto watched over and assisted our progress through scenes of difficulty and trial to our present state of prosperity, and humbly solicit that he will continue to us his benificent care and protection.

The example of my predecessors will not justify me in detaining you on this occasion to give you my views upon those measures of public policy which I think should receive your attention during the present session. I shall avail myself of an early opportunity to do this, satisfied that your patriotism and enlightened judgment will give to them that consideration and reflection which their importance demands.

Second Inaugural Address *

December 21, 1855

GENTLEMEN OF THE SENATE
AND HOUSE OF REPRESENTATIVES,
AND FELLOW CITIZENS:

The proof of the confidence of my fellow citizens, manifested by my re-election to this important office, fills me with emotions of gratitude which I find it difficult to express.

I enter upon its duties with a determination to use my best efforts in their service, with a full confidence that they will justly appreciate my motives, and that my public acts will be viewed with that indulgence which I have hitherto received at their hands.

Having so recently communicated to you the condition of the Government, and recommended for your consideration such measures as I thought expedient, I shall not detain you, at this time, with any thing further on the subject.

I feel, however, that this occasion is not an improper one, for saying a few words upon political subjects, since our late election for State officers is the first that has been decided by our citizens upon political issues alone.

The sages of the revolution adopted the policy of encourageing immigration, and with that view, naturalization laws were passed at an early day, which enabled immigrants, within a short period after their settlement, to obtain all the privileges of original citizens. The policy of their successors has been equally liberal to the inhabitants of those countries which have been, from time to time, incorporated into the Union by treaty and by annexation.

Those great and good men also adopted the policy of leaving all forms of religion untrammelled and absolutely free.—They fondly hoped, when they exempted the rights of conscience and the functions

---

Journal of the House of Representatives of the State of Texas, Sixth Legislature (1855), pp. 264–66.

of religion, from civil jurisdiction, that they had banished forever, from this fair land, that religious intolerance under which the people of other countries had so long suffered and bled.

By a firm adherence to these liberal and truly American measures, our growth has been rapid, beyond the example of any other country, in territory, population, intelligence and wealth, and in all those arts which tend to elevate and improve the condition of man. Each successive change in our institutions has increased and extended the rights and influence of the people, and restrained the powers of government, until we, now present the sublime spectacle of thirty millions of freemen whose government, deriving all its powers from their own consent, is administered solely with the purpose of contributing to their happiness and prosperity.

It has been reserved for a modern political party, to discover danger to our institutions and our liberties, from the operation of these measures, under which our country has attained its present exalted position among the nations of the earth.

The citizens of this State have, in their late election, exhibited their devotion to those great democratic principles which have hitherto exercised so salutary an influence upon our destiny, by discarding the heresies of this new political party, and I have an abiding confidence that they will find as little favor with the majority of the citizens of the other States as they have with their own.

The rise of this party has given new vigor to the freesoilers and abolitionists of the Northern and Eastern States, who compose its principal strength in those sections, and whose dangerous and disorganizing attempts to resist the execution of the laws of Congress, threaten the peace and permanency of the Union.

I trust, however, that the good sense of the people of every part of the country will, as it always has in past emergencies, come to the rescue, and forever extinguish the hopes of those fanatics who, for the fancied advantages of freedom to a race who are incapable of appreciating or enjoying it, would put at hazard the existence of a government upon which rests the hopes of the friends of the rights of man throughout the world.

It is my ardent desire, that the labors of your session may redound to the welfare of our common constituents, and that our favored country may continue to receive the superintending care of the Author of the universe, upon whose will alone the destinies of States and Nations depend.

V

Hardin Richard

RUNNELS

1857–1859

Courtesy of Archives Division, Texas State Library

HARDIN RICHARD RUNNELS (*August 30, 1820–December 25, 1873*) reportedly was born in Mississippi and migrated with his mother to Texas in 1842. The family established a cotton plantation in Bowie County.

From 1848 until 1855 he represented Bowie County in the Texas legislature. In 1855 he was elected lieutenant governor. In 1857 Runnels won the Democratic nomination for governor and defeated Know-Nothing candidate Sam Houston by a commanding margin.

He was sworn into office and delivered his inaugural address on December 21, 1857. He sought reelection in 1859, but was defeated.

Inaugural Address *
December 21, 1857

About to enter upon the discharge of the high and responsible duties which will now devolve on me, as Chief Executive Officer of the State, custom requires that I should make use of this occasion, to return the most sincere acknowledgements of a grateful heart, for the confidence reposed in me by my fellow-citizens. Conscious of the responsibility, and aware of the onerous task it will impose, it is not without emotions of true embarrassment, and apprehensions of difficulty that I shall enter on their discharge. Indeed, when these considerations present themselves, enhanced by a knowledge of the diversity of opinion incident to the population of most newly settled countries, of the conflict of interest which may be expected to arise between different localities and divisions of the State, I may scarce hope to meet that ordinary share of public approbation which has been awarded to my predecessors, and could well wish that a charge of so great importance to the future interest and well being of the country had been confided to abler and more experienced hands.

In the ordinary course of events, it might not have been expected, that one with aspirations so humble as my own, would ever have been called to a station of such high honor and trust. It is a circumstance which should inspire with hope and encouragement, the humblest who bows in sincerity and truth at the shrine of patriotism and duty, in the illustration it furnishes of the character and genius of that Government with which the American people are blessed, the truth of which has been so often exemplified in the workings of its system, that honors and promotions are not the prerogative of rank, station, or high degree. As a representative of the people, my first and greatest aim has ever been, a just reflection of the sentiments of those with whom my fortunes have been cast; their interests have been my interests, linked together by one

Proceedings at the Inauguration of Hardin R. Runnels, Appendix to the Journal of the House of Representatives of the State of Texas, Seventh Legislature (1858), pp. 6–14.

destiny, and both alike inseperably connected with the prosperity, happiness and welfare of the entire State. As I am not conscious of having indulged any motive inconsistent with their maintenance in times that have passed, I surely can have no other now. If it has been from such an apprehension of my fellow-citizens, that I am indebted for my present position, I have only to assure them, that no effort shall be spared to promote the best interests of the country, and however much I may distrust my own ability, that I shall shrink from no responsibility which attaches to my position.

The recent political contest through which this State has passed, forbids my passing it by without a notice. Early in May last, the Democratic party met in Convention at Waco, and according to long established usage, adopted its platform, and presented nominees for the different offices to be filled at the ensuing election in August. The principles set forth were those of the National Convention at Cincinnati, in 1856, and in substance the same as those under which the Democratic party made its first advent to power with their great author, Mr. Jefferson, at its head, with the single exception of the doctrine of nonintervention as incorporated in the Kansas bill. The news of the action at Waco had scarce transpired, when the name of a citizen prominent in the rolls of his country's fame, was announced in opposition, and a canvass actually begun, the most remarkable, perhaps, in the annals of political warfare. The celerity of the movement, the electric rapidity with which its intelligence was communicated, and the alacrity with which it was endorsed by the entire opposition, furnish the most indubitable evidence of the preconcerted design to distract and if possible to destroy the identity of the Democratic party. Happily the effort failed, and it must be gratifying to all sympathizing with the party from a devotion to principle that victory should have perched on its banner, under circumstances so well calculated to destroy unanimity and confidence. The result affords full and ample assurance of the enduring affection of the great body of our fellow-citizens to the principles of civil, religious and constitutional liberty. Since the first defeat of ancient Federalism, it has been the practice of our opponents, at different intervals, to disguise themselves with new names, and promulgate new platforms of principles. The last assumed has surely excited a greater share of deserved ridicule, while the principles have been more dangerous than all that have preceded it. This fact is evident in the proof of their voluntary abandonment.

I would gladly, if I could, in justice to the occasion, avoid an allusion to the questions growing out of the institution of Slavery, which is now made to act so conspicuous a part in the politics of the nation. Silence, however, might be misconstrued.

The first great issue on this subject, arose on the introduction of Missouri into the Union in 1820, when the restriction of 36° 30' was applied to her Territory, and the slave holder prohibited from the right of joint occupation north of that line with his property. Although this line was not originally intended to extend beyond the limits of the territory of Louisiana, on the annexation of Texas, the principle was applied to it north of that line, and acquiesced in by the South. But when after the acquisition of additional territory, by virtue of the treaty with Mexico, it was again proposed in the formation of a Territorial Government for Oregon, the binding efficacy of the principle was denied, and hence the series of enactments, known as the Compromise Measures of 1850. By that Legislation, California was admitted into the Union as a State, regardless of all the forms of law, under a Constitution which for ever excluded the Southern Slave holder. Next in the series, came the Act creating the Territorial Governments of Utah and New Mexico. In these territories, which comprised the remainder of the territory acquired from Mexico, and also that of Texas, by virtue of annexation and cession of boundary, the principle of non-intervention as a measure of compromise, was expressly recognised and enunciated as the future policy of the Government, touching legislation in the territories. Under the soothing influence of that legislation, it might have been expected, that agitation on the dangerous subjects involved, would cease, and the controversy be forever put at rest. But not so—for notwithstanding that a large portion of the territory comprised in these bills, was subject to the restriction under the articles of annexation, when it was proposed to recognize the validity of the non-intervention principle in the Kansas bill, and leave the people free to make their own selection of their institutions, the right was most bitterly contested, and the attempt denounced as a violation of plighted faith, by those who had hitherto refused in every single instance to respect it. Could insolence and hypocrisy go further, an example might be found in the declarations of the opposition in our own section, who have denounced the abolition of the restrictive line as a surrender of slave territory to free soil, in the face of combinations of Anti-Slavery men, and of Emigrant-Aid-Societies who in the name of religion and free Kansas, were preaching a crusade against the slave power, and sending forward the vilest dregs and slough of their population to rescue her from slavery, or drench her plains with blood. With the aid of Southern sympathizers and misrepresentation, it is greatly to be feared that the efforts to abolitionise have been but too successful.

Painful and humiliating as it must be to every true-hearted Southerner, it is not to be denied, that if abolition propagandism has succeeded in Kansas, it is not alone attributable to the lawless armed bands who have marauded the territory, nor yet to military organizations, headed by renegades and desperate adventurers, acting in open hostility to all Federal and Territorial authority; but it is owing first to the course of those who have in plaintive notes, bewailed the repeal of the Missouri Compromise and thus "given aid and comfort to the enemy," and more recently to the course of Robert J. Walker, (Governor of that Territory,) that so deplorable a result is mainly chargeable. Instead of exercising the authority with which he was vested, to ensure the faithful administration of the laws, he has been engaged in the miserable attempt of conciliating public offenders, by concessions and compromises, utterly inconsistent with the principle of non-intervention incorporated in the organic act, a portion of which is in terms as follows: "It being the true intent and meaning of this act, not to legislate slavery into any territory, nor to exclude it therefrom, but to leave the people thereof perfectly free to form and regulate their institutions in their own way, subject only to the provisions of the Constitution of the United States." The principles of the act can afford no security to the people of the slave-holding States, unless its provisions are to be respected by the agents of the Executive as well as the Legislative department of the Government. Gov. Walker, seems not to have so regarded it, or if so, he has violated the high trust confided to his keeping. For immediately on his arrival in the territory, he commenced a system of intermeddling intended and fully calculated to interfere with the just expression of the legal voters of the territory, in dictating the terms on which it could be admitted into the Union, and in declaring that if the Constitution was not submitted to the whole people, (including, it is to be presumed, those tainted with the high crimes of rebellion and treason) he would aid in having it rejected by Congress; although the right to determine such a proposition belonged alone to the Convention chosen by the legal voters of the Territory. Again, in attempting to prescribe the qualification of voters in contravention of the positive law of the territory, he is believed to have been guilty of an usurpation without parallel or example in the history of free governments. It now remains to be seen what shall be the contents of the chapter that is to follow, in recording the history of a question which has thrice brought the Government to the verge of dissolution. The present and future interests of Texas, are deeply interwoven with the issue, come when it may, be it what it will. As a member of the confederacy of States, Texas possesses a common interest in maintaining the force of the compact which binds it together so long as the administration of its conditions continue to secure the objects for which the compact was intended, *but no longer*. There is no proposition clearer, than that the obligation of parties to a compact ceases, when the instrument has been broken and violated. Recent decisions of the highest tribunal in the land, have defined and established that construction of the Constitution for which the South contends. She should be content with no less than its observance in future. Nor in the fulness of our joy at the gratifying evidences which greet us of an increasing conservatism at the North, should we be unmindful of the fact that he who is not for us, will probably be against us, and that more than two-thirds of the non-slaveholding States yet remain abolitionised. Year by year the South is becoming weaker, the North growing stronger. That equilibrium has been destroyed which afforded the only sure and permanent guarantee of protection against abolition innovation. If the argument has not been exhausted, it has become powerless and impotent from the lips of Southern men. For the future, to the North must be left the management and control of a question which involves union or dissolution, peace or war. In view of these facts, it behooves us earnestly and calmly to look forward to the impending danger, for the problem may soon be solved of the adequacy of the Constitutional restrictions and "paper guaranties" to interpose sufficient barriers to the lust of an aggressive and dominant sectional majority. Should this proposition be decided in the negative, I do not hesitate to believe that the determination of Texas will be taken, to assume the guardianship of her own destinies, and bid adieu to a connection no longer consistent with the rights, dignity and honor of an equal and independent State. "For while disruption would be a great calamity, it is not (in the language of Mr. Jefferson) the greatest that could befall us: there remains one yet greater—submission to a government of unlimited powers." Under these apprehensions prudence would dictate that our house should be set in order, and due preparation made for the crisis, that seems to be foreshadowed by coming events; this should be done not for offence but for defence only. No reasonable effort should be spared to secure that thorough military organization and training, indispensable to the liberties of every free State; as auxiliary to this, a liberal course of policy should be pursued to ensure the organization of volunteer companies—in pressing forward to an early completion the works of Internal Improvement, indispensable to the wants of Commerce and Agriculture, and again in dissemminating information among the masses, through the medium of our systems of Education. These are all-important in constituting our people prosperous, happy and independent.

There is now left but one reasonable hope for preserving the Union, and maintaining the rights of the States in it, and that is upon a rigid adherence to a strict construction of the Federal Constitution. Our opponents preach hostility to our institutions from every quarter, alike from the pulpit as the hustings. With but a single exception, and for the first time, the Southern States have marched in line, and congregated upon the platform of the Constitution, there to fight the battle for their rights under it. That platform is the same in New England as in Texas: its adherents there, though over-whelmed by numbers, are standing firmly to the doctrines it teaches. Let us, by our own thorough organization, offer them assurances of our warmest sympathy and cordial cooperation in support of the glorious cause it is their mission to follow. That cause commends itself to our confidence, because, amid the vicissitudes and changes of half a century, it presents the only record, unblemished by mutation and change. If weakened by defections, time has invariably "recovered for it more than its lost strength;" if occasional departures from the doctrine of strict construction have occurred, truth and investigation have as invariably combatted the error and established it still more firmly in the minds of the American people, as the only true and reliable exponent of our institutions. The tempests of passion and fanaticism have assailed it, hitherto, with no other effect, than to remove the rubbish with which it was encumbered, and exhibit more clearly the patriotism and virtue of those who remain faithful to its cause. It is at that altar alone that the man of the South discovers the arcana of his present and future security, and there alone, that patriotism can take her humble abode, hoping to perpetuate a constitutional government and preserve to futurity those model institutions, alike the purest, the greatest and best that have ever entered into the conception of man.

VI

Sam

HOUSTON

1859–1861

Courtesy of Archives Division, Texas State Library

SAM HOUSTON (*March 2, 1793–July 26, 1863*), the son of a bridge inspector, was born in Rockridge County, Virginia. Houston's family moved to Maryville, Tennessee, and there he attended school for a few terms.

At the age of twenty, Houston enlisted in the United States Army, fought in the Creek War, and was wounded in battle at Horseshoe Bend. In 1818 he resigned his commission, began reading law, and opened a law office in Lebanon, Tennessee.

Houston served as congressman from Tennessee from 1823 to 1827. He was elected governor of Tennessee in 1827, but resigned in 1829 after separating from his first wife.

He established a trading post among the Cherokees near Fort Gibson and became a tribal citizen. In 1833 he settled near Nacogdoches, Texas, and represented that community in the Independence Convention of 1836. He was elected first president of the Republic of Texas in 1836 and served until his term expired in 1838. He served a second presidential term from 1841 until 1844.

Following the annexation of Texas to the United States, Houston was elected to the Senate, serving from 1846 until 1859. He was defeated in the gubernatorial contest of 1857 in which he was a Know-Nothing candidate. In 1859 Houston ran successfully as a Union Democrat. He took office on December 21.

When Texas joined the Confederacy, the Secession Convention declared the office of governor vacant. Lieutenant Governor Edward Clark assumed office on March 16, 1861, to complete the remaining months of Houston's term.

Inaugural Address *
December 21, 1859

GENTLEMEN OF THE SENATE AND HOUSE OF REPRESENTATIVES:

Called from retirement by the voice of my fellow citizens, to the responsible position of the Executive of the State, I am not insensible to the delicacy and importance of the duties which devolve upon me. Having been withdrawn for years past, to the discharge of Federal duties, as Senator of the United States, I have not had the advantage of participating in the local affairs of the State, and have much to inquire into concerning its interests. I am aware that our local interests are varied and important, and feel pleasure in assuring my fellow citizens that my object will be to promote and advance every interest without regard to section, and use my best endeavors to develop our resources. To effectuate this object, and to meet the just expectations of my fellow citizens, it will be necessary that I should enjoy and realize a hearty cooperation on the part of the people's representatives in consummating these desirable objects. My purpose, as well as my desire, will be to sustain such measures of policy as may have been introduced promotive of the public good, and to inaugurate and advance such others as will conform to the best interests of the community.

Our insular situation imperatively demands the construction of railroads on an extended and practicable scale, commensurate to the growing importance of our settlements, as well as to the production and commerce daily increasing in our country; at the same time a policy should be adopted and pursued which would secure the State against all imposition and insure the fulfillment of every charter granted and the accomplishment of every contract to which the government may be a party. The munificent grants made by the Government, hold out

*Amelia W. Williams and Eugene C. Barker, eds., *The Writings of Sam Houston: 1813–1863*, Vol. 7, *November, 1824–March, 1860* (Austin: University of Texas Press, 1942), pp. 379–85.

every inducement for the investment of capital and the employment of enterprise; and it is but justice to it that all fair requirements in its behalf should be exacted and conceded in return for its liberality. The improvements of our rivers so far as can be effected at a commensurate expense so as to render them navigable, where it is practicable, seems to me to be an object demanding fostering care of the government. Nature has provided these channels of commerce and when improved they will supply the necessities and wants of communities, which railroads cannot accomplish for a length of time. True economy dictates that we should realize from them whatever advantage they possess.

Having treated of the physical economy of our State, it is proper that I should advert to the intellectual and moral improvement of our people. It is a truism that "to maintain liberty, intelligence is indispensable." To attain this object, education is all important; it should not be confined to classes, but disseminated throughout the whole community. How to accomplish this object, to the greatest perfection, seems to be a subject yet left for solution.

The Constitution evidences that its framers regarded education as a primary object, and in that instrument ample provisions were made for the endowment of Universities and the support of common schools. The improvement and perfection of common schools suggest themselves to me as the foundation upon which to erect the best system of education, and when the foundation is firmly laid, it will be easy to erect thereon materials for a University, if the voice of the State should, at some future day, require the establishment. To me it seems both wise and expedient that all reasonable encouragement should be extended to all educational institutions now in existence, which have been established and sustained by individual enterprise, and to promote the establishment of others in various portions of the State, thus rendering them more able to extend their usefulness, and increase their advantages to the community. In the attainment of these various objects, it does seem to me that two important desiderata must enter into the plan of their accomplishment: Economy in relation to the finances and the public domain, and strict accountability on the part of all public functionaries should be held indispensable. It is for the legislature to enact such laws as are necessary to attain this object, and secure the public treasury from imposition and fraud. So far as is dependent on my official action, I can assure my constituents that in the appointment of official functionaries, I will entrust no man with office in whose integrity I have not entire confidence that he will discharge the duties of the trust confided to him with fidelity. I have confidence that my constituents, in the exercise of their discernment, will not fail to discriminate between that which was desired to be accomplished, and could not be done for want of unity and a cooperation of the different parts of government, and that which falls within the constitutional power of the Executive. As regards the public domain, the intelligence of the legislature whose attention has been called to it, is capable of devising a system for its future disposition, and such an one will embrace a liberal policy towards the settler. From the inception of the Government of the Republic of Texas a provision was contained in the Constitution providing for sectionizing the public domain; and if such a policy had been carried out, it would have prevented a vast amount of litigation which has since that time occurred. If the legislature of the State should, at any time, adopt such a measure, it would have a tendency to dispel a thousand anxieties which the settler now entertains, because, when he would then settle upon a tract of land, he would know his metes and bounds, and that he could assuredly repose in the guarantees which the State afforded him for the occupancy of his homestead.

In an inaugural address it is not expected that subjects which would be more appropriate in a general message to the legislature, which I contemplate making, should be embraced; yet there are subjects which demand of me attention. The subject of our frontier defenses is of absorbing interest. Where it is possible for the Government to give protection to its citizens, it is a duty which cannot be disregarded. The extent of our frontier, stretching as it does, from the Red River to El Paso, on the Rio Grande, and from thence to the mouth of that river, comprises a distance of but little short of two thousand miles. One half of that distance is exposed to Indian depredations, and the other borders upon Mexico, which is in a state of anarchy. Depredations by the Indians are so frequent that to hear of them has almost ceased to excite sympathy and attention in the interior of our State. We have a right to look to the Federal Government for that protection which, as a part of the Confederacy, we are entitled to. The Federal Government has stationed troops on our frontiers, but they are Infantry, and not calculated for that effective warfare which should be carried on against the Indians, they escape, and the Infantry cannot overtake them. Were a force authorized by the Federal Government of Texan Rangers, who understood the Indian mode of warfare, and whose animals would be capable of subsisting upon prairies, without other forage, the expense would be less to the Government, and their efficiency greater in protecting our frontier, than any other description of troops. The misfortune which has attended us is the fact that annuities paid by the United States to tribes that infest our borders, are received by these Indians by way of Arkansas, and not by way of Texas, which causes them to believe that they violate no treaty stipulation by marauding upon Texas, because the people of Texas are not identified with those of Arkansas. If annuities were paid to the Indians upon our borders it would exercise a salutary influence upon them. We must look beyond mere physical means for defense. There must be a moral influence exerted upon the Indians, and I earnestly hope that will be exerted by the President of the United States, having full confidence in his desire to promote the well-being of the whole country, and that he will not withhold any means in his power to protect our bleeding frontier. The various tribes on our borders, if they were invited to meet at some place convenient on our frontier, and a treaty were made with them to give them a trifling annuity compared to the amount required to afford us but partial protection, would give us peace to our borders. This policy at the time of annexation, gave security to our frontier. Of the future it is fair to judge by the past. In the meantime we must not neglect the demands of emergency; but must ourselves provide means for the immediate defense of our settlements.

Our entire boundary upon the Rio Grande, from the anarchy which prevails in that country, is in an exposed and excited condition. The utter disregard of all law and order in Mexico, has communicated its unhappy influence to this side of the Rio Grande, and a portion of our citizens, at this time, are in a most deplorable condition, and in what it is to eventuate it is impossible to conjecture. The federal arm has been extended there, and I hope will give security and restore tranquility to our people. I will deem it my duty, if sustained by the Legislature, to institute a proper inquiry into the causes which have led to the recent disorders and adopt such measures as will prevent the recurrence of similar outbreaks. I am satisfied they have grown out of local causes, and that no premeditated insurrection was contemplated.

Whilst your representative in the Senate of the United States, being well apprised of the hopeless condition of Mexico, I introduced a measure for the purpose of establishing a Protectorate by the government of the United States over Mexico. The measure was received with disfavor. Aware of the State of Mexican Affairs, I believed the Mexican people utterly incapable of framing a government and maintaining a nationality. This has been demonstrated since their separation from old Spain. Their history is a catalogue of revolutions, of usurpations and oppression. As a neighboring people to us, it is important for the main-tainance of good neighborhood, that law and order should exist in that country. The Mexicans are a mild, pastoral and gentle people; and it is only by demagogues and lawless chieftains, who with armed bands have robbed and plundered the people, that the disorders in the country are continued. A guarantee given to these people, for the protection of their lives and property against such, would cause them to rejoice and they would hail with pleasure any measure which might be adopted by any foreign government that would give them peace and security. As a border state, our own security must to a great extent, depend upon the condition of things in Mexico, and the restoration of order, and the establishment of good government in that country. This is a subject for the consideration of the federal authorities, and, no doubt will command their gravest reflection.

Should no change take place in Mexico, restraining their disorders, and should they extend to this side of the Rio Grande, it will demand of the Executive of the State the exercise of its fullest powers, if needful, to protect our citizens, and vindicate the honor of our State.

In concluding this Inaugural, I am irresistibly led to reflections which I hope will be heard with no disadvantage to any of my audience. When Texas united her destiny with that of the government of the United States, she took upon herself duties and responsibilities for the faithful performance of which we are pledged as a State. She entered not into the North, nor into the South, but into the Union: her connection was not sectional, but national, and however distinct or diversified her interests may be, as compared with those of other States, she relies upon the same Constitution as they to secure her in the enjoyment of her rights. Making that Constitution the guiding star of our career as a State, let our rivalry be to approximate more closely to it than any of our sister States. It inculcates faithfulness to the Union, let us be faithful to it. Let us, in our relationships with the General government, and with the States of the Confederacy, allow none to excell us in our desires to promote peace and harmony. When our rights are aggressed upon, let us be behind none in repelling attack; but let us be careful to distinguish between the acts of individuals and those of a people, between the wild ravings of fanatics and that public sentiment which truly represents the masses of the people. It is in the diversity of opinion that Democracy may rest securely. The right to think adversely, to us is a guarantee of American Republicanism, and though this privilege may often be carried to extremes, and to our detriment, yet the very safety of our institutions depends upon our maintaining it as a republican principle. When thought becomes treason, the traitor is as much the enemy of one section as of the other. Its overt acts we must repel. Its expression by those inimical to our institutions, where they do not exist, need affect us nothing. The alarm at their endeavors is needless and but strengthens them,—the eternal din which has echoed to that song of hostility to the South is music to their ears. Their aim is to array sectionalism upon their side, and thus promote strife and confusion. We should meet their clamor with the contempt of a people who fear no invasion of their rights, and instead of feeding the flame of discord, which a few in both sections have kindled, lend our endeavors toward quenching it altogether. How happy would have been the result if the attention of Statesmen North and South, had been as much directed towards promoting harmony between the States, and cementing those fraternal bonds which can alone hold us together as a people, as towards promoting the strife of sections, and the antagonisms which are fast dividing us. Half the care—half the thought which has been spent to meet sectionalism by sectionalism, bitterness by bitterness, and abolition by disunion, would have made this people, today, a happy, united and hopeful nation.

Elected by the people, I am responsible to the people alone. Indebted to no clique or caucus for the position that I occupy, I shall act alike beyond the wishes and control of such. Looking to the people in their broad conservatism and their patriotism to sustain my endeavors, I shall pursue the course which will best conduce to the prosperity of Texas. Regarding my election as an endorsement of the sentiments enunciated by me when I yielded my name to the people, I shall feel as the representative of the popular will, an additional incentive to make my administration accord with those principles. Should my endeavors to turn the attention of the Legislature toward these questions, whose solutions bear the prosperity and happiness of the people of Texas to the sacrifice of those national abstractions which should have no place in our councils, fail of success, I have but to look to the people to sustain me. My hopes point me, however, to the honorable body before me, believing that in so much wisdom and intelligence there cannot fail to exist, at the same time, that amount of virtue and patriotism necessary to meet any emergency.

VII

Francis Richard
LUBBOCK

1861–1863

Courtesy of Archives Division, Texas State Library

FRANCIS RICHARD LUBBOCK (*October 16, 1815–June 22, 1905*), the son of a planter and merchant, was born in Beaufort, South Carolina. He attended private schools but was forced to leave school at the age of fourteen when his father died. He was a hardware clerk and later managed a cotton warehouse. In 1834 he moved to New Orleans and opened a drugstore. He moved to Texas in 1836 and operated drugstores in Velasco and Houston. Later he engaged in the mercantile business, farming, and ranching.

Lubbock served in the Texas militia and fought against Mexico and Indians. In 1837 he became clerk of the Republic of Texas House of Representatives. Later he served as comptroller of the treasury. In 1840 he was elected district clerk of Harris County, a post Lubbock held for sixteen years. In 1857 he was elected lieutenant governor and served one term.

A Democrat, Lubbock was elected on November 4, 1861, in an election held without party affiliation. He took office on November 7, 1861.

Inaugural Address *
November 7, 1861

GENTLEMEN OF THE SENATE AND HOUSE OF REPRESENTATIVES, LADIES AND MY FELLOW CITIZENS:

The time designated by the Constitution, that you, gentlemen of the Senate and House of Representatives, shall meet and enter upon the important duties assigned you, having arrived, permit me to congratulate you that you are here assembled today for that purpose, in a free land, untrammeled and unpawed by the mercenaries of despotism; and let me congratulate you, fellow-citizens, that while some of our sister States have been and are now being invaded, the soil of our beloved State is free from the presence of our enemies, except such as are prisoners in the hands of our brave soldiers.

A generous and confiding people, by their suffrages, have called me to the Executive chair of a great and sovereign State, a member of a proud and powerful Confederacy. I feel deeply conscious of the great responsibilities attaching to the position at this important crisis. Much has already been done by the retiring Executive to place Texas side by side with her sister States in the present struggle; but, gentlemen, it must be borne in mind that we have as yet but seen the beginning, and I am resolved, with your aid and support, so long as I occupy the position confided to me by the people, that her footsteps in the career of honor and patriotism shall be onward, and the precious interest entrusted to my keeping be rendered back at the appointed time uninjured and untarnished.

It is useless at this time, gentlemen, to discuss the causes which led to the present state of affairs. The history of our wrongs is a long and bitter

House Journal of the Ninth Legislature Regular Session of the State of Texas (1862), pp. 11–15. (This House Journal was compiled and edited from manuscripts in The Texas State Archives [1964]. The inaugural address was retrieved from *The Texas Republican* [Marshall, Texas], December 7, 1861.)

one, and has been so often discussed and reviewed by the great minds of the country, that it has become familiar with you all. You, together with a large majority of our fellow citizens, have long since decided that grievances to such an extent existed as to warrant the necessity of separation from those with whom for so long a period we have been politically connected.

That separation was consummated by us after mature reflection, in view of all the attendant dangers and difficulties.

Many had hoped that we would be permitted to part in peace, and that those with whom we could not live in brotherhood would at least allow us to retire from a co-partnership that had become onerous and oppressive, and take with us our institutions that had become so hateful to them.

This fond hope was not to be realized. Those who had heretofore professed friendship for us, and a willingness to stand by our constitutional guarantees, become our most vindictive foes, vieing with the Abolitionists who should be first in the field for our subjugation.

The war was inaugurated by our enemies, and our once peaceful and happy land is now the scene of this inhuman struggle.

The Lincoln government vainly boasted that the base and hireling soldiery would overrun and subjugate the South in sixty days. Eight months have past away and we find this wicked and boastful government, after warring for that length of time against a power not half their equal in numbers, forced to pursue on every line of military operations, a defensive policy. Their armies defeated on every battlefield, and their hireling soldiers flee panic-stricken before our army of citizens.

In all this, a kind Providence has hovered near our armies, giving us victory after victory over our enemies.

In portions of our country heretofore subject to casualties that have caused the earth to fail in its productions, genial showers have fallen upon the land; abundance has been given to us, our granaries are filled, and plenty prevails in our midst, and the people feel that the great God who presides over the destinies of nations and "sits on the throne judging right," is on our side, and will bless us in this struggle.

Thus far our efforts have been crowned with success. Let all praises be given to our gallant soldiers who have defended the integrity of our soil.

It has been said, gentlemen, that this is a war for slavery. I tell you it is a war for liberty! Upon the issue of this war must depend on our status in all time to come. We must maintain our liberties by our strong arms and stout hearts, or we must consent to be the most abject slaves of the basest, most corrupt, and vulgar despotism that ever clutched in its unhallowed grips the liberties of a free people.

I know, gentlemen, that in your hearts you have already determined that this war should be carried out with promptness, vigor, and ultimate success.

I call upon you, therefore, in the name of patriotism, honor, and all that you hold most dear, to devise and carry out such wise and efficient measures as will strengthen the arm of the Confederate States, and aid them in speedily achieving for us our independence, pledging to you my most cordial approval and co-operation in every such measure.

I trust you will see that those gallant men, who have served the State well and faithfully, be fully provided for, and that no Texian soldier shall charge his State with ingratitude. They deserve well of their country; they have and will continue to sustain the reputation of their State as the home of a chivalrous and warlike people.

Gentlemen, to the ladies of our country, we owe much; in our trials and troubles, they too have been with us. To prepare comforts for the soldiers, their busy needles have been plied incessantly; their smiles, their tears, and their prayers, accompany the soldiers to the battle-field. They yield up to the cause of their country, right bravely, husbands, brothers, sons, and lovers. They gave up ease, luxury, and elegance, for the soldier's benefit. Can a people thus supported and encouraged, be subdued by the base Hessians of a corrupt and fanatical government: no! never, while one bold heart is left to combat.

Gentlemen, I am pleased to know that at the head of the Government of the Confederate States, we have men of ability, integrity, and patriotism; and while I have every confidence, and feel satisfied they are doing everything in their power to secure our liberties, and chastise our insolent and remorseless foe, it is nevertheless our duty to see our State is put in an attitude of self defense, from the seaboard to the hills, and our soil defended against the polluted tread of abolition hordes.

Our frontier must also be guarded, at every cost against the ruthless Indian foe; the lives of our men, women and children, preserved from the tomahawk and the scalping knife.

Texas must pay punctually to the Confederate Government her portion of the war tax; and I have no fears but that our people will promptly respond to this sacred call of patriotism; and, in addition, they will cheerfully meet such taxation as may be necessary to carry on our State Government with efficiency.

I trust that every citizen will feel that he must perform his part in the great struggle now going on; that prudence and economy will enter into the administration of every department of Government, and that every servant will look well to the welfare of the country.

Let me say in conclusion, that I am here in accordance with the wishes of the people; that I bring with me to the Capitol the kindest feelings toward all good men, having no prejudices against this party or that party, this man or that man. I come here determined, as far as in my power lies, to see that the laws are enforced impartially, and to carry on the State government for the people with honesty and economy.

I enter upon the discharge of my duties free and untrammelled, bound by no pledges, only to a faithful performance of every trust confided in me.

I trust every citizen in this broad land will see the necessity of lending his aid in sustaining the glorious cause in which we are now engaged, that of securing to millions yet unborn the right of self-government.

Let us all stand upon the Constitution that has been adopted by our own people, presenting one unbroken front to tyranny in every shape it may present itself, with the determination never to place our liberties in the keeping of the dastard foe that now seeks to conquer us.

I hope, gentlemen, that our session will prove harmonious, and that your every act will redound to your praise, and the good of our country.

For the present, I have done, at a future day I will take pleasure in giving you my views more in detail.

Ladies, for your attention, I thank you, and from my heart say— God bless you.

VIII

Pendleton
MURRAH

1863–1865

Courtesy of Archives Division, Texas State Library

PENDLETON MURRAH (*1824–August 4, 1865*) was a native of South Carolina. The exact date of his birth and place of birth are not known. He was educated by a charitable society of the Baptist church. He graduated from Brown University in 1848 and later studied law. He was admitted to the bar in Alabama.

Shortly after becoming a lawyer, he moved to Marshall, Texas. In 1862 he was appointed to the Quartermaster's Department of the Confederate States Army for Eastern Texas. He was an unsuccessful candidate for Congress in 1855 but in 1857 won a seat in the state legislature.

In the 1863 gubernatorial election, a contest without political parties, Murrah, a Democrat, won by a comfortable margin. He took office on November 5, 1863.

When the Confederacy collapsed, lawlessness and panic swept the state. Civil authorities lost control, and on the night of June 11, 1865, Murrah fled the country to Mexico. Lieutenant Governor Fletcher Stockdale completed the remaining months of Murrah's term, which expired on June 16, 1865.

From June 17, 1865, until August 9, 1866, the governorship was held by Andrew Jackson Hamilton, who was appointed to the post by President Andrew Johnson.

Inaugural Address *

November 5, 1863

GENTLEMEN OF THE SENATE AND HOUSE OF REPRESENTATIVES, LADIES AND YOU, MY FELLOW CITIZENS:

I have been chosen by the people of Texas chief executive of the State for the next two years. The office of Chief Magistracy of a great, sovereign State like Texas is at all times one of great importance and responsibility; but now when war is waged upon our common country, and danger threatens the State upon every hand, and when so many grave questions of policy are to be met, its importance and responsibilities are greatly magnified.

I fully appreciate the fact that a majority of the suffrages of the people have been cast for me at a time when all that is sacred to us is involved in the issue of a war of such magnitude, and of such virulence in character and when the perilous condition of the country requires of the Executive so much discretion, watchfulness, soundness of judgment, and firmness in the discharge of the duties of his office.

I most sincerely thank the people for the distinguished honor conferred upon me, and for their manifestation of confidence under circumstances so marked and significant; while I distrust my ability and my experience in public affairs, I can promise, without reservation, a will and a determination to discharge the duties of this high trust with a firm hand, and as nearly as I can in accordance with the wants of the State.

I indulge in the hope that a zealous devotion to the great interests of the State in these times of peril will plead, not unsuccessfully, and excuse for my shortcomings and want of wisdom in this high position,

House Journal of the Tenth Legislature Regular Session of the State of Texas (1863), pp. 53–61. (This Journal was compiled and edited from the manuscripts in The Texas State Archives [1965].)

and that a generous constituency will be slow to desert or abandon a public servant faithfully laboring for the public good.

If statesmanship and ability—the power to distinguish and the disposition to observe the true character of our political system—be essential qualifications in the officials of the Confederacy, they can be no less so in the officials of the state government. Texas in allying herself to the other states of the South for general purposes, and for the common weal surrendered not her sovereignty, or the complete control over matters of local concern; and it follows, as a matter of course, that a wise and judicious administration of the affairs pertaining to the local, can be of no less importance to the welfare of the people, than the proper administration of affairs pertaining to the general authority. A full appreciation of this simple fact and a rigid observance of its practice will have no little influence in producing sober and correct views as to the scope and object of the Confederate authority, and in modifying tendencies to partisan organizations and partisan strife, founded alone upon differences of opinion as to the extent and object of that authority.

But the responsibilities of position, in a government like ours, and especially at a time like this, when the services of all are needed, should not deter the Citizen, through timid apprehensions of evil consequences to himself, when called by the voice of his country, from yielding his services to it. The life of the state is threatened, its welfare being at all times an object near the heart of the patriot—and all selfishness and merely personal consideration should be banished, and the Citizen in private life, and in public station, should be guided alone by the most exalted patriotism, discarding from every act and utterance having reference to public affairs, all baser motives.

We are struggling through the perils of bloody fields for the preservation of the institutions inherited from a glorious ancestry, and it surely behooves us to heed their voice, to be instructed by their experience, and to study well the condition and means by which they are not only to be maintained by the sword, but perpetuated and wisely administered. For the machinery of government of all machinery is most intricate and most difficult of adjustment and management; the science of government, of all sciences, has claimed from mankind the greatest share of their attention, and yet has secured from them the least uniformity of opinion as to its true mission, and as to the principles which should be embraced in a perfect system.

Though the builders were master builders, the complicated and refined character of our political system, together with the absence of experience and precedents as guides, gave rise from its very origin, to most serious and delicate questions in the adjustment of state and federal authority—questions often involving the most bitter party strifes, and most alarming excitements in the public mind, bringing at an early day to the minds of the original framers, grave apprehension of the long duration of the workmanship of their hands.

Our bleeding and struggling country warns the people of the dangers of holding to the differences of opinion vital in their character, as to the true nature of the government of their own formation, and of yielding themselves up blindly to partisan organizations and partisan strifes, for the purpose of building up theories at variance with the government, as written and ordained. Instructed by experience and guided by the lights of the past, it is hoped and believed that if we are true to ourselves, we may escape such dangers for the future, and from the beginning of our new political career, not only understand, but put in practice the government according to its true theory.

The objects and the ends of the State and Confederate governments are so distinct, the powers to be employed by them so well distinguished and defined, that it becomes a matter of wonder how they can be involved in confusion and uncertainty.

The strength and beauty of a Federal system of government, its value and completeness as a government, its harmonious and energetic action, absolutely require in both the general and local authorities, a rigid observance of the boundaries of power lying between them and marking out their appropriate spheres of action.

This simple **rule** forbids alike the usurpation of authority upon the part of the general government, the infringment upon local authority, and the denial on part of the State to the general government the exercise of authority clearly granted in the Constitution. These observations are not deemed out of place here, for the reason that the extraordinary events daily transpiring in our country, together with the universal demands of this war upon its energies and resources, are trying both strength and character of the State and Confederate organizations—the extent of their authority, respectively, bringing into action a large class of powers, which in ordinary times, and especially in times of peace, lie dormant and unobserved in the organism of a complicated political system.

A distinction will of course be observed by every intelligent and just minded man, at a time when necessity forces upon the government the employment of so many agents for so many varied purposes, between deliberate acts on the part of the governments at variance with the

Constitution and mere irregularities in the exercise or execution of authority on the part of officials, which may be promptly arrested and corrected by appeals to the proper tribunals.

To make such irregularities the foundations for factions and organized opposition to the government would be at all times unjust and unwise, but in times like these madness and folly.

It is not apprehended by me that the Confederate government will either inaugurate or persevere in a line of policy that will touch the sovereignty of the States—infringe upon the rights and privileges of the citizen, violate the compact between these States, or fail to rebuke and punish usurpations of authority upon the part of officials when properly brought to its attention. Its disposition is conceived to be the reverse of this, and it is believed that the State and Confederate authorities, not only may but should, in their own organism, work harmoniously together in uniting and directing the energies of the country in this deadly conflict for freedom and humanity.

For while this contest shall continue for national existence, our main business must be war. To its demands all other considerations must yield, just as a man yields all else for the preservation of his life. The destiny of Texas for weal or for woe, and by her own volition, is connected with that of the Southern Confederacy, and she has pledged herself to her sister states of the South, that their triumphs shall be her triumphs, and their fall her fall—their glory her glory—and their sorrows her sorrows.

She has pledged life and sacred honor, that the Lone Star banner around which cluster so many glorious memories sacred to the cause of civilization and well ordered government shall never be a banner of treason to the Southern Confederacy or her own plighted faith.

Texas can, of course, as other states, act but a subordinate part in the conduct of this war. And yet the line of policy to be pursued by her as a sovereign state, under existing circumstances, may not only be essential to her own liberties, but to the liberties of the Southern Confederacy.

Up to this period in this bloody drama, Texas has discharged her duties full and nobly—even beyond the legal demands made upon her energies and resources.

Whenever danger has been incurred, or glory won upon the field of strife, her sons have poured out their generous blood freely, and won for themselves, their State, and their Common Country, imperishable renown.

But dangers thicken around us, and make still greater demands upon her patriotism and power. The fall of Vicksburg and Port Hudson, the consequent imperfect correspondence with the states east of the Mississippi River, and with the government at Richmond, has rendered the Trans-Mississippi Department to a very considerable extent self-dependent, not only for Counsels, but for the means of prosecuting the war, and defending itself. The people of Arkansas and Louisiana are flying by thousands with their property to our borders to escape the presence of an insolent and insulting foe; and a large portion of the territory of those states is already within the Federal lines. Under these circumstances, it will be admitted that Texas occupies a large place in the Trans-Mississippi Department. Her territory is vast, her geographical position favorable, her resources great—her credit has been used but to a limited extent, her people have not been driven from her borders—murdered upon her soil, or her property destroyed as has been the case for her sister states.

She will own these advantages—appreciate her grave responsibilities and, rising with the occasion that demands still greater effort, make full preparations to put forth her strength to the best advantage when the occasion shall present itself. The glories of San Jacinto—the horrors of the Alamo, and the tyranny of Mexico, are too fresh to her memory—her sacrifices in this war are too great, and her experience too bitter for her to fail or falter in this, perhaps, the darkest hour of this dark con quest, the spirit of her departed heroes—of Clough, of Dickson, of Burnes, of Carter, of Terry, of Lubbock, and of thousands of others who offered up themselves freely upon the altar of their country cry aloud for vengeance and for still greater sacrifices on the part of the living in the cause for which they fell. A young giantess as she is almost of the forest, with limb unfettered and spirit erect and free, that never stooped to disgrace or tyranny, Texas has not forgotten or forsaken the faith involved in the issues of secession—she owns the presence of a divinity in a wild storm of human passion that rocks this continent and finds the true interpretation of this, as of all great revolutions in human affairs in the mysterious ways of an All-wise and Overruling Providence.

As a matter of course, the conduct of the affairs of the state and its legislation, should have reference, in main, to our condition in a state of war. But we know not how long these clouds shall hang over the land. In the midst of the embarrassments and dangers of war, we should not forget that the essential end of government, and of all struggles for governments, is the protection of society and the securing its welfare physically, morally and mentally. The laws therefore should be upheld and honored and as far as consists with circumstances surrounding the state, rigidly enforced, so as to visit speedy punishment upon the offender against the mandates, and check the wild tendencies to anarchy and violence, resulting from the demoralizing agencies at work in these times of evil. We shall strive in vain upon the field of blood, if in the meantime the bands of society are to be broken asunder—the habit of obedience to law and the authority of government forgotten and abandoned—human life and individual rights left unguarded or exposed to the caprices of the mob, and the matured and youthful mind accustomed and familiarized to the fearful and dreadful scenes which always occur when lawless passions hold their sway. We claim to read in the northern mind a downward course to the dark abyss of confusion, anarchy and hopeless tyranny, which but too often marks the destiny of nations involved in protracted wars, and bloody revolutions. Warned by ruin and misery that seems to overhand their society, and by the instructive voice of history, we should not in these times of excited passions—of jealous apprehensions, and of real dangers—overlook the importance of a frequent recurrence to the fundamental principles of security lying at the foundation of society and of government, of trusting to the regularly and legally constituted authorities and tribunals, and of laboring zealously, watchful and systematically, and with proper foresight, to make them fully adequate to the punishment and suppression of crime, and to the protection of society from the wicked offender against its peace—its welfare and its life. We should accord our conduct with the spirit of the Constitution and the theories of our government, and make the law a shield to every man, and cause every offender to be punished according to law.

In the midst of this revolution, the education and training of the rising generation appeals with peculiar force to the whole society and to the authorities of government so far as they have control over the subject. We are losing many men by the casualties of war, and many others are absent from home beneath the banner of their country contending with the foe, some of whose sons cannot be educated unless they receive aid from the state through that system which finds its foundation in the Constitution. The lapse of but a few years will introduce the youth of the land upon the stage of active life to act their part in society for good or for evil. Every consideration as to the welfare of society and of government, under our institutions, requires that they should be trained, educated and prepared for the stern and varied duties that lie before them as citizens.

The establishment of manufactories for the leading articles of husbandry and of daily consumption so as to relieve the people from a dependence upon a foreign, irregular, and uncertain and corrupting trade, is a consideration that will be owned by all to be of the highest moment.

The consummation of this desirable end rests mainly with the people, limited and prescribed, as the government is, in its power over the subject. They own the Capital, the labor—the raw material—the most useful metals lie embedded beneath our soil, our geographical position is favorable to the introduction of the necessary machinery. What can be accomplished in this line by association of individuals and of capital, by enterprise and resolution, can only be determined by persevering, systematic effort.

The necessity and the inducements for effort cannot be overrated. It is far better and far more economical, as I conceive, to make Capital yield its profits, not only during the war, but after its close, to make it an enduring monument of a lofty, well-reliant spirit in the people by investing it in permanent and useful manufacturing establishments than to squander it away forever in purchasing goods from nations perhaps indifferent to our fate, or from a foe who is striving by all the appliances of war to subjugate and enslave us. Besides, the uncertain duration of this trade should be impressed upon the public mind. We know not how soon the direction of war may close the trade across the Rio Grande, and leave us not only without a market for clothing, but without the machinery necessary to the manufacture of material for them.

It is gratifying to learn that the public mind, to some extent, is being awakened to the importance of this subject and that combinations are here and there being made for developing the mineral resources of the state and for the introduction of machinery for manufacturing purposes. Let the spirit of enterprise be diffused, and let the good work go on until every man, woman and child in Texas, if need be, be clad in homespun or in domestic manufactures, and until every field shall be ploughed with iron from our native ores.

The first act of my introduction into this high and responsible office, is the taking of a solemn oath to discharge its duties according to the Constitution and the laws, established in accordance with its provisions. This oath forbids me to make it the law of my official acts as it is the law not only to the government but to all of its officials. Where its provisions are plain, difficulty is at an end, and wherever sanctioned by time and experience.

I should with the more apprehension take upon myself the administration of the affairs of the state, were I not to be aided through the coordinate branches of the government. I indulge the hope that the officials of the various departments of the government may labor harmoniously and energetically together, with the single purpose of securing the welfare and the highest interests of the state—trusting that the God who has thus far sustained our cause and given victory to our army upon a hundred bloody fields, will vouch-safe His guidance to all those engaged in the administration of the public affairs of the country.

IX

James Webb
THROCKMORTON

1866–1867

Courtesy of Archives Division, Texas State Library

JAMES WEBB THROCKMORTON (*February 1, 1825–April 21, 1894*) was born in Sparta, Tennessee. His father was a physician. He received a common school education. In 1836 his family moved to Fayetteville, Arkansas, and five years later to Fannin County, Texas. Subsequently, the family relocated to Collin County, Texas.

At the age of nineteen he studied medicine with his uncle in Princeton, Kentucky, and began a private practice in McKinney. He volunteered to serve in the Mexican War and was commissioned as a second surgeon. In 1849 he began to study law and upon completion was admitted to the bar.

Throckmorton served in the Texas House of Representatives for two terms from 1851 to 1856 and in the Senate from 1856 until 1861. During the Civil War he was a captain and a major in the Confederate Army and in 1864 was a brigadier general of Texas troops.

He opposed secession and attempted to organize the Union party. Seeking the governorship as a member of the Conservative party, Throckmorton was elected governor on June 25, 1866, in a special election. He took office on August 8, 1866.

On July 30, 1867, he was removed from office by the federal military commander in Texas as an "impediment to reconstruction." Former Governor Elisha M. Pease was appointed governor and remained in the position until January 1870.

Inaugural Address *
August 9, 1866

Fellow-citizens:

Called by the people of Texas, with an unanimity of sentiment rarely equalled in the history of Republican Governments, to preside over their destinies at a period so critical, when the future of the country appears so gloomy, when so much prudence and sagacity are required and expected, I can but be most profoundly impressed with the respon sibilities of the task before me.

About to take upon myself the oath of office as Chief Magistrate of the State, and entering upon a term of service that must prove eventful in the history of the country, I am frank to confess that I feel greatly wanting in the ability necessary to the occasion; and, feeling thus, I cannot withhold the expression of my regret that the choice of the people had not fallen upon some one more worthy and capable.

During periods of profound peace, when the State was undisturbed in its domestic concerns, and in its relations to the Federal Government, the administration of its political affairs was attended with much difficulty, and required a high order of administrative ability. At a time like the present, when we have just emerged from the most terrible conflict known to modern times, with homes made dreary and desolate by the heavy hand of war; the people impoverished, and groaning under public and private debts; the great industrial energies of the country sadly depressed; occupying in some respects the position of a State of the Federal Union, and in others, the condition of a conquered province, exercising only such privileges as the conqueror in his wisdom and mercy may allow; the loyalty of the people to the General Government doubted; their integrity questioned; their holiest aspirations for peace and restoration disbelieved, maligned and traduced, with a constant misapprehension of their most innocent actions and

---

*Journal of the House of Representatives of the State of Texas, Eleventh Legislature (1866), pp. 18–25.

intentions; with a frontier many hundred miles in extent, being deso-
lated by a murderous and powerful enemy, our devoted frontiersmen
filling bloody graves, their property given to the flames, or carried off
as booty, their little ones murdered, and their wives and daughters carried into a captivity more terrible than death, and reserved for tortures
such as savage cruelty and lust can alone inflict; unprotected by the
government we support, with troops quartered in the interior, where
there is peace and quiet; unwilling to send armed citizens to defend the
suffering border, for fear of arousing unjust suspicions as to the motive;
with a heavy debt created before the late war, and an empty treasury;
with an absolute necessity for a change in the laws to adapt ourselves
to the new order of things, and embarrassments in every part of our
internal affairs; under such circumstances, with such surroundings,
when so much depends upon prudence, and so great an amount of
patriotism and intelligence is required, I feel sadly oppressed with the
difficulties which lie before me. Under the most favorable attitude of
affairs it is impossible always to meet public expectation. Situated as
we now are, I beg of my fellow-citizens to form no hasty judgement of
my actions, but take time to consider of them and witness their effects
upon the country. Doubtless errors will occur. It is impossible for
human foresight to avoid them. I feel that I shall greatly need the generous indulgence of the country, and confidently anticipate a large measure of its forbearance and charity.

Notwithstanding the difficulties which beset us, and the untoward
direction given to measures proposed for the settlement of the grave
questions growing out of the late unhappy contest between the
Government and the Southern States, and notwithstanding the measures
so proposed have received the sanction of the National Legislature, yet,
my fellow-citizens, with proper conduct on our part, I do not despair of
receiving liberal and generous treatment from our Northern countrymen. I am not yet prepared to believe that the land of Franklin and
Hancock, of the Adams', of Hamilton and Jay, of Webster, and so
many other worthies of pure unsullied patriotism, is no longer a land of
good and great men, or that the lessons of unselfish devotion to country, taught by these illustrious and venerated fathers, have been wholly
forgotten. The wild hurricane of passion, engendered by fanaticism and
misguided philanthopy, augmented in its fury by the flames of civil war,
may sweep over the country, the warning voice of patriotism may be
unheeded, and hushed for a time, but when the storm subsides, and its
fury is expended, reason and justice, tempered with magnanimity and

a generous regard for every section of the Union, will resume their sway.

The true men of the country who have embalmed in their hearts the noble work of the founders of the government, who look to the sacred teachings of the constitution as the ark of safety for the American people, and who earnestly desire to perpetuate republican institutions, are the men to whom we must look for safety. Such, we have reason to believe, are yet in the land. They are already beginning to give tone to public sentiment, and soon we may anticipate that they will guide the councils of the nation, and control its destiny. How inviting the task for statesmen and philanthropists to renew, and place on an every enduring basis, the government erected by the toils and sufferings, and consecrated by the wisdom of Washington and his illustrious compeers! What a noble incentive to the pure, just and magnanimous in heart to enter upon the glorious task of restoring peace and harmony to the late fiercely contending sections of the American Union, of binding up and healing the ghastly wounds inflicted upon the country, of re-uniting in the bonds of affection and mutual confidence the hearts of countrymen estranged by war. A more inviting field was never presented to the consideration of the friends of freedom.

The good work has already been inaugurated. With a magnanimity of spirit that bespeaks a noble purpose, and a sagacity of mind indicative of the truest statesmanship, the President has extended to the people of the South liberal terms of restoration. His generous policy has endeared him to the great mass of the people, in every part of the country. This liberality has deeply touched the tenderest chords of the Southern heart. Sentiments of love and veneration for the government of our fathers have been aroused by it, which had long slumbered. Kindness and mercy have been far more potent in promoting fidelity to the Union, in a few short months, than could have been effected by bayonets, confiscation and the gallows, in long years of oppression. I am confident in the belief, my fellow-citizens, that the great mass of our Northern countrymen desire to treat us as brethren, and wish to see us restored to all the benefits of the government. I shall regard it the chiefest of my duties to foster and encourage this spirit, and shall inculcate among our own people the necessity of so demeaning themselves, that the breath of suspicion shall not sully their reputation for fidelity to the government, and, in this regard, shall labor to remove any erroneous impressions that may have been made as to a want of good faith and sincerity on the part of the people of the State.

Under the most trying circumstances, the people of the South have shown a constancy and devotion, rarely equalled, to a cause considered by them as sacred and holy. When they were isolated from the world, girdled around and penetrated by armies and navies, more powerful in numbers and the appliances of war than were ever before marshaled against one people, threatened with servile insurrection, suffering for food and clothing, with smouldering ruins and burning districts on every hand, the contest was continued, until almost every household mourned its dead, and until its mightiest chieftans and their most devoted followers had fallen, or succumbed to numbers they could no longer resist or evade. When all was lost, save honor, they yielded. Terms were offered and frankly and unreservedly accepted. We were invited to renew our allegiance to the government. As an evidence of sincerity, with hardly an exception, the Amnesty Oath of the President, authorized by Act of Congress, was taken by the people. The abolition of slavery has been recognized in our fundamental law. The people abide by and support the acts of Congress, and the Proclamations of the Executive of the Nation on this subject. And although much has been said and done by unfriendly parties, to breed disturbance and distrust, yet the people are pursuing the even tenor of their way, and giving proofs of fidelity to the government that will, in the end, convince all who honestly desire peace and restoration.

Having been a resident of Texas for a quarter of a century, familiarly acquainted with all her prominent citizens, having served in the Councils of the State for fifteen years, and shared the dangers and toils of the late war with her soldiers, recently mingled much with the people, and corresponded with them in every section of the State within the past few months, I claim to know something of the actual and truthful condition of affairs. I do not hesitate to declare that the great body of the people are earnestly desirous of performing all their obligations to the General Government. A people who have won the respect and admiration of the world for their chivalry, high daring and fortitude, will not be doubted by generous and brave spirits when they assert their loyalty.

In the administration of the affairs of the State, it shall be my constant endeavor to recommend and aid in carrying out such measures as will insure exact justice to all classes of men, of every political faith, religious creed, race and color. The changed relations, so suddenly brought about, of the white and black races, will require of us much thoughtful consideration. It is a duty we owe alike to ourselves and to humanity, to enact laws that will secure the freed people the full protection of all the rights of person and property guaranteed them by our Amended Constitution. The day is not far distant, in my judgment, when the black people will be convinced that their truest friends are those with whom they have sported in youth, and who have cared for them from their infancy. I shall give the subject the closest attention, and shall not fail, from time to time, to make such suggestions as experience may dictate, in order to render this class of our population useful to themselves and the country.

The condition of the frontier shall receive my serious attention. At the earliest moment, I shall endeavor to secure from the General Government adequate and permanent protection, and will, at the same time, use every exertion to have such treaties, made by the proper authorities, as will insure future security to the people. In the event, a sufficient number of troops cannot be procured from the Government, for the protection of the frontier, I shall not hesitate to urge expenditures by the State for this purpose. The people of that region, have already suffered with a patience and fortitude truly commendable. They are a bulwark to the older settled portions of the country, and if they give way, and are broken up in their homes, the loss of life and property, so long borne by them, will fall upon sections now enjoying peace and prosperity.

The prompt and efficient administration of the laws, their enforcement, and the protection of the life, liberty and property of the citizen; due obedience to the Constitution and Laws of the General Government, with a firm and just maintenance of the rights of the State; an early redemption of liabilities already incurred, contracting no new ones, without making adequate provision for their payment, with an endeavor to place the credit of the State at the highest possible standard; reforms in the laws, regulating the assessment and collection of taxes, so as to place the burthens of taxation equally upon the people; retrenchment in the expenditure of the public money in every branch of the Government, where it can be done with propriety; requiring the interest due the School Fund to be paid, with as much leniency to Railroad Companies as a prudent regard for the fund, and the general interest of the country, will allow; the re-organization of the common school system, and the establishment of a State University, at the earliest period compatible with the depressed financial condition of our affairs; liberal encouragement to internal improvements; fostering the charitable institutions, provided for the alleviation of the suffering, and the improvement of the afflicted and unfortunate portion of our population; an earnest desire to assuage party rancor engendered by political differences, and to promote harmony and good feeling among the people; and a determination to satisfy the authorities of the General Government, that the people of Texas are loyally disposed, earnestly desirous of an early restoration, and worthy of it on just and liberal terms; animated by such sentiments, I shall endeavor to conduct the affairs of the Government so as to promote the happiness and general welfare of the people in every section of the State.

It is known to my fellow-citizens, that I was opposed to the secession of the Southern States from the Federal Union, and exerted what influence I had to prevent it, and, as a delegate in the Convention of 1861, voted against the Ordinance which declared the separation. It would be a useless consumption of time to enumerate the reasons that impelled me to this course. Devoted as I was, and still am, to that Government which the blood of my ancestors had contributed to rear, for the protection of the rights of man, and accustomed, from earliest boyhood, to look upon the Flag of the Union as the proudest symbol of freedom, I turned, with horror, from the bloody vision of civil war that crowded on my sight. But while I regarded secession as impolitic and ruinous, I looked with scarcely less dread upon that docrine which asserted an undefined and unlimited power in the General Government to use its military force against the States of the Union. When the appeal to arms, was made, however, I pursued what seemed to me the path of duty. I followed the fortunes of a majority of my fellow-citizens, and shared with them the fate of the conflict. Others, who entertained sentiments similar to my own, took different views of their duty. I accord to them, motives as pure and patriotic, for their action, as I claim for myself. Now, that the contest is over, I have felt it to be the most sacred duty of patriotism, to labor in restoring peace and harmony to an afflicted and suffering country. The people of this State are alike impressed with this sentiment, and should it be the unhappy fortune of our common country to continue estranged, I am sure it will not be the fault of Texas.

Gentlemen of the Legislature, for the accomplishment of an enlightened and judicious policy of State Government, and a cordial restoration of our Federal relations, your earnest co-operation is confidently expected. The career of Texas has been eventful. She has had her days of darkness and sunshine, of suffering and prosperity. In all the vicissitudes of fortune she has borne herself proudly. A long list of heroes, patriots and statesmen adorn the pages of her history. We have their wisdom and example to guide us. Let us profit by their teachings, emulate their virtues and rival them in unselfish devotion to the country.

We are to-day, gentlemen, entering upon a new era, contributing another chapter to the already checkered and remarkable history of the State. The surroundings are uninviting—the future appears inauspicious. But the patriot should not despair. Let each one of us perform our allotted parts, with an honest and sincere desire to restore the country and promote its future quiet and good order. Moderation and forbearance on the part of those in power will have the happiest effect. If we act with propriety, we will be heartily sustained by our own people, and at the same time, disarm those who would oppress us, and strengthen those who desire to assist us. A suffering people are to be relieved—a great nation is to be saved. It will require the loftiest patriotism, and the purest devotion to principle. An enlarged and liberal charity should be exercised toward those who may differ with us in opinion. Great ends are to be accomplished, not by vituperation, and abuse of opponents, but by dignified appeals to reason and the nobler impulses of the heart.

Fellow-citizens, I cannot conclude what I have to say, on this occasion, without acknowledging to the people of Texas, the profound obligations under which I am placed by the high and unexpected honor conferred upon me. I know that I shall be unable to serve them with the ability which their situation demands. But nothing that energy and fidelity can supply, shall be wanting, on my part, to retain the confidence so generously bestowed.

Relying upon the intelligence and patriotism of the people, and expecting an enlightened assistance from their chosen counsellors, invoking the aid of the Great Ruler of Nations in our behalf, trusting that He will incline the hearts of the American people aright, and finally, restore our afflicted country to perfect peace and prosperity, I enter upon the duties before me.

X

Edmund Jackson

DAVIS

1870–1874

Courtesy of Archives Division, Texas State Library

EDMUND JACKSON DAVIS (*October 2, 1827–February 7, 1883*) was born in St. Augustine, Florida, and at the age of eleven moved with his widowed mother to Galveston, Texas. He studied law and after admission to the bar practiced law in Laredo, Corpus Christi, and Brownsville.

From 1850 to 1852 Davis was deputy collector of Customs headquartered at Laredo. He served as judge of the Rio Grande Valley District from 1854 to 1861.

Because he was defeated for election as a representative to the Secession Convention in 1861, he became alienated from the southern cause. During the Civil War Davis organized a regiment of Unionists who had fled to Mexico. After being captured by Confederate forces and narrowly escaping hanging, he led an unsuccessful Union attack on Laredo in 1864.

Davis was a delegate to the 1866 Texas Constitutional Convention and served as president of the 1868 Constitutional Convention.

In a special four-day election from November 30 to December 3, 1869, held under the direction of the federal military commander, Davis, a Radical Republican, won a narrow victory over his opponent, a moderate Republican supported by the Democrats. Also in this election, the people ratified a new state constitution, which, among other things, set the term of office of governor and other high officials at four years.

Davis assumed office on January 8, 1870. Texas was fully readmitted to the Union in March 1870 and on April 16, 1870, the military commander transferred all authority to the civil government.

Inaugural Address *
April 28, 1870

MY FELLOW CITIZENS OF TEXAS:

This day the government of your State and the control of your destinies is handed over to you. What may fairly be termed the second annexation of Texas is now consummated; but, a Texas very different from that of 1845 is found assuming her functions as a State. That Texas brought with her single star also her thousands of slaves, this Texas knows no bondsmen on her soil. We may differ in our opinion of the manner of bringing about this great change, and the necessity for it. We live too near (in time) the scene of this struggle to ever agree that Providence may have directed the issue as part of the great work of improvement and progress of the human race. But sensible men can even now agree to accept the situation as they find it, and after ten years of war and civil disorganization, take a fresh departure in political affairs.

It may be said that the American revolution, opening in 1776, with the proclamation "that all men are created equal," had its verification, and made its promise good only in 1870. But it is fair to admit that few on either side either calculated or desired the full result when entering this closing struggle. While on the one side, the aid of the God of battles was confidently asked to sustain a structure, of which the very corner-stone was a denial of the truth of this declaration, when applied to those whom habit had divested in our minds of their share of humanity; on the other, the sword was mainly taken to preserve a glorious nationality. We did not see then, and it required those years of misfortune to show us the foundation of our trouble. Let us accept this result as an indication and lesson that there is no safe neutral ground for human judgment between right and wrong—that we cannot afford to be unjust to the weakest of God's creatures. Let us be wholly right.

This struggle has, too, taught us a further lesson in self-government.

House Journal of the Twelfth Legislature, State of Texas (1870), pp. 14–16.

It had been fondly imagined that our government, in the name and form and as carried out by the general government and the respective States, was perfect; that no human device could improve it. Our education in this belief had been so decided, that we were not even inclined to try to improve it. But we can now see that this, like all other edifices of human creation, had its imperfections, and required repair and improvement. It was designed to, but as time progressed we discovered that it did not "promote the general welfare and secure the blessings of liberty," in all parts of the union, even to the class which esteemed itself the special object of the provision. While the general government was restrained from all violation of the right of life, liberty and property, it was conceded that the local government had no such restraint, accordingly local despotisms often flourished under the name of State government. There, free speech and thought was limited by the will of the majority, until individual freedom disappeared. It is not so now, and cannot (it is sufficient to say) be so hereafter.

While local self-government still remains, it is within the just bounds, that there is a supervisory power over all, far withdrawn from local prejudice and bias, which will temper State action within the limit of security, freedom, and justice to all. This will prove the better government, and under this, freedom at the North or South, on the lakes or on the Pacific, or the Gulf, will be one and the same. Through the length and breadth of the land, free speech and liberty of mind, as well as person, henceforth prevail.

In this faith let us enter upon the great work before us of re-organization, and let us take a survey of the position we are called to occupy. We find that we are about preparing a government for, and shaping the destinies of a territory larger than most of the great earthly powers. Let us realize that we control a part of our globe, large and fertile enough to hold a greater population than the millions now owing allegiance to the National Government. That as it were, we are the advanced guard of this mighty host, and that as we prepare the way for them, so will they find it will be industrious, prosperous, intelligent, law-abiding, temperate; or immoral, lawless, degraded and miserable, as we now plan and devise.

We have it in our hands to place our great State at once among the foremost in wealth, population and civilization, and if we can be made fully sensible of the extent of this, our opportunity and responsibility, we will not fail in the performance of our part. Let us recollect that, in coming years, when time has softened our prejudices and dissipated the memory of the jealousies and party contests of to-day, our reminiscences of this epoch will be pleasant or the contrary, as we now labor for the good of our fellows and the State, or for our own gratification and aggrandizement.

The time has come for us to learn other distinctions than loyal and disloyal. Let us hereafter know no other than that of the good and bad citizen. Let us cultivate a belief that our neighbor who differs in opinion with us, may so differ honestly, and devote ourselves only to emulate him in attachment to the right, and in determination to promote the public good. We must divide into parties, and differ in regard to public policy; and fit and proper is it, in a free country, that this should so be, but let us have this variance with mutual toleration.

Fellow-citizens, the disease under which our political system labored was a severe one, and required a sharp remedy. It unquestionably could only be cured by the application of the national sword. Strange to say, the military, the recognized right arm of despotism, was here summoned to the aid of liberty, and, against our will, has secured it to us. The day is not distant when we will all assent to this; now the heat of the struggle is too strong with us. In no other land has this phenomenon been seen, and, no where but among people educated from infancy to place the civil superior to the military law, may we expect to see what we now witness—the military coming forward (after tasting for years the seductive sweets of unlimited power) with alacrity, as to an agreeable duty, to surrender into the hands of the people a power always temperately executed. No where else than in a republic, where the military are of and from the people, can they be as here, the defenders of freedom. Let us give them, without stint, the credit and honor which is their due. We must, as fair-minded men, concede so much, though this employment of the military may have been totally against our will.

All, too, can agree that it was an unpleasant necessity which forced upon the Republic the coercion of her citizens; all may grieve that this necessity existed, and all now join in the hope that the same has passed away, never again in our history to return. That with enduring peace, will return the respect for order and the forms and majesty of civil law, which, inherited from our forefathers, has followed the English language to all parts of the world.

XI

Richard

COKE

1874–1876

Courtesy of Archives Division, Texas State Library

RICHARD COKE (*March 13, 1829–May 14, 1897*) was born in Williamsburg, Virginia, where he received his common school education. At the age of twenty he graduated from William and Mary College. He studied law and was admitted to the bar in 1850. That same year, he moved to Waco, Texas. In 1859 Governor Hardin Runnels appointed him to an Indian Commission.

At the outbreak of the Civil War, Coke joined the Confederate Army as a private and later served as a captain in the Fifteenth Texas Regiment.

In 1865 Coke was appointed a district judge and the following year was elected as a judge of the Texas Supreme Court. He was removed from that post in 1867 by the federal military commander as "an impediment to reconstruction."

In the December 1873 gubernatorial election, Coke, a Democrat, defeated incumbent Governor Davis by a commanding margin and took office on January 15, 1874.

Governor Davis declared the election law unconstitutional, refused to vacate the office of governor, and appealed to President Grant for troops. Grant refused to intervene.

Coke proceeded to organize his administration, and for a period, Texas had two state governments. However, Davis was soon forced to abandon his effort.

Coke won a second term on February 15, 1876, in a special election which also ratified the new state constitution. He delivered his second inaugural address on April 25, 1876. He resigned the following December to begin a term as senator to which he had been elected. Lieutenant Governor Richard B. Hubbard completed Coke's second term, which ended on January 21, 1879.

Inaugural Address *
January 15, 1874

FELLOW-CITIZENS OF TEXAS:

After passing through many vicissitudes and trials, and being chastened in the ordeal of adversity, you at length have reached the haven where the rights and powers of self-government are yours, and the duties and responsibilities of that condition are devolved upon you. Today, for the first time since she emerged from the ruin and disaster of the great civil war, Texas sees the inauguration in her Capitol of a government chosen by the free and untrammeled suffrage of her people, having their confidence and looking to them for support and accountability. Let the heart of the patriot throb with joy, for the old landmarks of constitutional, representative government, so long lost, are this day restored, and the ancient liberties of the people of Texas re-established. The virtue and intelligence of the country, no longer ostracised, now wield their legitimate influence, and the government of Texas henceforth is to be administered in the interest and for the benefit of the people, and to reflect their will. I congratulate you, fellow-citizens, upon this grand consummation, upon your restoration to that which is the birthright of the people of every State in this great Republic—the right of local self-government, a right reserved by each of the several States when they formed the Union and created the Federal government, that right which reserves to the States respectively the power to regulate and control their internal and domestic affairs, and so to shape their policy and direct the operations of their government as to give scope and development to the inclinations and genius of their people. The wise founders of our government foresaw that over so vast an expanse of territory, so diversified in climate, soil, production, and population, perpetual jarring and discord would ensue, arising out of the different and, in many cases, conflicting interests and views of the various States, if the notions of proper public policy of any one or

*Archive and History Department of the State Library, ed., *Governors' Messages: Coke to Ross (Inclusive) 1874–1891* (Austin: A. C. Baldwin and Sons, 1916), pp. 1–9.

more of the States should be enforced on another State, contrary of its own opinions of what was best for its interests. Hence the fundamental idea, which underlies the Federal constitution, is a recognition of the perfect right of each State in its own way to work out its own destiny, and seek the prosperity and happiness of its people, subject only to the requirement that its government shall be republican in form, leaving to the general government the care and control of all matters pertaining to the common interest and general welfare of all the States. This wise distribution of power leaves in the State governments respectively, which are immediately under the influence and control of the people and reflect directly the popular will, jurisdiction over the nearest and dearest rights of the citizen to regulate his conduct, the use, possession, title, and descent of his property, his duties as a member of society, in fine, to govern him and his family, his home and his fireside, in every particular wherein the interests of society require that they shall be governed. How indispensable to the liberty of the citizen it is that the government which thus controls and deals with his person and property should be near him and directly accountable to him. On the other hand, to the Federal government, which is more remote, inaccessible, and therefore not so directly accountable to the people, is delegated power over matters that do not so nearly concern the people, in which they are not so directly and personally interested, but in which the people of all the States have a common and general interest. Under our Federal constitution these two powers are so adjusted as to work in perfect harmony, each achieving in its appropriate sphere the desired result, and the two combined constituting that grand fabric of free government which is the pride and boast of every American citizen. In this plan of government, the wisest ever devised by the ingenuity of man, the right of local self-government, so indispensable to a preservation of the liberties of the people and to their material prosperity, is the fundamental principle. In virtue of it, each State, being free to pursue its interests and the happiness and prosperity of its people according to its own ideas of proper policy, possesses opportunity and margin for development and advancement, which is limited only by its resources and the wisdom of its government and people. Having an equal voice through its representatives in the administration of the Federal government; sharing its burdens and its benefits alike with its sisters, and having with them a common interest and a common pride in its greatness and power, and its beneficence and care, each State may in the career chosen by the will of its own people speed onward to the fulfillment of its destiny, while the Federal government, uniting in itself the combined efforts of all the States, receives momentum from its constituents and represents within its constitutional sphere the aggregate greatness and power of them all. The adoption of the thirteenth, fourteenth and fifteenth amendments to the Federal constitution, which are as binding as if promulgated in the original instrument, has taken from the States and vested in the Federal government powers, formerly residing in the State, and it is true that in the operative agency of the Federal government there is a natural tendency to an absorption of power from the States, which tendency was greatly stimulated during our civil war and has grown constantly since. Still the essential principles of local self-government remain to the States respectively untouched, and now that slavery and secession are dead and buried beyond the possibility of resurrection and no sectional question disturbs the public mind, since the States recently undergoing reconstruction have been restored to their constitutional relations with the Federal government and the people remitted to their original rights and duties, since a true and lasting peace has come and the power and authority of the Federal government, within limits which cover all the issues of the war, have been amply vindicated and are acknowledged by all, since it is the inherent right of every American citizen to do so in the interest of good government, has not the time arrived when, without being obnoxious to the charge of disloyalty, we may recur to original principles on which the government was founded, discuss them among ourselves and base our political action upon them? Is it inconsistent with a patriotic devotion to the Union and the constitution to do so? Is it not rather the highest duty of the citizen to study and understand the principles of the government under which he lives, and in defense of which, if necessary, he would lay down his life? If, while perpetuating the Union, we, at the same time, would preserve the right of local self-government in the States from the dangers which menace it in the constantly growing process of centralization, we must exert such political influence as we have for the protection of that priceless heritage, and this we can only do by recurring to the principles of the constitution, invoking a strict adherence to them in the administration of the government and making them the basis and guide of primary popular action. If the original framework of our government and the fundamental canons of the constitution are to be preserved and handed down to our posterity, as we received them, we must appeal to the virtue and intelligence of the voting masses of the people. They sometimes, under the influence of excitement, passion, or feeling, go astray, but their sober second thought is the perfection of human wisdom, and ever brings them back to the maintenance of correct principle and good government. In every section and quarter of this great republic evidence of this fact is being given in manifestations of popular enthusiasm and determination for a return to honesty and economy and the limitations of the constitution in the administration of the government. In this disposition of the American people to return to old constitutional landmarks so soon after the subsidence of the great civil strife, which caused a departure from them, we recognize the popular instinct which tolerated what the necessities of the times demanded, but keenly appreciate the fact that the necessity no longer exists and demand a restoration of government, based on fixed principles. The patriotic believer in republican representative government finds in this manifestation abundant cause for rejoicing, because he sees in it that conservative quality of the popular mind and heart which is the surest guaranty of the stability and permanence of our institutions. Opposing political parties, aspiring to the control and direction of the government, have existed under every limited government in the world, and will always exist. In a government like ours, they are a necessary consequence. When based on principle and the advocacy of great measures of public policy, when they demand popular confidence and support on account of the excellence of their respective theories of constitutional construction, when "Measures, not men," is in truth their controlling idea, they constitute the staunchest prop, the most powerful element of support, and the most effective preservative of constitutional government to be found in the organization of our society. The masses of the people are educated by them to an understanding of the principles of the government. But when abandoning or ignoring principle, political parties become the mere partisans of men in their scramble for power and place, they are hurtful and demoralizing to government and people, and a bane and curse upon the country. This is not a country for personal parties and personal issues. In the empires and kingdoms of the old world, where opposing dynasties marshal their adherents in contests for crowns and sceptres, each claiming to be master of the people by divine right, such parties are legitimate, because in full accord with their theory of government. But here where the people are sovereign and the government constitutional, where all men are free and equal, and where, in a great measure, the preservation of our peculiar form of government and with it the liberties of our people depend upon the policy and measures of administration and the principles which guide and control it, no party should be trusted with power which does not boldly avow and blazon on its banners its leading principles and measures of policy, and ask for them the popular indorsement and approval. The great civil war with its madness and passion is a thing of the past, while patriotism, broad and comprehensive as our common country, now possesses the hearts of the people. Reason and cool, unclouded intelligence have resumed their sway. Henceforth acrimony and bitterness and appeals to prejudice and hate in political contests must give way to enlightened discussion of the element and the principles of government, and the party which would propitiate popular favor must achieve that result by appealing to the sober judgment and intelligence of the people and through the excellence of its principles and plan of administration. Hence, I repeat, the time has arrived when the people of Texas, recurring to fundamental principles and drawing new inspiration from them, should base their political action on them and demand of their servants a strict adherence to, and observance of them in their official conduct. The limitations of the constitution observed, and the rights of local self-government preserved, as it now exists, from further encroachment, the future is bright with promise of stability for the government and happiness and prosperity for the people. Let the people be true to themselves, and exercise with intelligence, with watchfulness and care their elective franchise demanding, as a condition to a bestowal of place and trust and power, capacity, unsullied honor and integrity, and unswerving devotion to the principles of the inner spirit of the constitution—and our government, the freest on earth, will go down and carry its blessings to our remotest posterity. Under it, the inestimable boon is now ours of seeking the progress, development and advancement of Texas, and the happiness and prosperity of our people in our own way. The genius, tastes, sentiments, feelings, and will of the great mass of the people of Texas will find expression in the administration of their State government, and the destiny of Texas, her glory and her history, will be the work of her own people.

We have the fairest land that the sun of heaven shines on, rich in all the elements of greatness, in vastness and extent, in fertility of soil, in variety of climate and productions, in ore and mineral, in beauty and grandeur of scenery, and in salubrity and healthfulness, and richer still in the heroic history of its people. This glorious land is ours. Forgetting the troubles and adversity of the past, except the lessons of wisdom to be drawn from its bitter experience, and remembering only its glories, let us in the spirit of true statesmanship look to the future which lies bright before us, beckoning us on to a higher and more advanced civilization, to progress, development, prosperity and greatness, and by seizing the opportunities in our reach show that we are worthy of our magnificent country and of the heroes and statesmen who won and transmitted it. With firm reliance on the capabilities of our people, an unfaltering faith in the greatness of the destiny of Texas and a determined purpose to reach the highest excellence in all that pertains to her development and to the material prosperity, and moral, intellectual and political advancement of her people, let us mould the action of our government to the achievement of these grand results. Let our watchword be progress,—and I mean by progress that vigor which may be imparted to the natural growth of Texas by skillful and generous cultivation, the policy which is broad and comprehensive enough in its sweep to discern and utilize all the resources of the State, which leaves none of its wealth unmined and none of the elements untouched which may be used in building up its greatness, that healthy, steady, sturdy advancement which is born of intelligent, considerate, persistent effort to be up and abreast with the times in all that is good and great, and which carries along with it increased and increasing prosperity and elevation to both State and people. The great purpose embraced in this idea should animate our people and pervade all departments of our government. We should mature, adopt and pursue an educational policy, an internal improvement policy, an immigration policy, and a financial policy, each to be improved as time and experience may suggest, and as the changing conditions of the State may require. With a common free school system which shall secure to every child in the State an education fitting him for the high duties of American citizenship, an immigration policy which shall make known to the world the unrivaled advantages of Texas, her liberal homestead laws, and the cheapness of her rich and productive lands, the remunerating prices of labor, the healthfulness of her climate, the magnificent rewards of thrift, energy and industry, within her limits, and by appropriate legislation stimulate and increase the steady and swelling tide of enterprising, thrifty and intelligent population, now pouring into her borders from every quarter of the old and new world; a wise and liberal policy, which shall invite the investment of capital in works of internal improvement, especially in the construction of railroads, by giving ample margin of profit and by friendly and just legislation inspiring confidence in the good will of our people towards such enterprises, now so absolutely essential to the growth and development of Texas, reserving at the same time such powers over them as will surely subordinate them to the will, interests and supremacy of the people; and with a financial policy running parallel with a strictly economical and thoroughly honest administration of the government, which shall reduce taxation to the lowest figure adequate to the expense of the government, the prompt payment of the public debt and the preservation unblemished of the credit of the State—to these I will add a system which will supplement the efforts of the Federal government for the protection of our suffering frontier, and give that protection to the inhabitants of that portion of the State to which they are clearly and justly entitled, thereby opening up an area of magnificent territory to settlement and productiveness, while discharging a high obligation to the frontier people; with the inauguration and steady, judicious prosecution of these lines of policy, Texas will develop, in the near future, a greatness truly magnificent. Wealth, population and political power will flow in upon us, and every interest and industry will be buoyed in the rising tide of the country's prosperity. Let us be true to ourselves and posterity and use with wisdom the munificent gifts bestowed upon us by a kind Providence, and we will reap the rich reward of our efforts in the prosperity and happiness of our people and the greatness and glory of our beloved State.

We must remember that this is an eminently practical era, that abstract principles, barren of practical results, find no favor in the popular mind. The people demand facts, results. The world is moving around them and if they stand still, the party in power will justly be held responsible. They cannot see the excellence of principles which keep them in the rear while others are advancing in the general march of improvement. Hence the political party which would commend its principles to popular favor must show by its works, by the results it accomplishes when in power, that it stands upon no platform of dead abstractions, but upon living, moving principles, in full harmony with the spirit of the age, having the power of expansion and adaptation to the changing conditions of society, fully capable of meeting its wants and responding to its demands in all the phases it may assume. A government adhering in its operations closely to constitutional restrictions, marked by vigor of administration as well as the strictest honesty and economy, giving perfect protection to life, liberty and property by a vigorous enforcement of the laws, advancing the moral and intellectual condition of the people by means of common free schools, filling the country with population by means of an immigration policy which shall actively promote the object, liberally fostering by friendly legislation the construction of railroads which shall give rapid and cheap transportation to the production of the country, and maintaining the honor and credit of the State by paying the public debt, and incurring no debt in future without at the same time providing a specific fund for its payment, is demanded by the times and the people of Texas, and nothing less will satisfy them. Let us respond fully to this call of duty and patriotism, and prepare to acquit ourselves of the duties and responsibilities now devolving and to be devolved upon us, in such manner that hereafter, when the great tribunal of the people shall pass judgment upon our acts, it shall find not only their liberties preserved, but their material prosperity and the power and greatness of the State advanced.

The attainment of these grand results need involve no accumulation of public indebtedness, or the imposition of further burdens upon our people. On the contrary, a careful administration of our government, added to a prudent husbanding of our resources and due attention to proper retrenchment of all unnecessary expenditures, will enable us to secure not only these but other blessings to our State and people, and at the same time enable us to take from their shoulders a large portion of the load of taxation now resting on them. The healthy development superinduced by a wise administration of these essential measures will add new sources to our revenues each day, and thus in a manner furnish the means necessary for their due execution. Demanded alike by the exigencies of the hour and the united voice of our people, their successful inauguration must command our early and assiduous attention and our most untiring energies. Standing today in the threshold of a new era in the history of our State, our thoughts naturally recur to the past with its checkered vista of storms and sunshine. We remember the privations, hardships, struggles and victories of the fathers, the gradual advancement of civilization and the building up of waste places, the development of our resources, the increase of population, and we look around us today and find, as a reward for steadfast devotion and constant toil and effort, a State, the peer of any in this proud commonwealth of States. We love Texas because we have, day by day, watched her growth and contributed in part to her development. It is the home of our nativity or adoption, and we cheerfully lay upon her altar the purest treasures of our heart's devotion. Her government and the administration of her laws receive our most zealous watchfulness, because committed to our hands by her people. But we do not forget that a part of our sovereignty is lodged elsewhere, and that as patriots we owe duties and obligations to another authority which in its sphere equally demands our loyalty and devotion. As Texans we stand by Texas, as American citizens we stand by the Union and are prepared to peril our lives in defense of our national government, its interests and its honor, as Texans have done before. Its interests are ours, its prosperity is ours, and to us belongs a part at least of its glory and its greatness. Side by side with our sister States, we have labored for the achievement of a common result—the development and advancement of our common country. And Texas will prove no laggard in the race, but with the stride of a young giant will press forward to the fulfillment of her every duty.

Fellow-citizens of Texas, this day I assume the high trust to which you have called me. Chosen by a portion of my fellow-citizens of one political belief, I am not unmindful of the fact that others of a different faith are citizens of Texas and equally entitled to the benefits and blessings of good government. We must forget the passions and prejudices of the past, and vie with each other only in a generous emulation to subserve the true interests of our glorious State. Invoking the charity and forbearance of my fellow-citizens, and humbly asking the favor and guidance of Almighty God, I announce to you my acceptance of the responsible duties devolved upon me, and my unwavering determination, so far as in me lies, to so discharge them that the interests and liberties of our people will be protected and preserved, and the honor and glory of Texas advanced.

Second Inaugural Address *
April 25, 1876

FELLOW-CITIZENS AND GENTLEMEN
OF THE LEGISLATURE:

After years of trial and struggle, the people of Texas have at length inaugurated a government made in all its parts by themselves. Its faults and errors, as well as its blessings, have no uncertain paternity. The highest exercise of sovereign power of which a State in the American Union is capable, is that through which the people of Texas have swept out of existence the old government and enacted in its stead that which today has been put in operation in all its departments. Thus has a great revolution been accomplished, without violence or disorder, and with no other conflict than the attrition of opposing opinions in the field of argument and discussion, preparatory to the grand arbitrament of the peaceful ballot. Free discussion by press and people, and a free ballot, have eliminated from the aggregate mass of popular sentiment and opinion the sovereign will of the people, and given it expression in the new instrument of fundamental law under which we are now assembled. This is the sixth time in the history of Texas that this sovereign right has been exercised. The Constitution of 1836, the work of the fathers of the Republic, of the heroic age of Texas, of the men who bared their bosoms to the storms of war in defense of the right of local self-government, and by their wisdom in council and valor in the field achieved the independence of Texas; that of 1845, which merged the glorious Lone Star of the Republic in the constellation of the American Union; the Constitution of 1861, born amid the muttering thunders which presaged the coming of the great civil war, and expiring in 1865 under the heel of the conqueror; that of 1866, rudely thrust aside and ignored under the reconstruction laws of Congress; and the Constitution of 1870, just superseded—all

*Archive and History Department of the State Library, ed., *Governors' Messages: Coke to Ross (Inclusive) 1874–1891* (Austin: A. C. Baldwin and Sons, 1916), pp. 167–73.

these, in the respective periods of their adoption and enforcement, represented the will of the people as moulded and fixed by the circumstances surrounding them, and in turn have been discarded as changed conditions of State and society have required corresponding changes of government. A comparison of these instruments of organic law with the last expression of the popular will, now about being enforced, will furnish another exemplification of the great truth that change is the one inexorable condition of all human government. There must be growth and advancement, or retrogression and decay. Government can no more be stationary than can society or the members of which it is composed. The constitutions of governments in the American States have, until a few years past, been mere outlines and landmarks, and declarations of principle purely fundamental, leaving the inner details of the structure to be moulded and fashioned, altered, amended or abolished, as time or cotemporaneous circumstances might require.

In the more recently framed constitutions we plainly see a wide departure from the beaten track of constitutional structure, and in none of them is this more apparent than in the new Constitution of Texas.

The accepted theory of American constitutional government is that State constitutions are limitations upon, rather than grants of power; and as a general rule, not without its exceptions, that powers not prohibited exist in the State government. Hence, express prohibitions are necessary upon the powers the people would withhold from the State government, and as time and circumstances and experience suggest their wisdom, these restrictions upon the powers of government have multiplied in the more recently created instruments of fundamental law. Many causes have conspired to produce these great changes of constitutional theory, and prominent among them are the enormous amounts of capital concentrated in few hands, operating under charters which perpetuate its power; immense railroad systems, which drive off competition and monopolize the carrying trade of the country; the wonderful growth of towns and cities, whose immediate local governments are peculiarly subject to abuses and malign influences, general extravagance, and frequent corruptions of all departments of government, of late years becoming so alarming—all producing results which necessitate a clearer definition and closer guardianship of the rights of the people; and, for their protection, constitutional barriers not demanded by the conditions of society a quarter of a century ago.

Steam and electricity, invention and enterprise, have wrought such changes in the conditions surrounding the country, have pushed its wealth and progress forward with such rapidity, have diversified its industries and enlarged its interests to such an extent, that government must expand to embrace within its regulating control the vast and frequently inharmonious relations which have been created, and while protecting them in their commerce with each other, must protect the public interest against them all. In doing this, the result has been the formation of instruments of organic law more voluminous, more detailed, containing more numerous limitations, and asserting, for protection of the people, more extensive powers in the government than did constitutions of the olden time. Instead of being obnoxious to the charge of descending into the details of legislation, made against constitutions, thus departing from the old standard, these instruments simply respond to the demands of the times and the exigencies of the State. They are keeping pace with the progress of society, and conforming to its conditions; meeting the attacks upon the rights of the public, which in the growth and diversification of interest, each struggling for its own advancement at the expense of all others, are constantly being changed. The constitutions of Texas of 1836 and 1845 do not more fully represent the demands of the country, the requirements and exigencies of those periods, than does our new Constitution, amended, as public sentiment already demands it shall be, those of 1876.

In this instrument we see mirrored the result of issues made in the politics of the State, in the halls of legislation, and in the primary assemblies of the people during the last decade; and we see faithfully reflected in its restrictions upon the power of government, as in its assertion of powers, the dangers of the past, a recurrence of which is so well guarded against in future. The instrument presents in its fundamental and leading features a basis on which a government may be reared, eminently conservative of all the purposes for which government may be reared, eminently conservative of all the purposes for which government is instituted; and adapted to a sound and healthy growth and development of the State. It may possibly be, in some respects, too restrictive; but when such is the case, the error is on the safe side, and while temporary inconvenience may ensue, no permanent injury will result. On all questions of principle, affecting the great leading interests of the State, the wisdom of its provisions is conspicuous. In portions of its administrative machinery, however, are to be found defects which, it is believed, will enfeeble the efficiency of the government in its practical operations, which the best interests of the State require shall at once be remedied. Upon the threshold of the first administration of the new government, the time and circumstances are propitious for the correction of errors, which have not yet fixed themselves in our system, and created relations which later would require more violent disruption; and as we value the great reforms so much needed, inaugurated in our new plan of government, the more ready we should be to correct mistakes, whose consequences may mislead the public mind as to their source, and bring undeserved reproach upon wise and wholesome changes. It should be remembered that popular reactions are usually sweeping, and that the public mind does not discriminate nicely between causes when a great evil or burden must be removed.

History is filled with examples of great changes and revolutions in government set in motion by trivial causes, but acquiring momentum in their progress, and reaching in results far beyond the ostensible design which incepted them. Nor should it be forgotten that reforms—those measures of public policy whose object is the prevention of abuses—are usually silent in their operation, attracting no attention from the general public, who frequently, while enjoying the immunities from evil and benefits they bring, lose sight of the source whence their prosperity comes; while vices in government, especially those which meet and assail the people, and are before their eyes every day in practical life, in the judicial and executive administrations, are trumpet-tongued, and proclaim themselves throughout the length and breath of the land. Let us take care that defects like these are not permitted to fill the popular mind and create public opinion as to the merits of the new Constitution. Let us heed the voice of experience, and while the mind of the country is in a frame to discriminate clearly, supplement the good work already done with still another effort which shall make it more perfect.

At no time in the history of Texas have the exigencies of the State more urgently demanded the highest efforts of her public servants, and the coolest reflection and most deliberate judgment of the people, and he who can write his name highest on the list of those through whose efforts the common weal has been secured, will, indeed, be a public benefactor, entitled to the honors and gratitude of the country. While it may not be reserved to any one to achieve a singular distinction in this regard, an earnest and assiduous devotion and an honest effort will meet its appropriate reward and to this we can all aspire. The country and people whose welfare depends upon our deliberations and action need and expect a government light in its burdens, effective in administration, and certain in its securities for person and property. Naught else is necessary to ensure prosperity and continued progress and advancement. With such government the elements of greatness so abundant in the noble State we represent, in the hands of our intelligent adventurous and enterprising people, will combine, and evolve from the womb of the future a destiny of grander proportions than the most gorgeous dream of the enthusiast now pictures. By the natural increase of present population and the influx of immigration in the ratio it is now coming, within one decade more the population of Texas will number not less than four millions. Twenty years from today not less than eight, and possibly ten, millions of people, more than the present population of the great States of New York and Pennsylvania combined, will inhabit the two hundred and seventy-four thousand square miles of territory within the boundaries of Texas. With a commanding commercial position in her Gulf ports; with capacity to produce cotton enough to clothe the world; her western plains unrivaled for wool-growing and stock-raising; her millions of acres prolific of all the cereals, and producing every variety of fruit and vegetable; her southern alluviums unsurpassed for sugar and rice; her inexhaustible resources of copper and iron, and her wealth of the more precious metals; her rich and extensive coal-fields; her splendid university and common school endowment; her genial climate, balmier than that of Italy; with freedom of debt, low taxes, and free homesteads, offering an asylum to the overburdened people of other States; and with a history which in a life of forty years commemorates achievements, and a line of heroes and statesmen of whom centuries might proudly boast, Texas, in the great future which shall witness her development, if her people be but true to themselves, will stand among the States of the American Union a very colossus; the greatest and most wonderful of them all, and her voice will be mighty in controlling the policy and shaping the destinies of the Union.

The causes are now in active operation which will produce these results, and grown men now within the sound of my voice will live to see them realized. But one danger menaces this grand consummation, and against that the statesmanship of the country and the patriotism of the people must provide. It is the spirit of sectionalism; the selfish and unhallowed ambition; the greed for power which, ignoring the interests of the great mass of the people for whose benefit the government was instituted, would rend into fragments, insignificant and petty, our splendid empire State, strand its fortunes, and forever blast its hopes. Let us stand unflinchingly by the glorious integrity of Texas, by her past history, by her present, buoyant with hope and promise, and by the mighty future assured by her undiminished unity. Let the government of Texas deal wisely and justly with the different sections of the State, and the weaker feel the generous concession of the stronger. Let our Constitution and laws so operate as that no portion of the State will be sacrificed in its interests, or wounded in its pride; and when conflicts arise, let us remember that the highest statesmanship will be revealed in their satisfactory compromise—that power, numerical strength in legislative bodies, as elsewhere, may be unwisely and oppressively used. Let each legislator be in truth, as in the theory of our government he is, the executor of a special trust for his immediate constituents, and of a general and equally obligatory trust for the whole State, and be possessed of a comprehensive patriotism and sense of duty which shall embrace within its guardianship and protecting care every interest, every square mile of territory, and every inhabitant of the State.

While resolving unalterably that the single star which rose from the historic field of San Jacinto, the emblem of a new republic, born of the valor of heroes and the brain of statesmen, shall forever, in undiminished luster, remain the sign and type of undivided Texas, let us endeavor to emulate the wisdom of the sages who transmitted us the heritage, and as they did, by just and equal and beneficent government and sagacious, far-seeing policy, bind by the ties of interest, of common brotherhood and of patriotic pride, the whole people of all the sections of the State to one glorious standard.

Secured against this danger, the future greatness of Texas, under a wise administration of her government, is assured. Let us contribute all that earnest effort in our respective positions can accomplish to the achievement of the grand result. No higher goal ever beckoned on the just ambition of men than that which through the paths of peace, the rivalry of intellect, the emulation of patriotic and exalted purpose, invites the statesmen of Texas to put forth their best powers, their greatest and noblest endeavors, in advancing the progress of their State to the great destiny which awaits her. Nor should we be unmindful of other relations and obligations imposed upon us, no less by considerations of interest and patriotism, than by those of constitutional duty. Texas is one of the various States which under the indissoluble bond of union forged in the Constitution of the United States forms a component part of our great Federal republic. Our duties as citizens of Texas, and as officers of her government, demand of us not only a hearty and sincere discharge of our obligations to the national authority, but an assiduous cultivation to the extent of our influence of that patriotic love for and pride in our common country which in former days was the distinguishing characteristic of the American citizen of every section, and the restoration of which in all its ardor is so dear to every patriotic heart. The people of Texas have an interest in the common government of this Union equal with that of any other State; they have rights not inferior to those of any other, and their share of the glories of its history is no less brilliant than that of the others. Let critics carp, and evil men, for selfish or party purposes subversive of the public good, destructive of patriotic devotion and fraternal feeling, seek to tear open the healing wounds of internecine strife, and erect perpetual barriers of separation between those bound together by all the ties of country, race, religion and laws; but let our better and nobler part be to strive for the restoration of peace and good will, a feeling of common brotherhood, and a sentiment of all embracing patriotism among the re-united people of this great country, love for its institutions and honest pride in its greatness and glory. As Texans, our first duty is to Texas: let us build up her material interests and develop her splendid resources; give her good government and prepare her for the grand part she is to perform in the future history of this country. As American citizens, let us lay our sacrificial offerings on the altar of the American Union, and while standing unyieldingly by the principles of government we believe to be correct and maintaining inviolate the faith, that is in us, let us put our foot upon every narrow and sectional feeling and embrace in our efforts and aspirations the glory and advancement of the whole country. We own an equal and undivided interest in every foot of its soil, in every page of its history, in every ray of its glory. The wisdom of our fathers helped to create, to shape and direct it; their blood helped to sanctify it; their valor to establish it; let us as rightful heirs enjoy it, and with true hearts and willing hands, aid in building up, improving, and perpetuating it.

Fellow-citizens, again invested by the generous confidence of a noble and gallant people with the duties and responsibilities of the office of Chief Executive of the State, I assume them under the inspiration of but one ambition, and that is, by the blessings of heaven, which are humbly invoked, to stand by and maintain the Constitution and laws, and through them to advance the honor and interests of the State, and the prosperity and happiness of the people.

XII

Oran Milo

ROBERTS

1879–1883

Courtesy of Archives Division, Texas State Library

ORAN MILO ROBERTS (*July 9, 1815–May 19, 1898*) was born in Laurens District, South Carolina. While he was still a child, the family moved to northern Alabama. He was privately tutored and graduated from the University of Alabama in 1836. The following year he was admitted to the bar.

He engaged in private law practice in Talladega and Ashville, Alabama. He served one term in the Alabama legislature. In 1841 Roberts moved to St. Augustine, Texas, where he continued his private law practice.

In 1844 he was appointed judge of the Fifth Judicial District of the Republic of Texas; in 1846 he was appointed to the same position for the newly annexed state. He held this position until 1851. From 1857 until 1861 he served as associate justice of the Texas Supreme Court.

He served as president of the Texas Secession Convention in 1861. The following year, he raised the Eleventh Texas Infantry Regiment for the Confederacy and served as colonel.

During 1864–65 he was chief justice of the Texas Supreme Court, a position he would later occupy again from 1874 to 1878. In 1866 he chaired the Judiciary Committee of the 1866 Constitutional Convention. That same year he was elected to the United States Senate but was denied his seat by the Radical Republicans. He practiced law in Tyler and conducted a law school in Gilmer.

Roberts, a Democrat, contended for the governorship in the election of November 1878 against National Greenback and Republican opponents and won by a commanding margin. He took office on January 21, 1879. He won a second term in 1880 and was inaugurated on January 18, 1881.

Inaugural Address *
January 21, 1879

FELLOW-CITIZENS, SENATORS AND REPRESENTATIVES OF THE LEGISLATURE:

Called by the voice of the people to preside over the destinies of our large State at this important period of its history, I accept the position with a full appreciation of the responsibility resting upon me. Had I much more experience in public affairs than that given me by a long career in its service in different positions, mainly judicial, I should feel diffident of my ability to meet successfully the demands of the hour. The State, emerging from the ruin of the civil war and from the consequent difficulties of its changed condition, has already advanced in the work of reforming its institutions and in resuscitating and husbanding its resources. Still, much remains to be done in that direction to establish permanently good and efficient government, economically administered. This is the impending necessity of the day; and whatever energy, influence and power I may have will be directed to that as the leading object. In the effort to accomplish it I confidently rely upon your lead in the matter as the legislative department, and upon the intelligence, patience and patriotism of the people of Texas. The democratic party stands pledged to that policy, as announced in the late canvass, and their large majority at the late election for state officers fully indorses it. Nor did any opposing party dissent from it. It may, therefore, be taken to be in accordance with the common sentiment of the country. The democratic party, being now in full charge of all of the departments of the state government, is responsible for its being carried out as far as it is practicable under existing circumstances.

However certain this may be, the policy of the incoming administration of the state government demanded, by a common sentiment, an examination into its details will show it to be environed with intrinsic

Journal of the House of Representatives of the Sixteenth Legislature of the State of Texas (1879), pp. 106–15.

difficulties to be surmounted, and extraneous matter relating to the past, present and future to be considered in both of the branches into which the propositions must be divided—which are, first, that the laws, organic and ordinary, should be so reformed and rigorously executed as to more certainly and speedily protect the rights of persons and of property; and, second, that the expenses of the government should be so reduced that they can be paid by the taxes which the people are reasonably able to pay, and which may be collected without increasing the public debt of the State annually.

Under the first branch it may be found necessary to amend the constitution so as to remodel or at least improve the judicial department, which is generally conceded to be inadequate to the wants of the country; also, the revised and digested codes, submitted to the Legislature, embracing the whole body of the statutory laws, civil and criminal, may, when examined and adopted, be expected to remedy many defects, which have long been accumulating upon our statute book. This is the department of the government that acts directly upon the people in the suppression of evil and in the maintenance of the right constituting their actual government, and it should be organized for efficiency, and maintained in full vigor at all hazards, and at all necessary expense that can be borne by the country. This is the first and highest duty of this or any other State. There has been a tendency, from several causes, to weaken this arm of the government, which should always be strong. It is not infrequently seen in our courts that the greatest strength of legal ability stands in the bar, instead of sitting on the bench. And, worse still, the State's counsel is seldom equal to cope with the body of the bar that he has to meet. In the determination of rights in a free country, learning and intellect should match each other, at least on equal terms, and if there is a difference, that which rules should be superior to that which is ruled. A false idea of economy, and a supposed acquiescence in popular will, have brought this about.

Another cause of weakness, delay and inefficiency is found in positive laws, limiting or cutting off judicial discretion from the apprehension of the abuse of power. This likewise limits or relieves from responsibility, making no one to blame if things go wrong. To make the practical operations of government efficient, responsiblity must be imposed and assumed. They can not be made to move by inflexibly fixed rules like an automaton. The tendency of legislation has long been too much directed towards that end, the evils of which are now continually perceived in the practical administration of the laws.

There are powerful influences operating upon the country which should induce an increase of this direct force of the government, rather than permit a diminution of it. The large emigration from other countries, the former spirit of speculation and subsequent monetary depression and want of profitable employment, the extension of our frontier and the changed condition of a large colored population, have all contributed to generate and exhibit an amount and character of crime and civil wrong entirely unprecedented in this country. The very inadequacy of the power of correction has provoked, and many continue to provoke, outrageous wrongs as a substituted remedy, without and against law. This inadequacy is also increased by the present habits of the people, in which their pursuits and avocations are more closely and constantly followed and their time considered more valuable than formerly, by which they have more indifference and even reluctance in giving their aid in any way in the execution of the laws, except on full compensation in money. All this has brought forth and exhibited a new feature of government here that few might commend, but all acquiesce in upon emergencies, which is a frequent call for the military to aid the civil authority in the execution of the laws, and the giving rewards to officers to make arrests. This is a radical departure from the principles of local self-government, planted in this country and derived from the common law of England and decided leaning to the practices of civil law countries, in which the people look to a police force, rather than to their own participation, for their protection. This growing sentiment of looking to an extraneous power and means to regulate local self-government throughout the whole State should be nipped in the bud before it is too late. The remedy is to infuse into our judicial department a power of action that shall inspire the people with confidence in its capacity to govern, and then the people will crowd to its aid, instead of holding back as they now do. "God helps those who help themselves," and so do the people the world over. Although we may not be able to do all that may be necessary, it behooves us to do whatever we can to accomplish this most desirable object.

There are exceptional cases wherein extraneous aid at the command of the government is necessary, as in occasional uprising combinations or party feuds, which may happen in communities ordinarily capable of self-control; and in cities where a police force is necessary, being in effect a quasi military power to aid the civil authority; and in a sparsely-settled stock-raising country, such as we have upon our western frontier; for the civilization capable of republican local self-government begins and ends with the plow. So it has been and is. An agricultural population, sufficiently contiguous for co-operation, must predominate or hold the balance of power to establish and permanently maintain local self-government as known in the history of the past in this country.

For this reason there should be a greater check than now exists by law upon the organization of new counties on our stock-raising frontier. The assumption that underlies the proposition to organize one of our unorganized counties on the frontier is that there are in that territory a sufficient number of settlers with fixed, permanent habitations in reasonable proximity, possessing intelligence, integrity and property sufficient to keep the peace and execute the laws, and also to defray the expense of a local government within it. And if any county already organized should, from any cause, permanently fall below that standard of capacity for local self-government, so as to require a standing military police through a number of years, it should be abolished and attached to a county that can govern itself locally. So long, therefore, as we have a vast area of country not settled by a population at least partly agricultural, the State may need a small movable police force to aid occasionally in the execution of the laws, the sooner it can be dispensed with entirely as an auxiliary the better. For a reliance upon it and the use of it all over the State would, in time, fundamentally change our free institutions by the creation of a central power that might be used despotically to the destruction of local self-government, which has so long been the protector of our rights and our liberties and the object of our political pride.

In connection with this subject, the penitentiary system as a mode of punishment must be considered. It was adopted on two grounds—one for the reform of the convict, and the other to secure a more certain conviction of the guilty than could be procured by the old plan of whipping and hanging. It may be doubted whether our plan of leasing and working the convicts outside of the penitentiary is favorable to reform any more than whipping and hanging. Still the other ground holds good even under our defective plan, and it would be contrary to the spirit of the age not to continue in the effort to perfect it as far as may be found practicable, so as to accomplish both of its leading objects. This should be done as far as practicable in such a way as would incur as little expense to the State as possible. In this connection, also, are laws for properly imposing and collecting taxes. Our system of taxation is founded on the correct principle—that as the leading objects of government are the protection of persons and of property, so an *ad valorem* tax should be levied upon property and a poll tax upon persons. An occupation tax should hardly be supposed to be levied as a drawback imposed upon one occupation in preference to another equally lawful, but rather as a means of taxing property of a transient nature passing through the hands of those taxed in such manner as can not generally be reached and identified in the ordinary way of levying an *ad valorem* tax. There is an unusually large amount of such transient property that is a fruitful source of litigation and consequent expense to the government that is not adequately reached either by the occupation tax or by the *ad valorem* tax assessed upon property owned on the first day of January every year. The tax designed to be levied upon the annual production may not, and actually does not, reach the bulk of it, because a large portion of that which is produced, such as cotton, wool, wheat, beef canned, cattle and other marketable stock is transported out of the State before the first day of January. From the habits of trade, since we have railroads, the stock on hand of a grocer merchant on the first day of January, is not an accurate, or even an approximate criterion of the amount of property that passes through his hands and is consumed during the year. This may be verified by reference to the assessment of goods, wares, etc., in any county. In Galveston county, for instance, it is only $1,751,782, which amount may be sold annually by one or two houses in the city of Galveston. It might not be proper to reach this transitory property in both wholesale and retail houses, nor by taxing both, that which is produced and that which is consumed during the year, because that would to a considerable extent result in a double tax upon the same values. This deficiency in the tax laws operates to the prejudice of the agriculturist whose capital is invested in land, improvements and farming stock permanently kept on hand, and is reached by his property being assessed on the first day of January in each year; whereas the retail merchant and grocer, from the present habit of ordering and paying for additions to his stock monthly or quarterly during the year after the first day of January in each year, escapes taxation upon the bulk of the property which he sells and is consumed during the year, which very property is generally more expense to the government in its protection than the more stable and permanent capital of the agriculturist. The transitory property is not adequately reached, therefore, by either our occupation tax or *ad valorem* tax. Virginia, it is reported, is successfully reaching it by a tax upon the retail of liquors according to the quantity sold, and this may lead the way to reaching it by a tax upon the property annually consumed, rather than upon that produced, which our tax laws now ineffectually attempt to do. That would also distribute the burden more generally than it is now done, because there are a great many more consumers of such property that is retailed than producers of that which is now taxed.

There is also a great deficiency in the payment of the poll tax, a correction of which demands the most rigid remedy that it is practicable to apply. The amount of land bid in by the State and held up indefinitely also demands a remedy. Any man who is able to pay his taxes, and wilfully fails to do so, is receiving protection and, if a citizen, participates in the rights and privileges of citizenship without rendering a consideration to the government therefor, and imposes an undue burden upon other persons, which is a gross injustice that should not be tolerated in this or any other state. There is another class of persons, the special protection of whom incurs expense, which has not as yet been adequately compensated for by any mode of taxation that has been adopted here. They are those who travel for business or otherwise, on railroads and steamboats, who might be reached by an occupation tax on common carriers of passengers, assessed by their number, or by the length of travel within this State. This protection to the traveler is a thing of real value which the government holds itself bound to furnish by the remedies afforded for injuries and losses for traveling on railroads and steamboats, which have largely increased the expenses of the government and which is not compensated for by the ordinary tax on railroads and steamboats, it being no special benefit to them. These common carriers pay taxes on their property as other persons for their own protection, and not for the protection of the rights of the persons whom they carry. This subject has not until lately been of sufficient importance to deserve attention. In our present emergency it is proper for the government to require compensation for its protection, general and special, wherever substantial rights are protected that necessarily increase its expense. Though it may be difficult to make the protection and the compensation for it exactly equal, it is certain that if we stand still and rely only upon our old modes of adjustment amid the new industries and accrual of rights and developments of wealth, we will fall short of a full appreciation of the progress of the age, and close every year with crippled resources, entailing upon us an accumulating debt, which has already reached over five millions of dollars since the late civil war, with a large defficiency bill every session of the Legislature to foot up.

The enactment of proper laws and the proper execution of them in the courts of the country, and in the collection and disbursement of taxes, together with the operations of the executive departments, constitute the government proper. If our attention could be devoted to them solely or even mainly, as was the case in our former period of cheap government and low taxes, we would have no difficulty with a proper adjustment of occupation and poll taxes in sustaining a vigorous government with an *ad valorem* tax of twelve or fifteen cents on the one hundred dollars worth of property instead of the fifty cents now imposed.

Gradually, and much more in the last ten years, the State has been assuming other and extraneous burdens beyond the capacity of the productive wealth of the country to sustain, as is plainly evinced by the country to sustain, as is plainly evinced by the constantly accumulating public debt. Some of these burdens are due to our frontier position in the Union and our extensive territory, and others of them are taken on to an extent not common in young and intrinsically feeble states. Reference is here made to the protection of our frontier and our police force; to the penitentiary and its enlargement; to our free common school system; to our schools for the blind and the deaf and dumb; to the establishment of an agricultural and mechanical college, so styled; to our lunatic asylum; to our quarantine establishment; to our pensions to Texas veterans and to our immigration bureau, formerly.

These are things which caused our public debt to be contracted, and which now cause a large amount of taxes to be assessed and collected annually. We are numerically a very poor people as compared with older states that have assumed these or similar burdens; much poorer, indeed, than the $300,000,000 worth of property appearing on the assessment rolls would, by its mere amount, indicate in reference to our capacity to support a government. Because an immense amount of that sum is made up by unimproved lands all over the State, which is dormant property, but is only estimated to be valuable because of its prospective value in the future. Its taxes have to be paid from the proceeds of productive property. The State in that regard is like a man who owns and pays taxes on a league of land and cultivates only one hundred acres of it. Because also our population is sparsely scattered over a large territory, which itself largely increases the expenses of government beyond that required in a state with the same population occupying one-third or one-fourth of the same space, as most of the states do. Because we have not yet piled up any considerable amount of permanent wealth as the fruit of the labor of many previous generations still producing values for the benefit of the present generation, which is the case in most of the older states, particularly in those of the north. Because also at the time of the annexation to the United States we did not, as Virginia, North Carolina and Georgia did, cede to the United States our vacant unoccupied territory, inhabited or roamed over by Indians, but chose to retain it and manage and protect it, at a large expense, to be annually paid by the tax upon the comparatively small amount of productive property. The chief benefit yet derived from it has been the hastening the building of railroads in a portion of the State by the donation of portions of the public lands thus reserved. Another great benefit generally expected to be derived is from the donation of lands set apart to the permanent common school fund. This, however, will prove delusive if it is expected to raise a fund in a distant future under the present management that will relieve the people from the taxes which they now pay to support the free common schools. For under the present mode of disposing of these lands the scholastic population will increase faster than the fund. And the same thing applies to the lands set apart for the schools for the deaf and dumb, and blind, and for the lunatic asylum. And the same policy will postpone indefinitely the building of a university, which should be erected at the capital of the state for the education of Texas youths, instead of sending them out of the State to be educated, and to return home strangers to Texas. Another benefit counted on is giving pre-emption to settlers, by which the frontier is extended. While this is a great benefit to those now no longer occupying the frontier, the fact that it is extended increases the expense of the government in proportion to the population thereby increased, and such is our experience for the last twenty years, and will be for the next thirty or forty years, until the whole territory shall have been filled up with a self-sustaining and a locally self-governing population. For until that time arrives the frontier must be protected, and the sparse population on its border must occasionally be aided in the execution of the civil law, under any line of policy that may be maintained. This necessarily follows from reserving territory to be governed by us. We have yet over thirty millions of public lands not appropriated that we are holding on to for the purpose of giving them away as we have done, while the people are struggling to pay nearly $400,000 annually in taxes on our bonded public debt, with a prospect of an indefinite increase of it, if there should be no change in the general management of the public affairs of the State. This debt is an obligation upon the State, the same as a mortgage upon all of the property and polls within it.

Now the question is, would it not be better as a business transaction to pay it with the property of the State not yet appropriated, by a sale of its land as soon as practicable, at a reasonable value, rather than from year to year to sell the lands of our citizens that they have worked for, and otherwise wrench from them taxes to pay the interest and ultimately the principal of the debt. There are other obligations imposed upon the government of the state by the constitution, of equally as high a nature, which are to devote one-half of all the public lands to the public school fund, and one million of acres to the university fund, and three millions of acres to the building of a capitol of the state. Under the present policy of procrastination these obligations will not be met, and the people will have to be taxed to perform them. I have reason to believe, from information that I have received, that the lands can be sold rapidly to persons both in and out of the State, for colonies of settlers and other purposes, if large tracts could be bought.

Another disadvantage imposed upon the people, in the payment of taxes to support the government, is that in the present scarcity of money, shrinkage of the value of property, and embarrassment in business, they pay too much generally to officers for the services rendered by them when compared to the attainable value of the same ability, skill and labor in other business pursuits of the present day. This is evidenced by the numerous applications for office, and by the anxiety and powerful efforts to obtain office in all parts of the State.

The true policy of the State, in my opinion, under the present juncture of affairs, is to retrench expenses from top to bottom, wherever it can be done consistently with the efficiency of the public service, and inaugurate the policy now of disposing of the public lands at a fair value as soon as practicable to any purchaser that will buy them in any quantity, so as to meet the various obligations of the government, increase the school funds and asylum fund, and thereby if possible relieve the present generation from the onerous burden of taxation imposed upon them for the dim prospect of a future good which will never be realized.

It was said in substance by one of the greatest of American statesmen, that it was the highest duty of government to subserve the interests of the present generation without imposing unnecessary burdens upon future generations. Justly take care of the present, and the future will take care of itself. Our present policy is violating both ends of this rule by imposing burdens of taxation on the present generation that might be relieved against by the means at command, and by imposing on future generations obligations that can only be discharged by heavy taxes.

The Legislature is the controlling power of the State, and the responsibility rests with them to determine whether or not we shall continue to drag along, mending up an old policy, unadapted to the times and to our present condition, or to at once inaugurate a practical policy that directs us to a definite end, promising a relief to the present generation, and a fair chance for prosperity to the future.

It may be objected that this policy will stop immigration. Not so, for the railroad companies owning millions of acres are the best immigration agents we ever had, and those that buy the lands who are not settlers will help them.

It may be objected that a land monopoly will be created that will prevent poor men from buying lands. Not so, for poor men, white and black, are now buying cheap lands all over the State, except in a few localities, from private owners, at more advantage to themselves than if they were to take them up by pre-emption, or were they to buy school lands, where they can be obtained either at this time or in the future.

It may be objected that this policy will stop the progress of railroads by exhausting the donation lands, and leave large portions of the State unprovided with them. Not so: for this result will soon follow under the present policy. But if the obligations resting on the State are satisfied in a reasonable time, and the people are relieved from these extraordinary burdens of taxation, then we can well afford to devote a part of the taxes derived from the railroads then already constructed to the building of other roads, in the shape of a loan, the interest on which could be turned over to the available school fund, and thereby give all sections of the State indirectly the benefit of the land donations, that will have already been made for the building of railroads long after all of the lands may have been exhausted. In some such way as this alone can the effects of land grants to railroads be continued and perpetuated so as to give all sections of the State the benefit of them.

It should not be supposed that I here now enter this plea for economy and the prompt discharge of the State's obligations because I am an old man desiring or expecting a return of the good old safe and slow times of twenty-five years ago. Far from it. He who looks back while the world moves on is turned into a pillar of salt. The steam power has entered our borders and spread its iron arms far and wide over our country. As soon might we stop the norther that sweeps down over our plains as to stop its progress until it spreads itself to our utmost borders, filling the whole country with wealth and intelligence, and implanting upon our soil a mightier and, if we properly appreciate and adapt ourselves to it, a higher civilization. I would that Texas, disinthralled from her burdens and prosperous, should enter safely into this new and more speedy progress of human affairs, in full plight to foster and cherish this power, as a friendly and befriended benefactor, and at the same time to direct and control it with justice and liberality in protecting the interest of society. For sooner or later will come to be solved the great problem not yet solved by the wisdom of the wisest American and English statesmen, as to how the transportation tax upon production and consumption shall be adjusted and regulated, so as to do full justice to all parties and still get the full benefit of the motive power of a higher and better civilization, that is driving us whether we will or not into a new era of human affairs. It is proper that we should fully recognize our relation to the country in the discharge of the duties assumed by us respectively. It may be truly said that it requires the highest talent, ability, experience and virtues in any country to make and carry on the best government of which it is capable. The allurements of federal office and the superior emoluments of private employments very often, if not usually at this day, prevent a state from obtaining the benefit of these in all of the different departments of its government. Notwithstanding this, it is with great gratification that I now see in both houses of the Legislature many gentlemen of ability and experience in the public councils of the State, and others of good ability who, like myself, may not have had any great experience in the positions they now occupy, but who, like those who have had experience, have now entered the service of the State with the resolve to give their time and best efforts to advance the public good. Upon those thus occupying the different departments the burdens and responsibilities of the government are thrown. I feel an abiding confidence that they have capacity, experience and patriotism enough to do a good work for the people of Texas now, if we will take hold of the matter before us with a strong grasp and courageously wield the power we have for their present and future benefit, according to our best convictions of the right, irrespective of all extraneous influences that may be arrayed to swerve us from the strict line of duty.

Having expressed my views freely in a general way, it will be my pleasure as well as my duty to execute to the best of my ability whatever policy in the administration of the state government that you may adopt. In you, as the legislative department, is vested the controlling power of the State. I, as the chief executive, but follow your lead and direction. But I hope and trust, whatever may be your policy, that the administration of the government will be shaped with a full recognition of the present hard times pecuniarily, and that there are aged men, crippled men, women and children who are working in the fields and otherwise all over this State, with scant living, to make the taxes which you will vote to maintain it.

Leaving behind us the difficulties through which we have passed and looking forward to the future, there is much in our condition to encourage us and to make us thankful. We have a large territory teeming with wealth in all of its parts, awaiting the touch of labor to bring it forth; a salubrious climate that is itself a source of wealth as well as of enjoyment; abundant crops that fill our marts and make ours a land of plenty. We have no conflict of labor and capital to excite the angry contest of classes, but all men here can find work and live, if they are not too choice in the kind of it. We have escaped this year a direful scourge that has sorely afflicted some of our sister states, for which we are indebted to Galveston, our beautiful city on the gulf, in the first instance, and then to other cities, in establishing a prompt and rigid quarantine. We have lately passed through an exciting political contest and election, in which an unobstructed free suffrage has been exercised and a peaceful acquiescence in the will of majorities has been exhibited all over our State. We are receiving annually a large emigration to aid us in driving back our extensive frontier and increasing our population. Industry and enterprise are starting up all over our State to develop our vast resources. We have a history of which we should be proud. It should be our pleasure, individually and collectively, to contribute our best efforts to direct its affairs so as to secure its material prosperity and the happiness of its people.

Standing in this place on the 4th day of March, 1861, as the president of the seceding convention, and acting by their authority, I proclaimed Texas a free and independent State. I did it in good conscience, believing it to be right. I now with the same good conscience, as governor of the state, declare Texas to have been in good faith reconstructed into the Union by the voice of its own people, marching steadily on with her sister states in the new progress of national development and standing ready to vie with any other state in advancing the prosperity and defending the honor of our common country. Having made it the study of the flower of my life to know how the rights and liberties of her people could be best preserved and her material interests advanced,

I now believe that the chief reliance should be placed upon building up a great State with all of its varied interests fostered, and the rights of all protected by a good state government, vigorously and economically administered, so as to secure permanently the confidence and love of her own people. Nothing less than a bold and determined strike for that end will accomplish it. The power, the responsiblity and the honor of the attempt are yours, and if my services shall substantially aid you in fixing it upon the country as its permanent policy, the end of my political ambition will have been attained.

Second Inaugural Address*

January 18, 1881

FELLOW-CITIZENS, SENATORS
AND REPRESENTATIVES IN THE
LEGISLATURE OF TEXAS:

In view of the eventful career of Texas in the past, long an unknown land to the civilized world, emerging into existence in the gloom of a far-off country; cradled in revolutions and wars, growing up with a history filled with sore trials and grievous sacrifices, alternated by glorious achievements, both civic and military; famous for her great men and chivalric people; and now rising up conspicuously into general view, with her vast proportions and magnificent resources; and fairly entering upon the grand struggle for their developement, I can but feel diffident of my ability to be equal to the task before me, as your chief magistrate, now for the second time called to preside over the destines of our beloved State. But sustained by an ardent zeal for her present prosperity and future greatness, I cheerfully and hopefully accept the position, at the behest of a generous people, who have manifested their desire to place their public interests under my care and direction, as they have done before. It is only by the wisdom of the Legislature, the harmonious co-operation of the executive officers, and the patriotic aid of the citizens, that I can hope to be equal to the grave responsibilities imposed upon me, in the effort to make Texas what she should be in the near future—the great and prosperous State of the American Union.

Sixty years ago Moses Austin entered Texas, then a Spanish province, to found a colony; which resulted in the first organized establishment of American civilization in this country, through the patient perseverance and wisdom of his son, Stephen F. Austin.

San Antonio and Nacogdoches were then on the track of the king's

*Journal of the House of Representatives of the Seventeenth Legislature of the State of Texas (1881), pp. 29–31.

138

highway—a mere mule-path, that traversed the province from the interior of Mexico to the United States, and which was then, and had been for an hundred years, the one great route of travel and commerce through the province. There were no towns on the coast for trade, but our ports and harbors had then but lately been the hiding-places for slavers and freebooters of the sea.

A few villages and settlements were situated south of and along the king's highway, near the Sabine and Red rivers. Small bands of Indians, from the tribes in the Southern States, were located below and above the king's highway. The great plains of Texas were the home of the roving wild Indians and buffalo, whose undisputed dominion had existed for unknown centuries. While its forests, wide-spread and fertile plains, and genial climate were as inviting then as now, they existed in the solitude of their native grandeur here, while, for an hundred years before centers of civilization had been formed and spread abroad, far and wide, fifteen hundred miles northeast and southwest of it. Why was this so? Simply because the waves and currents of the Gulf had heaved up bars of sand that closed our rivers and bays from receiving the vessels that transported civilization from Europe to America, as it was done on the Atlantic coast and at Vera Cruz in Mexico.

It had, with all of its slumbering resources and prospects of beauty, to await the spread from one or the other center, in its slow tread by land, and fortunately, and at last it came pouring down from the north and east, and now how changed the scene. Over a million and a half of people moving and pressing on to work out its magnificent prosperity, are settled within its borders.

The late rapid increase in Texas, with its being now the center of attraction for every species of enterprise, give promise of three millions of people in the next ten or fifteen years.

Already Texas is the foremost State of the Union in the production of cotton and beef-cattle, and soon will be in wool-growing. Here different productions fill the whole range of those in the temperate zone, and some of those in the tropics. She has a cotton region as large as any two or three of the other Southern States; a sugar region as large as Louisiana; a wheat region larger than Ohio or New York; a region for orchards larger than New Jersey and Delaware; a grazing country for stock of all sorts, extending through ten degrees of latitude and from one hundred to four hundred miles in width; an iron ore and coal region larger than Pennsylvania, with copper and other metals added. She has an abundance of good water power in the east and southwest; and timbers, from pine to bois d'arc, of every valuable variety; part of the largest gypsum bed in the world, soon to be reached by the railroads; an inexhaustible supply of lime-rock, and other building rocks and valuable earths. The railroads now traverse the State, in several lines, from north to south, and two of them will soon traverse the State from east to west. Wealth is springing up in cities, towns and country, far and wide over the State; and even on our coast, shut up as our ports are by sand bars, and neglected as they are and have been, an increasing commerce is flowing through them. And now, after Texas has been a far-off outside-country so long, she is upon the eve of being in the middle of the transit of the commerce of the continent by two Pacific railroads passing through it on the nearest and best routes from the Atlantic to the Pacific ocean, with the immense advantage of furnishing a half-way transportation by water, through our Gulf ports, when they shall be properly opened to the enlarged commerce to which our position entitles us.

This is not all that pertains to Texas now. Her government, and her actions therein, have been as peculiar and out of the common course, as her history and condition in other things have been. She recognizes the right of women to hold property in their own right, secures every citizen a homestead, if he earns or otherwise gets it, and gives him one if he will go upon the public lands and settle upon it, and enforces the fundamental principle of the just correspondence between taxation on the citizen and protection by the government. Texas joined the association of American States by voluntary annexation, and not as a purchased territory. She retained her vacant lands, and by liberal donations of it induced the building of railroads, thereby encouraging the settlement and promoting the prosperity of the country. She has endowed her public free schools with over forty millions of acres of school lands, each county with four leagues of land (17,712 acres) for the purpose, originally, of erecting and supporting a county academy; and university with 1,221,400 acres of land, enough of which have been sold to begin its establishment now; the asylums, Lunatic, Deaf and Dumb, Blind, and Orphan, with a large amount of lands, over four hundred thousand acres of which are still unsold; has set apart and surveyed three millions and fifty thousand acres of land for a new capitol and other public buildings; set apart over eleven millions of acres of land, one-half of the proceeds of the sale of which, are appropriated to the payment of the public debt, and the other half to the public free schools, and the whole of Greer county for the same purpose; and there is now still left over nineteen millions of acres of unappropriated lands.

Texas has a good body of laws, in the main, and they are as well executed for the protection of life and property as the condition of the country, with a population of strangers continually flowing into it, and the means and agencies employed will permit, with a prospect of gradual improvement. She has a system of public free schools organized, in which the scholastic population has been taught four months in the year, upon an average, over the State, and which permits incorporated cities and towns to assume control of their own schools, and, by consenting to tax themselves, may have their common schools taught as long as they desire; and in addition there are two normal schools, one for white and the other for colored pupils, who are supported at public expense, except their clothing, and an agricultural and mechanical college in successful operation; and she has quarantine laws that have for four successive years secured her people from yellow fever, that, during part of that time, has terribly scourged other portions of the Southern States; the taxes, though burdensome only on account of the large amount of unproductive property, in the shape of uncultivated lands, are still much lower than they are in most States of the Union; and she has a small public debt, a surplus in the treasury, and public credit equal to any State in the United States.

This condensed presentation of Texas, with her institutions, her varied and vast capabilities, and the provisions made already to give them direction, will give some idea of the weighty responsibilities resting on those, who are now, and may be hereafter invested with the control of the State government, and also of what deliberate judgment and political skill must be continually exercised by them to wisely manage these great affairs of State.

Those constituting the State government, who now, and hereafter are to have control of these great affairs of State, must bear in mind, that there is another government that acts directly and indirectly upon the same people within the same territory, and more or less upon the same great interests involved, which is the government of the United States, as it is now administered.

In the historic voyage of the States, it is well occasionally to make a reckoning of their true position, in order to judge of their future course.

The great and wise men, who devised and instituted the system of governments, of which Texas is now a part, provided for the general government to manage and promote mainly the exterior interests of all the States combined, as in commerce, war, and the like, under special powers delegated to it, and that each State should promote and take care of the private and public interests of its own people; and that each government, federal and State, should have and exercise the power to make and enforce laws over the same people, and in the same country, necessary to perform its duty, in the promotion of the distinctively, different interests confined to each government; and that thereby one of said governments would not undertake to do that which was entrusted to, and imposed on the other.

The system of those wise and patriotic men was thought to be wise then, in thus separating the powers of the government, in reference to the objects to be promoted by each one of them. This division has not been adhered to, as is demonstrated by the present state of public affairs in this country. Much of the business that engages the attention and action of the general government now, is to promote the interests of particular sections and classes of persons within the States. A State now, instead of being as originally intended, *regnum in regno,* is *regnum sub regno*—that is, all of its supposed deficiencies and incapacities to promote the private interests of its own people are supplemented or provided for by a superior power, according to its discretion, and to accomplish its purposes. The general government is now actually engaged in the business of hatching fish and sending them alive over the country, to furnish food for the people within the States, and at the same time giving to a particular class of citizens within the States a large bonus out of the public Treasury to export salted dead fish to foreign ports. It has been engaged in finding a way to stop the grasshoppers, that obscure the radiance of the sun in their flight, and eat up the wheat and other green things in the people's farms when they alight. The cotton worms, too, have engaged their attention, to aid the cotton planter and insure cotton to the cotton mills within the States. The farming interests of citizens are promoted by it in the cultivation of a model garden, and the collection and sending out seeds of peas and beans, and other things of utility and fancy.

These may be small matters, but they therefore the more plainly show how careful the general government is in attending to the private interests of the people within the States, wherein the State governments have failed to do it. Nor has it neglected their great private interests. It has furnished them with a circulating medium of bank notes, and legal tender Treasury notes, in the place of money coined. It has chartered railroads to be operated within the States, one of which is in our own State. It has so arranged the exercise of its powers, and now so professedly, that the manufacture of cotton and woolen cloths, and hats, shoes and other things, that are bought and used by the consumers, is paid a protectionist bonus, and a large one, too, for investing his capital and labor in that pursuit, and that is done to promote the private interests of some classes of persons within a State or States, so situated as to follow those pursuits.

Every pound of freight carried in a vessel from Boston or New York to Galveston pays, in the amount charged for it, a bonus or subsidy, in the way of additional charge on it, to the man or company that built that vessel, by reason of the fact, that he or they built that vessel within the territory of some State of the United States; that is to promote the private interest of the shipbuilders residing within some State or States.

The wool raisers of Western Texas, and elsewhere, are paid indirectly a subsidy upon every pound of wool they sell, while the cotton grower helps to pay it in the woolen fabrics which he uses. The very extravagance of the government in the exercise of its powers, and in doing things out of its prescribed sphere of action, puts money indirectly in somebody's pocket proportionately, and therefore, there is a perpetual influence brought to bear to encourage extravagance in everything.

Of late it is proposed to educate the children in the States, by the promotion of schools for that purpose, and, if not to assume entire control of them, at least to supplement the deficiency of States in their educational efforts, by an appropriation of an amount, estimated at seven cents for each child to be sent to school within the States. It should be remembered that the Agricultural Bureau at Washington, that now spreads its wings out to be seen far and wide, was hatched under the wing of the Pension Bureau. The avowed purpose is to elevate the personal capacity of the voters within the States.

The care of the general government has been extended to the management, promotion and protection of private interests through its courts, to make citizens and officers of States obey the laws of their own States. Even writs of *mandamus* and injunction have been issued to require governors and other executive officers to execute State laws in the discharge of their duties according to the construction of district Federal judges, and even further than that, State judges have been indicted and imprisoned by the Federal courts for deciding according to their convictions of right, in matters coming before them under State laws. Alfred the Great was in the habit of beheading his judges, and that is an English precedent of very ancient authority.

Many and various are the ways and constructions, by which the

Federal courts have extended their control over the private and public affairs of the State and its citizens, arising under the laws of the State. A law has even been passed to authorize a Federal court to decide a contested election between State officers; and that is to protect the right to vote of a class of citizens of the State in a State election held within a State. Thus every department of the general government is, and has been, step by step extending its assumption of right to regulate, control and promote the private rights and interests of the people of the State, which must necessarily result in complete centralism, if it should continue to increase. We need not look for that to be accomplished by the assumption of supreme power by a military dictator, but it is being accomplished by the gradual process under the operation of the general government in absorbing and appropriating to itself the powers and duties appropriately belonging to the States.

Thus, too, it will be seen, that the State government has a competitor within our own territory, for developing the private interests and protecting the rights of the people of Texas.

I believe, as did the founders of this system of associated governments, under which we live, that these local private and public rights and interests of the people of this State can best be protected and promoted, by the local State authorities, and that the means now left us are, to maintain a State government, so stable, and so powerful, in its capacity to fulfill its legitimate objects, as to exclude the necessity of interference with, or the supplementing of them by, the action of the general government, and to give encouragement to those pursuits, that will place our citizens, as far as practicable on an equality with the favored classes elsewhere, so long as such favoritism shall continue to be exercised in the government of this country.

One point in good government has been gained—the expenses have been brought within the revenue, and our public credit has been established. Let us hold on to that, which will now, as ever, be found no easy matter. Every great interest of State will now appeal to the Legislature for advancement and enlargement. Right now, at this session of the Legislature, is the turning point of its continuance and permanent establishment. Let us hold on to it with settled resolution, that admits of no failure, and strike for another essential point, not neglecting other great interests in the meantime. That other essential point is an improvement in the execution of the laws for the protection of life and property, both in their expedition and force. That is the imperious necessity resting upon us now. And while giving especial attention to that, we may maintain our public free schools, enlarge our means for their future improvement by the more rapid sale of its land, lay the foundation of an university, encourage our Agricultural and Mechanical College, establish additional normal schools, and thereby give an impetus to our educational interests generally.

The public health may be attended to by the organization of a State board of health, and an amendment of our quarantine laws.

Our railroad construction may still be encouraged, and their freights and fares justly regulated by our own Legislature.

It is useless to further enumerate the great interests already under our charge, none of which need be allowed to suffer abatement.

In addition to all these, we may now take steps by an amendment of the Constitution exempting from taxation for ten years property invested in the manufacture of our own cotton, wool and other raw materials, in utilizing our water power, in mining our coal, iron, copper and other metals by which we may invite capital and labor to develop our dormant or hidden resources, which a geological and agricultural reconnoissance of the State may make known to the world.

Thus, safely and securely, one by one, our great governmental interests may be advanced in succession, and crystalized on a permanent basis for their perpetuation, not allowing any of them to recede in the meantime, until they shall all have been raised to a standard of efficiency, resulting in an entire good government for Texas.

Texas will then be a great State indeed—an empire in its matured and varied capacity—indissolubly united, holding her own in an association of States, and capable of standing alone in the wreck of disintegration, should it come, with the lone star, whether associated with the galaxy of stars, or again hoisted alone, the emblem of Texas sovereignty, to be still the adoration of a united people.

XIII

John

IRELAND

1883–1887

Courtesy of Archives Division, Texas State Library

JOHN IRELAND (*January 21, 1827–March 5, 1896*) was born near Millerstown, Kentucky, the son of a farmer. He was educated in the Hart County "field schools." While studying law, Ireland served as constable and deputy sheriff of Hart County. He was admitted to the bar in 1852. The following year, he moved to Seguin, Texas, and established a private law practice. He served as mayor of Seguin. Ireland was a delegate to the 1861 Secession Convention. During the war, he enlisted as a private in the Confederate Army and rose to the rank of lieutenant colonel.

He was a delegate to the 1866 Constitutional Convention and that same year was elected district judge. He was removed from that position in 1867 during Radical Reconstruction.

In 1873 he was elected to the Texas House of Representatives and to the Senate the following year. In 1875 he was appointed associate justice of the Texas Supreme Court.

In the election of 1882, Ireland, a Democrat, defeated the Republican-Greenback Fusion party candidate and took office as governor on January 16, 1883. Two years later, he won a second term and was inaugurated on January 20, 1885.

*Inaugural Address**
January 16, 1883

GENTLEMEN OF THE SENATE
AND HOUSE OF REPRESENTATIVES,
AND LADIES AND GENTLEMEN:

In assuming the duties of Chief Magistrate of this, the most splendid commonwealth on earth, I do so with doubts and forebodings as to my capacity for the task.

Looking back a few years, we behold Texas a part of the Spanish kingdom. By the revolution of 1824 she became a part of the republic of Mexico. Mexico refusing to her distant territory that just and equal place in the family that was due to the people, and Texas having been sought by blood that knew what freedom and equal rights were—this blood, aided by many noble families descended from that of Castile—soon inaugurated the movement that culminated at San Jacinto and spoke a new nation into life.

For many years the Republic of Texas consisted of her ancient and noble settlement in eastern Texas, the lower Brazos settlement, and the Missions, including San Antonio. Her progress was slow, but soon the idea of annexation began to grow, and was made a finality in 1845. Her population was then about 150,000 souls, and as late as 1870 the total population was but little over 800,000. Up to near that period we had no disturbing questions about public lands. Our free schools consisted in what was known as the indigent system. We had no perplexing questions of taxation. The penitentiary was almost mythical, and our asylums were only known in name. The principal duty of the Executive was to sign patents and look to the frontier.

How changed the scene! Over two millions of population, and instead of the small settlements before mentioned, we find the entire country, "from the Red River to the Rio Grande, and from the coast to

Journal of the House of Representatives of the Eighteenth Legislature of the State of Texas (1883), pp. 38–39.

El Paso," peopled and yielding all the material products for the consumption of our race; while the Pan Handle supplies Chicago, New York, the Indian tribes and portions of Europe with beef—each section constantly struggling for the mastery and endeavoring to impress its ideas and laws upon the State.

The public lands are exciting that energy and calling forth that same spirit of gain that the gold fields of Australia and those of California did. The growth and settlement of the distant parts of our territory have demonstrated the fact that laws that are suitable for the Red River country do not prove beneficial to the Rio Grande, and those that the coast desire are not welcome at El Paso. With all these difficult and conflicting elements and interests must we deal. Shall we float along in the avenues of the sluggard, caring nothing for the future, or shall we deal with these great interests as though we, and not posterity, are to be affected by our action?

Prominent among the subjects that will challenge the attention of this administration are:

The preservation of our common school fund, including the lands set apart for that purpose, and the improvement of our school system.

It is known to the country that, prior to my nomination at Galveston, I severely criticised the practice of paying forty per cent premium for our bonds, and no amount of reasoning or financial skill can satisfy me that the practice is justifiable, either in retiring our bonded indebtedness, or as an investment for the school fund.

It seems to be admitted by all that the Constitution should be so amended as to permit the Legislature to levy and collect a school tax, without reference to the amount of the general revenue that may be necessary.

Another amendment to that instrument will be necessary with reference to the school fund—

The permanent fund belonging to the common schools can only be invested in bonds of the Federal agency, and of the State.

The United States are refunding at so low a rate that their bonds are not desirable for that purpose, and very soon we hope the State will have no bonded debt outstanding, and we must therefore seek some other mode of investing our permanent school fund.

Shall we guard, protect and increase this fund as a sacred trust, or shall we throw it away by paying forty per cent premium for an investment?

The University was early contemplated by those who have gone before. No one questions the usefulness or propriety of such an institution, and we suppose a retrograde movement, with reference to it, is not contemplated.

THE PENITENTIARY—WHAT SHALL BE DONE WITH OUR CONVICTS?

It would seem that experience has taught us that there are but few "penitents" and but few reforms accomplished in that institution, and, therefore, that it is probably misnamed. It will be for the wisdom of the law-making power to prescribe the proper management. I do not doubt but there are numbers sent to that institution for petty offenses, who should be punished in some other way; and for youths a house of correction or other place of confinement and punishment should be devised. I doubt the propriety of sending any, no matter what the age, to the penitentiary for short periods of time.

THE JUDICIARY.

Shall we amend our Constitution so as to enable us to have a judiciary equal to our demands, or shall we continue to multiply judges of courts of last resort? A little reflection will satisfy all that the evil in the system is radical, and we must begin the remedy in the trial courts.

TAXATION.

The earlier idea about occupation tax was that it should be laid on those occupations and pursuits that were to be discouraged; but the modern practice appears to be to raise money, even at the expense of those most useful and desirable. As to an ad valorem tax, there is no just power to take from the citizen one mill, if it is not absolutely required to carry on his government in an economical manner. What belongs to the citizen is his absolutely, and his agents have no right to demand more than is necessary. Again, no greater temptation and invitation to extravagance, and even corruption, can exist than a plethoric treasury. We need no other evidence of this than that offered in our landed system. After all the headrights, the augmentations, the donations and the bounties had been provided for, there still remained, say one hundred and twenty million acres of land. This was about the sum at the close of the war between the States. These lands then began to attract the attention of the capitalists, the land hungry and greedy, and scheme after scheme was resorted to to get hold of them. When standing in the Thirteenth Legislature there were a few—a splendid band—who protested against opening the door that was felt to be the first break upon these lands. These men stood amidst the jeers and scoffs of those who were clamorous for the golden egg, and casting a glance to the distant future and foreseeing that this rich field could not be longer guarded, as a last resort they introduced and had passed the law setting apart one-half of the entire public domain for educational purposes. They took the only step left them to secure to posterity a small pittance of that splendid educational fund; but the door was broken down and it has gone, until now there is but a remnant.

I think I see away down the corridors of time, this splendid territory teeming with millions. No more public lands; no more cheap homes—poverty and squalid want gathering fast and thick around the inhabitants; when some one of them will gather up the fragments of our history and read to the gazing and mind-famished multitude how this generation had in its power and keeping a fund that should have gathered like the snowball as time rolled on, and how, if we had been true to ourselves, to posterity, to *them,* they could have educated all their children, paid all their taxes, reared school houses, built roads and bridges—and then I see them turn with deep mutterings from the wicked folly that crazed our people from 1865 to 1882.

I know that there is a popular fallacy abroad that finds expression in such language as "damn posterity, let it take care of itself." I pity the heart can thus speak. Not so spoke our ancestors—the fathers. They saw not *to-day,* but looking with an eye of faith and wisdom, away in the distance, they saw *us,* and labored and toiled for us.

OUR COMMON HIGHWAYS.

Our laws on this subject are defective. There seems to be no reason why all who own property or reside near the roads should not contribute to support them. The youth, the aged and the non resident, having property that is benefitted by a highway, should bear a proper proportion of its burdens, as well as those within certain ages.

OUR RAILWAYS.

The constitutional requirement that the Legislature shall pass laws to regulate and control these institutions has been only partially performed. The people demand the fulfillment of this plain constitutional duty.

It is not the work of an hour, nor to be performed without mature study. These railways are our institutions; their value and utility to the country are not to be questioned; their management has challenged and baffled the highest order of talent, and whatever is done, it is to be hoped will be done in the spirit of justice and equity, that will prove adequate to our wants, without crippling or injuring the railways.

THE FRONTIER.

That the time is rapidly approaching when we will have no frontier, in the sense of an Indian border constantly subject to the incursions of hostile savages, is certain, and yet those familiar with our borders and the enforcement of our laws, will readily concede the fact that the time has not arrived for the disbandment of our State forces.

EXECUTION OF THE CRIMINAL LAW.

There are three things imperatively demanded to a proper execution of these laws:

1. We must have a good judiciary, which cannot be had—but in exceptional cases—without better salaries.

2. A salary to the prosecuting officer that will ensure talents and fidelity to duty, that will be equal to our young, vigorous and splendid bar; and

3. A higher sense of duty on the part of our juries.

CIVIL SERVICE REFORM.

This is a theme dwelt upon by statesmen of all parties, State and Federal; it goes forth in State papers of the most solemn character; we get it in prose and poetry, and no sooner has the party triumphed by the force of its logic than it dies, often a silent death, without so much as a prayer being offered at its obsequies.

Happily for the American people, the last and most glaring breach of public decency has been rebuked by an outraged people, in a manner so severe that we shall not likely, in the next few years, hear of a Hubbell organization or a cabinet minister tendered by the Chief Magistrate of our Federal agency for governor of a State, or of quarantine guards or revenue officials undertaking to conduct elections. While these things have been severely rebuked, it has not been done by a people unfaithful to the spirit of our institutions, for all governments here are the people's, no less that of the States than the Federal, and whether improper interference with the freedom of elections comes from those in authority in the State or Federal government, it is the right and bounden duty of the people to rebuke it—the more severely the higher the source from whence it comes.

In assuming the duties of this very responsible office, I do, to-day, although elected as a partisan, declare that the oath of office disarms the politician and leaves me free to deal with all alike, and whatever asperities may have been engendered in political contests, I thank God that I have moral courage enough to remember that I am the Chief Magistrate of a great people and State, and that it is their affairs, and not my own, with which I have to deal.

To those around me, charged with a portion of the same public trust, I have to say, that while a degree of individuality in all is a necessary ingredient, still I trust that we meet with that spirit of forbearance and concession that will render the aggregated will useful to our country, and in inviting their hearty co-operation, I deem it proper to say that they will find in me, at all times, not only a willingness to hear others and consult their views, but to make all necessary concessions in order that the incoming administration may meet the expectations of this splendid common wealth.

Fidelity to the Constitutions of our country, State and Federal, is the true test of loyalty, and he who tramples upon these or does other illegal acts in the name of law, is the vilest of law-breakers.

May we hope that our school lands and the common school fund will be guarded with that spirit of jealousy and devotion to trust and duty that the magnitude of the subject demands.

It is not unknown that the section of our State where these lands are situated feels a deep interest in this subject, and while the public servant must do nothing that can be avoided to retard or annoy any section, still I know that that gallant people will not require a guardian of a great public trust to lose sight of the fact that he does indeed represent all the people and all sections of our State, and that devotion to this great trust is of the first and highest consideration.

OUR INSANE.

Shall the institution intended for the treatment, care and cure of this unfortunate class be longer a thing in name, or shall we make it equal to the demands of justice and humanity?

These and many other subjects, not necessary now to enumerate, will receive more elaborate attention in direct communication to the two houses.

With regard to the management of our various institutions or appointments to office therein, I wish to say that the first great consid eration has, and will continue to be, the good of the public service, and when I do not think this service can be bettered, no removals will be made.

I believe in the fullest and freest ballot, and do not cherish the slightest animosity toward those who offered a manly opposition to my election, and as the Executive, I have no enemies to punish.

Second Inaugural Address*
January 20, 1885

I have repeated to day the oath of fidelity to the Constitution, and by implication to the people of the State, that I took two years ago. I then expressed some apprehension of my ability to give entire satisfaction to all the people. In taking the oath, I relied largely on the wisdom, patriotism and forbearance of my countrymen. In that trust I have not been mistaken or deceived. The generosity and zealous support extended to me by the two houses and the people has been thorough and full, to the extent, indeed, of filling me with gratitude and cementing my devoting to the best interest of the commonwealth.

True, I have not pleased all. I have not had public gifts in my keeping for all who have sought them—for self or friends. Sometimes I have found myself between the arms of the selfish and their goal. I now declare that no act or deed of mine has been dictated or done with any other view or motive than the general good of the people.

No one could more fondly seek the aid and assistance of his friends than I have done; yet when I have heard all, being responsible myself to the people, I have acted on my own judgment.

The stumbling block in the paths of our race, often as public servants and as private individuals, is the rugged boulder of self-interest. Just to the extent that we can divest ourselves of that, in the same ratio will our acts be promotive of public good, and satisfactory to ourselves. If I in a public capacity, find myself constantly trimming sail, or a member of either house is beset as a legislator, with consideration, self-imposed or thrust upon him, of private ends, our actions will be unsatisfactory and detrimental to the public service. When our public service is ended, if we can take a retrospect and feel that we have done our whole duty to the people and our country, we may well be satisfied.

With reasonable legislation our country will continue to grow and

*Journal of the House of Representatives of the Nineteenth Legislature of the State of Texas (1885), pp. 35–36.

prosper. The border will continue to recede, our new counties will continue to organize, the six-shooter and the Spencer rifle will disappear, and the people will be able to elect a local government that will afford protection to life and property without having to appeal to a central power to do that for which local officers are created. I feel sure that in the two houses will be found earnest public servants, and that when differences spring up they will be the result of honest motives. We want stability in our laws and form of government, and it is much better to conform to an awkward or improvident law, than to be constantly changing our system. We cannot have perfection, and legislators often deserve well of their country by opposing constant changes. When a few leading subjects have been disposed of, we always feel that we are ready to quit at any day. Whatever is done should tend towards requiring every person to let every other person alone in the enjoyment of what is his; to lessen the burdens of the people in the way of taxes, to afford speedy redress in the courts for wrongs; and finally, to leave the people free from any governmental control or supervision, except so far as may be necessary to accomplish the few great ends pointed out.

Since my late message to the two houses was penned, the knowledge has reached me of the perpetration of a series of horrible crimes, murders and thefts on Texas soil by incursions of predatory bands from Mexico.

Since it has become known that neither Mexico nor the United States will surrender one of their own citizens to be taken to the other government to be tried for crime, the people on the right bank of the Rio Grande have become emboldened, and they stand on Mexican soil covered with the blood of our women and children and their booty in sight of our people.

I have made repeated efforts, through the Secretary of State, to induce a discussion of the propriety of so amending the treaty of 1861 as to permit any one, no matter where his allegiance may be, to be extradited, but no results have followed. Commercial treaties and money affairs seem to be of more importance than the blood of our people.

In the last few days I have written to the President, giving him full accounts of the condition of affairs on the Rio Grande, and have also informed him that Texas can, if need be, protect herself, and minute companies and State troops on that border have been directed to protect our people without deference to nice points of international law. If the Federal troops, whose duty it is under the Constitution, are too tender to patrol that border, or if a few companies in the interior to make a show at dress parade are of more importance, it would seem that their presence on our soil is of but little practical use.

These remarks are not intended as a criticism of the commanding officers in Texas, but of the general management of the War Department.

It has been suggested that the members of the two houses may wish to visit the Cotton Exposition before final adjournment. If this conclusion is reached, I hope the adjournment will be without pay to either members or employees. If this mode is adopted, it would doubtless be satisfactory to the country. By a concurrent resolution the two houses may adjourn for fourteen days.

XIV

Lawrence Sullivan

ROSS

1887–1891

Courtesy of Archives Division, Texas State Library

LAWRENCE SULLIVAN ROSS (*September 27, 1838–January 3, 1898*) was born in Bentonsport, Iowa, the son of an Indian agent. His family moved to Milam County, Texas, when he was an infant. Later, the family moved to Austin and in 1849 settled in Waco. Ross attended Baylor University but was graduated from Wesleyan University in Florence, Alabama, in 1859.

In that same year, he was appointed a captain in the Texas Rangers and fought against the Comanches. Later he was appointed aide-de-camp and colonel by Governor Sam Houston. In September 1861 he entered the Confederate Army as a private; however, by February 1864 he had risen to the rank of brigadier general.

In 1873 Ross was elected sheriff of McLennan County. He was a delegate to the 1875 Constitutional Convention. In 1881 he was elected to the Texas Senate and served until 1885.

In the gubernatorial election of November 1886, Ross, a Democrat, defeated his Republican and Populist opponents and assumed office on January 18, 1887.

He won a second term in 1888 by defeating Prohibition and Farmers Alliance party candidates. His second term began on January 15, 1889.

Inaugural Address*
January 18, 1887

FELLOW CITIZENS, SENATORS AND REPRESENTATIVES IN THE LEGISLATURE OF TEXAS:

Every two years the people are called to select, from the citizens of the State, those who are to administer the affairs of their government. In making this choice, every political question that touches the honor, progress and well being of the country is fully considered: policies, laws and institutions are freely discussed. And as you have just come from the people, it is fair to presume that you are fully prepared to give expression to what may be termed the logic of the popular mind. Probably no legislature was ever confronted by graver responsibilities. Those who study the public affairs of our State, and consider the want of homogenity in its population, its industrial pursuits, business enterprises and social sympathies, are aware of the fact that it presents questions vastly more complicated and embarrassing than any other State; and the knowledge required to deal with them wisely, and work out safe issues, is immense.

I have a profound hope, not clouded with the slightest doubt, that these great and vital measures will be undertaken with commendable temper, moderation and fairness; and I feel confident that you will meet bravely, unselfishly and loyally, the great work confronting you. Recognizing a common obligation to do full justice to all, the humblest as well as the highest—and make stronger the bonds which should unite us, as a people, in a common, grand destiny—commensurate with a State boundless in its resources, infinite in its possibilities, and extending the largest freedom of pursuit in matters of religious concernment, social habits, and business engagements, with no respect of persons, in regard to rank or place of birth—in unison with that political creed which peculiarly distinguishes our system of popular government.

*Journal of the House of Representatives of the Twentieth Legislature of the State of Texas (1887), pp. 64–72.

The legislator has a peculiar province committed to his care, and is expected to meet the constant variations in the conditions of society, its interests and its securities. It is the experience and the wants of society, that teach what laws are necessary; and they should be enacted and framed according to these demands and exigencies. But the probabilities of frequent changes of policy, upon economic questions in our State, is, doubtless, a great disadvantage to its general prosperity. What it needs and pleads for is stability—permanency—something upon which the people may safely rely, as abiding. It is not to be expected that great enterprises will take that scope, or feel that vigor, confronted with the liability of radical change each two years, that it would could the assurance exist that a given policy would abide, so that men might be certain to reap the reward of their sowing. Experience demonstrates that frequent changes in non-essentials are more hurtful, in unsettling the minds of the people, than the small defects which these changes have generally proposed to remedy; to say nothing of the increased cost of legislation and the neglect of more important matters. Besides, it is possible to so complicate legislation as to render its effects nugatory, and to make the simplest provision a loop hole through which improper practices are possible; and it may not be deemed amiss to say that the practice has become quite too general, by which the most important business of each session, affecting laws and well established policies, is crowded into its last hours, thus constraining members, without time for mature deliberation, to either suffer measures to become laws, or incur the risk of subjecting the State and individuals to great loss and inconvenience.

In the philosophy of our government, we have a system of distributed powers, between the different departments thereof, so incorporated into the general system, and endowed with such functions as to enable them to act as checks upon each other. And there has been assigned to each, with great precision and certainty, its appropriate functions—wisely guarding the whole by expressly forbidding the exercise, by any one of them, of the powers assigned to either of the others.

It is further seen that the same admirable distribution of powers exists between the general and State governments, and while the nature and scope of the system is complex in its machinery, it is, at the same time, simple in its operation. According to this theory a very large portion of the functions of government is of a local character. The federal government takes cognizance of those matters of national interest and leaves the great mass of governmental powers to the States, which, in turn, largely distribute them out to the counties, and one important branch of the government—the judiciary—requires the aid of the individual citizen in the jury box. All, however, proceed upon the theory of self-government, and assume that the people of every locality are competent and well disposed to it.

This being true, it is important that the State shall be lacking in no essential quality to afford protection and security to person and property in every emergency, and present no pretext for the extension of the area of federal power, which, by express grant, coupled with an imperative injunction for its exercise, is given to those invoking it in the provision that declares, "No State shall deny to any person within its jurisdiction the equal protection of the laws." If, therefore, we would preserve the dignity of our State and make it sovereign with respect to its internal government, it must stand ready and willing to bring punishment to all those who seek to disturb society, or embarrass or obstruct its agencies for the preservation of law and order. Besides it is a fundamental principal of law that, while the citizen owes allegiance to the government, he has the right to demand, at any cost, protection for life, person and property, and the full enjoyment of free speech, a free ballot and a safe home. The obligations are mutual, and where you ignore or weaken this right you destroy or diminish the duty of allegiance.

It is not too much to say, then, that where there are extraordinary combinations to violate the laws there should be extraordinary legislation for its suppression, and the wisdom and statesmanship of Texas, I doubt not, will be found equal to the duty of prescribing remedies for every crime which the ingenuity of evil disposed men can contrive or invent. If our present laws are defective in that respect, they should be promptly amended; if new ones are demanded by public exigencies they should be enacted, and the officials charged with their execution clothed with ample power and authority to enforce obedience, otherwise they will be illusory in character and useless in action. The people expect their representatives to guard well the door of their treasury, and, under existing financial conditions, we are compelled to scrutinize our expenditures with the utmost vigilance, and endeavor by all fair and honorable modes to reduce the expenditures to the lowest practical amount consistent with a proper regard to the public interest and an effective administration of the government. But they do not demand an unreasonable stringency which would incur the peril of a disastrous recoil, superinducing the very state of things sought to be shunned, by a sacrifice of efficiency to a false idea of economy. We may boast in vain of our great natural resources, but we shall fail to impress the world by playing the giant abroad and the pigmy at home.

Our people are educated in law abiding habits, and their instincts and their interests are in favor of peace, order and justice. They present a higher evidence of thrift, economy, labor, wealth and prosperity—the natural results of obedience to law and order—than any other given section of the Union. And while insisting upon the exercise of a wise and just economy, they expect their representatives to infuse the necessary strength and vigor into every department of government, for they stand pledged to maintain the laws, foster progress, universal education and the elevation of the masses, protect labor, encourage capital and build up home industries, to the end that our people may be induced in a fuller measure to rely upon their own resources, and thus develop the greatest diversification of commercial and industrial enterprises to add to the wealth and production of the State, and the continued activity of those great and vital moral and economic forces which underlie true grandeur, and which tend to cultivate and enlarge an undying attachment to our State, its history and its institutions, and inspire a profound State pride, as well as a sublime veneration for the patriotic example of those who laid, broad and deep, the foundations of State government.

In every polity, whether civil or eclesiastical, the judicial system is a matter of the first importance, and needs to be adjusted with the greatest care and accuracy, to subserve the ends of government in the repression of wrong and the defense of right. Laws are mere abstractions, and cannot enforce themselves, but must be expounded and faithfully applied to serve their purposes; and it is quite possible to have a wise system of legislation, and at the same time, such defective organism for enforcement, as that the laws will be either too lax, or too tardy in their operation, as is supposed to be the case with our present system. The privilege of appeal is of small value to the citizen, where he is forced to wait long years before he can have his rights determined. The very lapse of time intervening working incalculable injury, and, in some instances, a practical denial of justice. Besides, it is impossible to compute the loss, in money and peace of mind, to the citizen where he cannot have his appeal heard, and his real or supposed advantages speedily realized.

The interests of every State needs, above all else, a strong bench, equal to the intellectual demands of the people, always remaining in justice and equity, in intellect and learning, in freedom and courage, the central orb of the highest civilization, and the sheet anchor of law and order. The rich and powerful, with an inexhaustible treasury, and a ready command of the best legal talent at the bar, can take care of themselves; but the surest, and often the only hope of the poor and weak, for the protection of person and property, is to be found in the able judge, who pursues the call of official duty, regardless of temporary frenzy, of popular passion or applause, or the corrupting influence of unbridled power.

But, after all, our laws must be sustained by moral sentiment, and personal effort must supplement official action. There are evils which statutes cannot reach or remedy; and when you have passed all constitutional laws appropriate to the situation and they have been faithfully executed by the proper officers, there will remain a great work for the people which comes not within the scope of legislation, and the reform that is called for in this direction is no small matter. It will take combined and continued effort, as well as wisdom, patience and courage. Where it is wrong public opinion must be changed; where it is false public sentiment must be corrected. We must begin at the fireside, keep it up in the school room, continue it in the press, urge it in the pulpit and complete it in the courts of justice.

The foundation of successful self government is a widely diffused education and a high average of moral culture. No people can be truly and permanently great, in the highest and best sense of the word, who do not provide ample home educational facilities for their youth. The wise statesmen who preceeded us recognized the fact that our Constitution rests upon the virtue and intelligence of the people, and when ever either one of these ingredients fails our government fails, and with lofty patriotism they placed our public school interests upon a substantial and permanent basis.

Though our common school books are in a more advanced state than those of any other part of the country, it is a matter of profound regret that our reformatory efforts, to save neglected and forsaken children, have not kept pace with our progress in common school education, and hence our state is now cursed with a large and rapidly increasing juvenile population growing up in vice and ignorance, and sure of becoming adepts in crime long before arriving at manhood. The minds and hearts of these children constitute a part of our State productive capital, of far greater value, in working out the noblest destiny of a noble people, than all its vast and varied natural resources, and it is not only worse than a waste of capital, but bad political economy, to suffer any of them to grow up to prey upon society.

The most inveterate offender has some rights which society must respect. It cannot be pretended that it is the object of punishment by the civil authorities that the individual punished shall receive the recompense of his crimes. This would not only be futile, but a usurpation of powers belonging to the Deity alone. It is not administered for vengeance, but for the prime object of the prevention of crime, and the incidental object of individual reformation. The most general and potent cause of crime is the result of neglected and miseducated childhood; and as this misdirection of faculty is amenable to discipline, and is easily modified by altered surroundings, and a judicious training which will show the disadvantages of a criminal life when weighed against the advantages of liberty and good repute. We, therefore, neglect our plain duty, so long as we fail to establish suitable industrial schools, or reformatory institutions where they may be taught respect for law and order, the necessity for virtuous principles, and to look forward to labor of some kind as their ultimate duty and privilege, while filling the weightier duties of citizenship with the patriotic devotion to the land in which they live.

The right to live, to own and possess property, and to exercise the civil and political franchises, are the dearest interests of mankind; and it is the highest duty of government to provide means to protect and secure every citizen in the undisturbed enjoyment of these rights. In every government allowing expression of opinion by vote, there have always been differences and sentiment, giving rise to political parties having the disposition of the honors of office, and attendant revenues. And in our country, the result rests upon the decision of the majority, legally ascertained, and announced as the will of the people, expressed under legal forms, and where all the citizens are of equal value. There should be, therefore, no loss of faith in the ballot as the infallible oracle of the public will, and the sovereign arbiter of political disputes, which would, in the end, result in the withdrawal of the respect due, and cheerfully accorded, by the people to their chosen rulers, ruinous to domestic content and the permanence of our institutions. For after all, their permanency is measured only by the heighth and depths of love and loyalty the true citizen bears to the government.

So jealous have been our law makers of the sanctity of this right of the people to have their will expressed at the polls without bias, and unawed by anybody, and afterward have that verdict legitimately ascertained by an honest count, that there has been a manifest reluctance on their part to amend our present election laws by the adoption of such inovations as would place them more in consonance with the advanced progress and thought obtaining in other States. It is a well recognized fact, however, that our law's slow delay has proven a prolific source of annoyance to the people; and there seems to be a popular demand that the eagerly anticipated answer, in the final decisions of our political contests, shall more speedily emerge from doubt into ascertained certainty, and there appears no good reason why we should hesitate longer to conform our laws, in this respect, to those of other States, which have stood the test of experience, and are eminently just and satisfactory.

While the enactment of penal laws are necessary and indispensable to quell disorders, detect, convict and punish those who outrage civilization and the peace of society, wise government will do all those just things to remove what any portion of its citizens properly deem to be grievances, for such action is quite as important as repressive measures. If you want a people to be orderly, give them a government under which the humblest citizen is not beneath the protection of the laws, or the highest above the reach of their authority.

Where there is found a just cause of complaint, we should, without delay, inquire into the nature and extent of the evil, and thoughtfully and wisely consider and apply the best and most practicable means of removing or lessening it.

The bill of rights declares in unequivocal language, that "perpetuities and monopolies are contrary to the genius of a free government, and shall never be allowed." And yet, our State has created, and is each year strengthening, a system of corporate power, relieved of all personal responsibility, and clothed with exclusive rights, powers and privileges in perpetuity, and it is apparent that influences vast and potential are at work to reduce the whole carrying trade of the country into a single monopoly and management, no matter how oppressive, and no matter how widespread the ruin and disaster it may bring to other industrial interests of equal, if not of paramount, importance to the people at large.

If this right be acknowledged and perpetuated, the great body of the citizens will have fastened upon them a bondage, compared with which the bondage of Isreal in Egypt was tender mercy.

These corporations were created by the people, in their legislative capacity, to meet an overwhelming need in bringing out the dormant wealth of the State and to supply its instant and pressing necessities; and it is not to be wondered at that they were extended extraordinary encouragement and facilities, nor is it strange that these privileges should have been accompanied with enormous land grants under State provisions. And while we proclaim our unqualified approbation of every policy, recognizing their importance as thoroughfares of travel, as carriers and distributors of products, and as an invaluable and indispensable means of developing and serving the country, it can hardly be questioned that these artificial bodies were created by the people as creatures of their power—the instruments of their convenience—and designed for their service and not their subjection. And it was clearly the will of the framers of our organic law, to throw them open to the laws of competition in every particular, making them evoke their own checks and regulators as the true theory for their management. But these constitutional inhibitions and statutory requirements are nullified by the simple will of corporations of our own creation, and possessing no powers except such as are conferred upon them by law.

It is the theory of our government that the Constitution shall be obeyed—that the laws made in pursuance thereof shall be executed—and until they are repealed, no party has the right to nullify them or deny their enforcement. If these laws, from inherent defect or absence of power in the State, cannot be executed, they should be eliminated from our statute books. If they are wise and just, they should result in securing the timely and efficient exertion of such control as the State may have the right to claim over these corporations, and no power on earth should be suffered to clog or impede its assertion. If they are to be operated in such manner that the products raised out of the soil, and the commodities created by the industry of the people, are taken from the producer and inure alone to those who receive their earnings, they become of small practical value to the people at large.

We should be unwilling to permit them, by an arrogation of authority superior to that exercised by the State, to abolish the wholesome laws of supply and demand, and advance or depress at will the price of every commodity raised by the people. It is the consumer, in every instance, who must pay for every factor that enters into the cost of a commodity, and it would, therefore, be ruinous in its results to the interests of the whole people.

We are endeavoring to induce capitalists to supply us with additional mills and factories, but prudent businessmen will not build them with so liberal a hand, knowing that this unbridled power can shut their doors and render them profitless at its pleasure.

The effects of such methods upon the lumber, cattle and cotton interests would be only a little less injurious. In regard to the latter, while these corporate and manufacturing companies are made rich by it, the producers waste their lives and fortunes in raising this article at a cost greater than its selling price, and yet it is an element of the largest manufacturing interest in the world, the most valuable article of commerce—a currency within itself—and the greatest boon to human industry.

These are all sources of wealth to our people, involving immense capital and supplying employment to an immense number of people, making it necessary, therefore, that the people shall have good public highways well kept, by improving, if possible our road laws, now so badly in need of revision. Turnpikes made the valleys of Virginia, Kentucky and Middle Tennessee, rich long before they had railroads. Good railways are worth more in inducing immigration and capital then all the speeches and publications that can be made about the undeveloped resources of our State. They increase the value of property and add greatly to the revenues of the State, stimulate production, by saving incalculably, in time and money to the producers, and all business and industrial interests are intimately involved in the matter.

The ownership of land is not only an element of great political power, but no class of people can make any very appreciable advance in civilization without its possession. There is but little to produce patriotism, or pride of country, in a people who are all tenants at will— the soil they tend belonging to others and of which they may be deprived of at pleasure—and even their labor worthless without the patronage of the strong. Government should, therefore, feel itself constantly bound to administer its public lands with schedule care, in order that the greatest number of its people may secure homes at a nominal cost, with security title. The problem confronting the people of Texas in this connection, comprehends the disposition of a vast commonwealth, as a great trust, created and assumed by the State Government, as a common fund to be held and administered for the best use and benefit of all the people. To divert these lands from that general object, to misapply or sacrifice them, to squander or improvidently cast them away, would be alike subversive of the interests of the people, and contrary to the plain dictates of duty, by which the State stands bound in the conditions under which it holds this public property, and for the fulfillment of which its faith is pledged.

Looking upon the lands remaining as a cession for the benefit of the special funds to which they have been dedicated as a productive capital, available for immediate use in bettering the fortunes and conditions of the present generation, as well as their posterity, by relieving them in some measure from the burdens of oppressive taxation—a sale to actual settlers, in volume of labor, and should receive the fostering care of the government, and not to be dominated by any single interest however important within the ligitimate sphere of its operation and usefulness.

Shall it be said that Texas has invited a power that can, at its will, deprive the citizens of the reward of his honest industry in his own State and at his own homestead, and the State's arm which he has toiled to nerve, cannot be extended to afford him redress? If so, it will be a confession that the wisdom and courage, which achieved political independence, has degenerated into that stupidity and unmanliness which forfeits material independence also. It would seem that these corporations ought not to be unmindful of the solicitude, so recently manifested, for their rights, privileges, and immunities, and should not wait to be admonished to do full justice to the people of Texas by a spontaneous act, as broad and general, as the circumstances warrant just and beneficent. And it behooves them to cultivate a proper respect for the law in the people, by an exhibition of proper respect for the law in themselves. If they do not propose to abide by the laws of our State with what grace can they claim protection against those who may assail their just rights?

For the first time in the history of our State, we have seen the laboring classes enlisting under the broad banner of innovation, determined to meet combination in a fierce and desperate conflict against the inexorable demands of a system deemed by them subversive of the philosophy of mutual rights in business; and, as we cannot afford to see our State made the battle ground of disorder and anarchy, while leaving nothing undone to repress violence, it is our solemn duty to remove all just grounds for its provocation, in order that we may restore confidence and establish a better feeling by providing, if possible, a remedy against oppression by capital, or riots by laborers. The more so, since in the contests between these waring factions, it is the innocent, in every instance, who suffer most. The farming class, and business of all kinds, pay tribute by being taxed in increased freight rates, to make good the loss in running expense and otherwise.

However desirable they may be to the development of our State, we can not have a railroad built by every man's house. It is all the more necessary [out] conjunction with leases of unsold lands, has become the avowed policy of the State. But as they clearly involve antagonistic principles, the great practical difficulty with which we are confronted is the adoption of a complex system by which each may be made to contribute its best result to the public benefit.

The celebrated Edmund Burke, in recommending that the forest lands of the British crown should be brought into market and converted into private property at a moderate price, laid down the following just and profound maxims of political economy: "The principal revenue which I propose to draw from these uncultivated wastes is to spring from the improvement and population of the kingdom—events infinitely more advantageous to the crown than the rents of the best landed estates which it can hold. I would throw them into the mass of private property, by which they will come, through the course of circulation, and through the political secretions of the state, into well regulated revenue." The history of the landed system of the United States furnishes the most convincing proof of the value of this policy.

Recognizing that the strength and wealth of the country consists not so much in the money to be exacted as the price of the public lands, as in the increase of population and the soil, and while regarding the public lands as a common fund and seeking to make what reasonably could be made of them as a source of revenue, it applied its best wisdom to sell and settle them as fast and as happily as possible—disposing of the soil in smaller and still smaller portions, with the view of enabling every industrious man in the country, however poor, to become a freeholder. In like manner, it has been the policy of our State, from the earliest settlement, to settle her domain with the tillers of the soil and others who would develop her resources; ever designing to make the settler the object of its fostering care. To this end, she gave first one league and labor of land to heads of families and one-fourth of a league to single men. This policy was continued, lessening the amount as the country was settled, until it was reduced to one hundred and sixty acres for heads of families and eighty acres for single men, always requiring, as a condition to the various grants, settlement, cultivation and permanent residence.

In the course of time, however, our law makers, becoming impatient at the slow but steady operation of these wise laws, which had been so successfully tested by experience, by improvident and reckless legislation, disposed of large bodies to the speculator and made enormous donations to corporations, thus arresting by law the extensions of further settlement of vast areas, so contiguous, important and valuable, and as a just cause of reproach to the State, by statutory prohibition rendered it an inaccessible solitude, which pioneer settlers may not legally disturb.

To lease land and at the same time reserve the right to sell it at any time without the consent of the lessee, operates as a snare and a delusion to both the lessee and the settler, and measurably defeats both sale and lease. Where there is a reservation of the power of selling the lands to others, regardless of all the lessee should do in the way of improving his leasehold, and this, too, without compensating him for his improvements or reimbursing him for the values swept away by the absorption of his range, and consequent removal at an inauspicious season, with possibly no place left to which he may go, or the danger of becoming the victim of a heartless extortion on the part of those acting under the fraudulent guise of actual settlers. We can hardly expect that a prudent man would be willing to invest his means upon such treacherous inducements; and yet this is the precise condition of that law which would lease land with the reservation of the right of sale.

It is not an uncharitable suspicion to say that it is clear that those who do thus lease, do so with the settled purpose of protecting their peculiar interests by the exercise of terrorism and lawless force, if necessary, and the apprehension of this danger defeats and hinders settlement by those who, in good faith, desire to embrace the purposes of the law, by the selection of the lands thus situated.

No better evidence could be required to establish this proposition than is found in the result of the sales made under the act of 1883. In addition to this, we have the experience of others, under the operation of a similar system of land laws, in force in New South Wales, Victoria, and Queensland, where there are unlimited areas, and where the laws, in one way and another, have enabled individuals to purchase the freehold of great tracts, or with sufficient machinery at his disposal, to keep himself informed of the situation, and to execute the powers granted him by law, to conduct these business interests upon uniform and prudent principles.

It is for the Legislature, in its wisdom, to determine what laws are appropriate, and its decision is binding upon every other department.

In a constitutional government, like ours, where the people have once delegated their powers to Representatives as their agents these Representatives cannot delegate the power entrusted to them to others, not selected by the people for that purpose. If the Legislature has the constitutional authority to delegate to a board any portion of their legislative functions, they have the authority to remit to them the entire mass of their legislative power. And the converse of the proposition must be equally true, that if they have no authority to delegate their whole power they are, in like manner, powerless to delegate any portion of it, unless the authority so to delegate is expressly conferred by the Constitution. And in this connection it should be borne in mind that the Constitution forbids any person, or collection of persons, being one of these departments, from the exercise of any power properly attached to either of the others, except in instances expressly sanctioned.

It is believed that under a judicious lease system, which will guarantee full protection to the leaseholder against encroachment, such portions of these lands as are not suitable for agricultural purposes, and susceptible of cultivation or in demand for settlement, can be made to contribute their quota of revenue to the support of the interests to which they were dedicated. The people are certainly not realizing the benefits intended by these munificent landed donations, and the public school system, especially, is becoming a grievous burden to them. The injustice of any proceedings which enable corporations, largely composed of non residents—who derive great profits from the products of their herds, while contributing but a small pittance to the support of our government—to arrogate to themselves the free use of these lands, needs no argument.

Every citizen in the State has a valuable and appreciable interest in these special donations, as well as in upholding the supremacy of the laws as one to hold immense blocks on long lease with very exclusive privileges. They were hired from the government, averaging ten shillings per square mile on long leases, and the leases were granted with certain reservations, chief among which was the right of any bona fide settler to choose for himself, and pay, by easy installments, for not more than three hundred and twenty-five acres of land. It was found, however, that this feature was the prolific source of interminable and bitter contentions between the settler and the lessee, disturbing the public peace and retarding both sale and lease. Finally, the government of Queensland found a satisfactory way out of the difficulty, by making only short leases, and by restricting the settler, in his selection of land, to well defined and surveyed districts, which could be extended from time to time to meet the demands of settlement—justifying its action upon the ground that it was neither violative of a wise policy nor a wrong to the citizen to prevent him from going into suitable or back country, where he would have either no chance of raising crops or would be too far from a market to sell his produce, and there picking the heart out of a "run" (lease) in order to compel the lessee to buy him out, or else taking up the land and ruining himself in sheer ignorance of the drawbacks.

A wise policy would seem to require that the State should, as soon as possible, ascertain definitely the precise classification and locality of her public lands, to secure a proper knowledge of their value, and to insure perfect security of title and certainty of boundary, necessary to avoid perplexing land disputes—the worst of all litigation—the distressing effects of which have been fatally felt by our people already. They should not, in any event be disposed of in large masses to individuals, thus leaving to them the time and manner of settlement, but should be sold under one uniform plan, by clear, simple and positive terms, in small bodies to actual settlers only, on known and moderate terms, long time, and at low rate of interest, so as to extend the blessing of cheap land to the largest number. They should be controlled by a single authority, by restoring the constitutional functions of the Commissioner of the Land office, whose responsibility being immediate, undivided, and direct, and whose wisdom and discretion would enable him, of the essential securities of civilization; and there should be stringent and resolute dealing with all those who defy the authority of the State. If it be known, therefore, that there is an extent of power and influence, as well as fixedness of purpose, on the part of any portion of the community, representing any special interest, which demonstrates that the local judicial machinery is inadequate to meet the emergency, which has erected itself into an open defiance that strikes at the very life of the State, while defrauding the revenues of these special funds, and if existing laws do not possess adequate punitive and remedial measures to prevent the use or enclosure of these public lands of any class, for exclusive occupancy, unless under the rights acquired as a leaseholder or purchaser, make them stronger and more vigorous, to be promptly executed by a firm hand, and if need be, with the forcible interposition of the whole power of the State government.

While the executive should proceed to the faithful and impartial execution of all the laws of the State, by use of all the means placed in his power and which may be necessary to that end, there is no real, true safety to our liberties and institutions, but in a strict adherence to the letter and spirit of our laws; and there is no danger to our peace and prosperity that we cannot easily escape, if we will conscientiously adhere to them. He should not, therefore, for the want of proper legislation, be left with the alternative of either seeing these special funds defrauded of their just revenues, or of becoming the sovereign judge of the emergency which would warrant him in marching an armed force into any community to strike down all civil law.

There is never, under any circumstances, any authority for him to break his oath or violate the law, or to take from the people at his pleasure that security of law which is their birthright.

In monarchies an appeal to the sword is justly called the last reason of kings. Such an exigency is a sign, not only of social demoralization, but of bad administration. If the people of our State can only be relied upon as obedient citizens when confronted by the soldier, with his hand upon the swordhilt, we have indeed fallen below the level of contempt from civilized people.

That no exigency should arise, if wise counsels prevail, is apparent to any one who is acquainted with the people of Texas. We claim to be law-abiding citizens, and this claim is borne out by our whole career as a State and Republic, and it may be set down as a maxim, that, if serious social disturbances should ever arise with our people, resulting in a defiance of lawful authority on the part of any section or class, the prime cause, if properly traced, will lead us back to defective or unwise legislation.

If, in any portion of the State, our laws relating to public lands are defied and set at naught, our first duty is to re-examine the laws, with the view of ascertaining what defects, if any, have produced this condition of society, and, upon discovery of any defect, to apply a remedy. Give the people just and wholesome laws and they will not only obey them, but aid their enforcement and execution.

Second Inaugural Address *
January 15, 1889

GENTLEMEN:

To the people of Texas, who have for the second time vested me with the authority of Chief Magistrate, I am unable to express how deeply sensible I am of the high honor which this mark of their renewed confidence implies. And standing upon the threshold of a new administration, with the retrospect in our possession by which we may in a measure estimate the accomplishments of the past and the possibilities of the future, I should be faithless to duty did I not recognize an individual obligation to administer the affairs of your government with the single-hearted determination to do all in my power to make the whole people more prosperous and contented, and strengthen the bonds which should unite them in a common grand destiny.

We have just emerged from a political contest involving the excitement of a presidential and State campaign, that justly agitated the entire State and stirred its people to the profoundest depths, and I congratulate you as their representatives upon the valid claim that there has neither been violence, evidence of fraud or diminution of the right of franchise; but, on the contrary, every citizen, without reference to former or existing conditions, who was entitled to vote has been accorded a free and unabridged exercise of this great privilege.

The spirit of subordination of our people to the laws and their prompt obedience to the demands of orderly government could not have been more forcibly exemplified. They fully appreciated the fact that the great fundamental principles of a popular government is the residence of power in a legal and properly ascertained majority, and the behests of the party ceased and the claims of country intervened in complete majesty, enabling them as patriots to lift themselves above the

---

Journal of the House of Representatives of the Twenty-first Legislature of the State of Texas (1889), pp. 88–90.

obligations of partisans in compliance with the truest principles of statesmanship, which consists in a ready and proper adjustment of affairs to the existing conditions.

Acknowledging no master but the law and the Constitution, and without fear of being despoiled of their political liberties by an unjust and unlawful interference of federal power to hold them in servile thrall, they simply claim the right as a sovereign people to regulate their internal and domestic affairs in their own way, being inflexibly opposed to such interference because they have seen and felt its injustice and know that it must end in the creation and perpetuation of sectional jealousies, prejudicial to that harmony and cordiality which is so greatly to be cherished and so important to their progress as a people.

No citizen of Texas will permit himself to forget that he is a part of the government, and that the highest considerations of personal honor and patriotism require him to maintain by all the power and influence he may possess, the integrity of the laws of nation and State. And yet it sometimes happens that the enactment of laws cannot be wisely undertaken when partisan interests and bitterness intervene to deny them that impartial consideration which alone can confer lasting benefit. But I feel assured that in the exercise of your official responsibility, fraught with consequences so momentous, you will temper your judgment with the keenest sense of discretion, controlled by a spirit of fairness, that will command the acquiescence of the whole people, and strengthen their confidence in the ability of their law-makers to preserve substantial justice between contending interests so far as it may be done in framing a code of laws.

It is needless to remind you that as legislators you have an important and peculiar province committed to your care, and the constant changes and variations in the conditions of society makes frequent legislation necessary to conserve and protect public interests, and yet it is a maxim as true as it has become trite, "that the least governed is the best governed State," and a few laws faithfully administered are far better than volumes of statutes amended beyond the comprehension of the people who are required to obey them, creating an immense public burden in having them expounded and applied. As the government is responsible to the citizen and not for him, he should not be placed under a sleepless espionage that takes cognizance of everything he does, while undermining a true spirit of manhood, and inspiring an element of unrest that becomes a constant menace to public peace and safety.

I am firmly established in that standard of political faith that holds to a plain, simple government, with severe limitations upon delegated powers, honestly and frugally administered, as the noblest and truest outgrowth of the wisdom taught by its founders, and which has proven through all vicissitudes the most valuable safeguard to public liberty, freedom of conscience, and a noble manhood, limiting the domain of its authority in the social compact to the preservation of public order through local agencies, and the administration of justice with the view of protecting every real and substantive right, while leaving all else to the unfettered enterprise of the citizen under the regulation of that moral power which springs from self-reliance, enlightened conscience, and a cultivated intelligence, crystalized into a devoted patriotism.

I have been led the more earnestly to these views because, in my judgment, one of the most serious perils threatening the integrity of our government lurks in the growing tendency on the part of the people to underestimate their duty and power and to call upon Hercules for aid, when their own shoulders are ample to move the wheels if applied with vigor and energy. How often do we see officials who are conservators of the peace, with a law abiding community subject to their direction for the vindication of the majesty of the laws, proclaim the want of reliance in a local community, and at the same time putting implicit faith in the ability of a half dozen rangers, clothed with the symbol of State power, to give needed protection and restore order, thereby probably unavoidably forming and encouraging the growth and spread of sentiments adverse to a proper feeling of self-dependence, self-reliance and self-maintenance, rather than a sturdy independence and manhood among the people, so essential for the healthy development and continuance of a form of government like ours.

This reasoning might be carried to a much greater length, and applied to the tendency of legislation toward destroying the individual enterprise of the citizen by an unreasonable extension and continuance of corporate powers and immunities for purposes that could as well be conducted by individual effort, taking under such protection all classes of business and every character of industry or enterprise, the greater part of which can with much greater safety to the community be confined to personal competition and liability.

It is conceded that many business ventures involving large capital justify corporate powers, but it is hard to understand the character of justice that exempts the corporator under these privileges from the same care and liability that is exacted from the individual citizen, and shields him in a failure, whether from want of care, extravagance or lack of attention to business, from loss beyond the amount of stock owned. The extent to which this power is drifting under cover of law seems to me to be hastening the growth of monopolies and moneyed combinations likely to become a heavy burden if not disastrous to the general public, and presents a serious consideration as to whether it is not the part of wisdom to curtail its privileges rather than to extend them further.

There is another feature involved in this line of thought with a more direct bearing upon the prosperity of our State, but which statutes, how-ever wise, cannot reach or remedy, mentioned with the hope of bringing our people to a fuller realization of the importance of that individual enterprise and independence which is so necessary to prosperity.

We have a State surrounded with exceptional advantages in climate and a soil fertile to exhuberance in the production of all the staple products and cereals, and peculiarly adapted to the creation of such wealth as is incident to the farm or stock ranch; and yet, the statistics exhibited by our agricultural department show that nearly seven mil-lions of dollars were expended abroad by our people for flour, bacon, lard and syrup, supplying us with an example, rich in undisguised and indisputable proof of the extent to which other people less favored with natural or artificial advantages are achieving the magnificence of their States and the prosperity of themselves at the expense of our own. This has its punishment in poverty, and every interest is suffering that pun-ishment which this improvidence, want of frugal habits, and depen-dence on others begets. Self-reliance is the great element of success in this world with States and individuals, and as self-preservation is a nat-ural duty binding upon all alike, and there being no constitutional amendment that I am aware of compelling our people to send to our Northern neighbors for everything we need, from a hoe-handle to a steam engine, without the least trace of hostility or bitterness, I would invoke them to a more perfect reliance upon the energies and the resources which they can find within themselves by the development of home industries, home markets, and individual enterprise. History does not record an instance of greater power to conquer adversity than our people have proven themselves capable of in times past when the neces-sity was upon them. It has been but a little while since our State was wholly prostrated in its material resources and overwhelmed by the rapidly succeeding waves of unprecedented reverses, political troubles, social disorders, and financial derangements; her works of internal improvements retarded or abandoned altogether; capital shunned her borders because of the unsettled condition, and sought safer and more prosperous channels of employment, leaving industry paralized and labor to contend at odds with want. But happily in course of time the superior intelligence and energy of the people made their impress and established their dominion, and the plowshare of industry was run deep among the smouldering embers of strife, turning them under the soil to be watered by the showers of material prosperity, and by methods of peace the wisdom of her rulers introduced into her governmental affairs, those patient, painstaking, economical habits which characterize the conduct of successful private business, and to capital and honest industry they promised encouragement, protection and the enjoyment of the highest freedom consistent with civil government, with exemption from heavy taxes and a happy home amongst a generous, brave and intelligent people. And to-day, as we take in the full measure of the picture and our hearts swell with exultant pride, we claim that the genesis of her prosperity has scarcely yet been written, and as we stand upon the Prisgah top from which we can view the inheritance of prosperity and political power that awaits her, no conceivable advantage that could inure to any class or special interest, nor even the increase of federal representation, would compensate for the loss of that prestige and power that exists in the presence of her united people with the strength born of unity.

XV

James Stephen

HOGG

1891–1895

Courtesy of Archives Division, Texas State Library

JAMES STEPHEN HOGG (*March 24, 1851–March 3, 1906*), the son of a farmer and a member of the Texas legislature, was born on the family estate near Rusk, Texas. Hogg attended the McKnight School, was privately tutored, and spent almost a year attending school at Tuscaloosa, Alabama. He studied law and was admitted to the bar in 1875. He practiced law and worked in newspaper offices.

Hogg began his active political career in 1873 when he was elected justice of the peace. Three years later he won the position of county attorney of Wood County. In 1880 he was elected district attorney and served two terms. In 1884 he moved to Tyler and established a law practice. Hogg was twice elected attorney general of Texas, in 1886 and 1888.

From this statewide elected position of attorney general of Texas, he ran successfully for governor, defeating his Republican opponent in the general election held on November 4, 1890. He took office on January 20, 1891. He became the first native Texan to be elected governor of the state and the first governor without a military service background.

In the 1892 election, Hogg won a second term which began on January 17, 1893.

Inaugural Address *
January 20, 1891

GOVERNOR ROSS, YOU HAVE MY HEARTIEST RESPECT AND ADMIRATION. FELLOW CITIZENS, SENATORS AND REPRESENTATIVES:

In taking the oath just administered I have, by the grace of a generous people, assumed grave responsibilities, the obligations of which bear heavily upon me. In return for the confidence bestowed I hope faithful service will be rendered by a grateful officer.

On this occasion I must eschew a discussion on state policy and of measures meriting legislative attention, for by message on tomorrow, God being willing, I shall present to the legislature my views on many important subjects with confidence that they may be duly considered to the advantage of public interests.

This government was instituted for the safety and happiness of the people, and the object of all laws should be to accomplish such ends. The splendid body of senators and representatives now in session with those objects alone in view will receive my hearty and earnest assistance in accomplishing the work that lies before them, while the people expect much of this administration, they can be trusted to wait for results, in which they will not be disappointed. Honest, faithful efforts on the part of their servants cannot fail of their approbation. There are no better judges of what is proper or of the efficient performances of duty than the great masses who, of right, do and should forever control this government. In them it is with pride that I confess my confidence. To them, before this imposing and welcome assemblage here to witness the beginning of my official service, I publicly acknowledge unfeigned gratitude. From penury in boyhood, all along life's rugged way, they

*Journal of the House of Representatives of the Twenty-second Legislature of the State of Texas (1891), p. 96.

have liberally shown me favors, and now from the summit of my political ambition I acknowledge their supremacy and dedicate my honor, my time and my abilities to the protection and promotion of their sacred rights and material interests.

In conclusion, I beg to tender to the senators and representatives the freedom of the department over which I am to preside, and to assure them that on no occasion will the doors be closed to their coming, for with them I join in a common work for the good of a proud and confiding constituency whose pride centers in the glory, the honor and the advancement of a great state.

I thank you kindly for you attention.

Second Inaugural Address *

January 17, 1893

Mr. SPEAKER AND GENTLEMEN OF THE SENATE AND HOUSE OF REPRESENTATIVES:

In good faith I have taken the oath just administered, and now with profound concern assume the grave responsibilities imposed by the office of Governor.

I have no further recommendations at this time to make to your honorable bodies than may be found in the message I delivered to you last week. The end and aim held in view by that message are the promotion of good government and the material interests of the people.

Prosperity, after all, gentlemen, depends upon the condition of labor and its profits. Every legitimate effort that tends to lighten the burdens of industry and to infuse into it life and vigor must in time receive the commendation of all patriots. From the farms, the ranches and the workshops, as a result of labor, springs the wealth of the government; and to their care and encouragement every leading legislative effort and measure should be directed. When last year over three million dollars were saved to the producers from traffic taxation alone, without diminishing the receipts of our transportation companies, the lesson was taught that this saving, diffused throughout industry in all its forms, marks the era of posterity in this State.

Consider well the beginning, gentlemen; add a few more touches to the work laid out by the platform demands, and your names will become enshrined in the hearts of your constituents and honored by those to follow. When the people speak, let their will be done. They have spoken, and I have confidence in the integrity, the intelligence and the fidelity of this Legislature. I thank you for your attention.

*Journal of the House of Representatives of the Twenty-third Legislature of the State of Texas (1893), p. 86.

XVI

Charles Allen
CULBERSON

1895–1899

Courtesy of Archives Division, Texas State Library

CHARLES ALLEN CULBERSON (*June 10, 1855–March 19, 1925*), the son of a United States Congressman, was born in Dadeville, Alabama. When he was a year old, his family moved to Gilmer, Texas. Five years later, the family settled in Jefferson, Texas. Culberson graduated from Virginia Military Institute in Lexington, Virginia, in 1874. He studied law with his father and graduated from the University of Virginia Law School in 1877.

Admitted to the bar in 1877, he opened a law office in Jefferson. In 1880 he was elected Marion County attorney but resigned the post in 1882. Culberson moved his law practice to Dallas in 1887. Culberson was elected attorney general of Texas in 1890 and served two terms.

It was from that political position that he sought the governorship in 1894. Running as a Democrat, Culberson defeated Republican and Populist opposition to win the position. He took office on January 15, 1895.

He won a second term in 1896 by defeating a Populist candidate. His second term began on January 19, 1897.

Inaugural Address*
January 15, 1895

These impressive ceremonies place me under profound obligations to the people of Texas. For the marked consideration which they have shown me no adequate return can be made. Their partiality and kindness, of which I am keenly sensible and justly proud, will ever be held in grateful acknowledgment and as the highest expression of appreciation my best energies will be consecrated to their service.

Under ordinary circumstances the assumption of the duties of this high office would carry with it serious responsibility and misgivings. These reflections are intensified by well known conditions which now confront us and it is manifest that the situation demands a clear and firm purpose, a large measure of forbearance and co-operation by the different branches of government and unyielding observance of public pledges. So far as I may be able to influence legislation or the administration of affairs the Constitution of my State, the avowed principles of my party and my public assurances shall guide and control, and the path thus marked out shall be followed withersoever it leads; for in this great presence and impressed by the solemnity of the occasion, it may be permitted me to declare that the confidence of the people in the integrity of deliberate and well considered promises is dearer to me than power or the glamour of office.

Loving Texas with patriotic devotion, warmly attached to her ennobling history and traditions, deeply concerned for the welfare and advancement of her people and anxious for the growth and development of her material interests, these grave duties are assumed with no thought distinct from her greatness, no higher aim than to maintain her honor untarnished and no nobler ambition than to contribute something to good government and the happiness and prosperity of her toiling thousands.

*Journal of the House of Representatives of the Twenty-fourth Legislature of the State of Texas (1895), p. 44.

This great audience, I feel certain, will unite with me in tendering Governor Hogg on his retirement from office assurance of the high esteem in which he is held. His has been a useful and remarkable career. Large of body and mind, great hearted, generous and brave, devoted to the masses, his place in the affections of the people is securely fixed and the great impress he has left upon our legislation is an enduring monument to his fidelity, his courage and his statesmanship. Wherever his lot and his fortunes may be cast, the best wishes of the people will attend him for his continued success and happiness.

Second Inaugural Address *

January 19, 1897

GENTLEMEN OF THE SENATE AND HOUSE OF REPRESENTATIVES:

Called the second time under extraordinary conditions to the highest office in the State, I am deeply sensible of the confidence of the people and the responsibilities of this great trust. The campaign through which we have just passed was the most virulent and vindictive in our history. Though lacking nothing in organization and equipment which irresponsible and unscrupulous wealth could command, falsehood and calumny were the chief reliance of the opposition. To have passed uninjured in character through that storm of malice and hate and political depravity and received decisive expression of the faith of a great people, is to me unpurchaseable and priceless. Proud of their loyalty and friendship, my deep sense of appreciation will be shown in a consecration to their service during my term of office and an unfading remembrance of their kindness. But above personal indorsement and vindication is the distinctive triumph here of the great party to which most of us belong, and the assurance of good government for the State. Whether the one shall be enduring and the other perpetuated through that agency may be influenced by your deliberations. Broadly speaking, what is demanded to further these results is that we act uprightly with the people. Not a single promise of legislation which we have made should go unredeemed, and no substantial public interest be disregarded. In a still larger and nobler sense, the ambition of all should be the advancement and the grandeur of Texas. Glorious in her infancy, rich in later memories, splendid in present achievement, and limitless in promise and in future, she offers exhaustless material for the betterment of mankind and the building of a mighty commonwealth. That you will be mindful

Journal of the House of Representatives of the Twenty-fifth Legislature of the State of Texas (1897), pp. 64–65.

of these considerations and act well your part is not doubted, and my duties are assumed with the single purpose of co-operating with you in whatever may contribute to the prosperity and happiness of the people and the glory of the State.

XVII

Joseph Draper

SAYERS

1899–1903

Courtesy of Archives Division, Texas State Library

JOSEPH DRAPER SAYERS (*September 23, 1841–May 15, 1929*) was born in Grenada, Mississippi. He attended Bastrop Military Institute from 1852 to 1860. From 1861 to 1865 he served as major of the Fifth Regiment, Mounted Volunteers, in the Confederate Army.

Following his military service, he practiced law in Bastrop, Texas, from 1866 to 1876. Sayers served in the Texas Senate from 1873 until 1878 and as lieutenant governor from 1878 to 1879. He served in the United States Congress from 1885 until 1898.

A Democrat, Sayers was elected governor in 1898, defeating the Populist candidate by a wide margin. He took office on January 17, 1899.

Seeking a second term in 1900, Sayers defeated both the Republican and Populist candidates. He began his second term on January 15, 1901.

*Inaugural Address**

January 17, 1899

My FELLOW CITIZENS:

He who undertakes the chief magistracy of this great Commonwealth will have no easy task before him, and without the earnest and hearty co-operation of his fellow citizens he cannot reasonably anticipate a satisfactory and successful administration of the public affairs. Therefore, at the very threshold of the duties imposed upon me by the oath, which I have just taken, I invoke the guidance of Almighty God and the aid of all my countrymen to enable me to so discharge every obligation as to best promote the prosperity of the State and the happiness of the people.

On an occasion like the present it will not be deemed out of place, I take it, to devote a few moments to the consideration of the purpose of government and its method of administration. Although the subject be old and indeed familiar, its importance makes it always worthy a reference before any audience. It will be conceded by all that a just and well constituted government will have no object in view other than to serve and benefit the entire citizenship, and that it should be conducted with wisdom, firmness, fidelity and without discrimination. No class or interest should be favored with special privileges, and to every one should be insured certain and complete protection to life, liberty and property. These are elementary propositions. They are recognized as indisputably true, and are so broad and comprehensive in meaning as to cover almost the entire domain within which the State may safely exercise authority. In their reasonable interpretation and application may be found to reside almost every necessary governmental power.

Faithful, honest and efficient administration is no less needful than wise and just legislation, and failure in either is always attended with unhappy consequences. Whatever the law—be it good or bad, popular or unpopular—it is the bounden duty of those to whom its execution is entrusted to enforce it, and no influence, however potent, should be

Journal of the House of Representatives of the Twenty-sixth Legislature of the State of Texas (1899), pp. 82–88.

heard to stay its steady and impartial operation. So long as it is on the statute book it is an authoritative expression of the popular will through the appropriate channel, and it should be respected and obeyed. Every infraction is an open defiance to the sovereignty of the people, and, if not followed by adequate penalty, begets dangerous distrust in the ability of the government to answer the purpose for which it was ordained. Disregard of the law through neglect of the executive branch of the public service to put it and to keep it in constant force, is as reprehensible as the exercise of power without proper warrant of authority. No deadlier blow can be given to free institutions than weak, loose and irregular administration, and such a policy, if policy it may be termed, cannot be too strongly condemned. The safety of society demands that the enforcement of the law should be uniform, steady and impartial, and that none should be so strong as to be beyond its requirements, and none so weak as to be beneath its protection.

In the earlier days of the Republic the sphere of governmental action was limited, and its appropriate functions were well defined. Individual freedom was then regarded as the very cornerstone upon which religious, civil and political liberty rested, and to which the progress of the race towards a higher and better civilization is chiefly indebted. The contrast between the legislation that was had prior to the Civil war and that enacted during the past three decades is broad and deep, and the most careless observer cannot fail to note this very obvious distinction between the two eras.

Formerly the greatest latitude, consistent with the welfare of society, was allowed the citizen, and he was taught to rely upon himself in the management of his personal affairs—thinking for himself and acting for himself. Nowadays it has become somewhat, if not largely, different, and the power of legislation is often invoked to suppress evils that were once thought to be beyond governmental reach, and to be corrected only through the operation of laws which are not artificial and which do not depend upon government for their efficacy.

This wide and radical departure from the long and well established policy of non-interference in such matters, except when the public good clearly and emphatically demanded, is in some measure due to and justified by the changed conditions in our social, commercial and industrial life, and the introduction of agencies that were previously unknown; but not altogether so. It has proceeded to a certain extent, from the tendency of the popular mind to over-estimate the power and enlarge the duty of the State, and to under-rate the ability of the citizen to successfully cope with the difficulties that environ him.

The effect of this tendency has been to cause the individual to lose confidence in himself, and to rely too much upon the government. But in the protection of property it cannot be well claimed that the duty of government is limited only to cases of open violence by the mob, or to the willful wrongdoing of the single trespasser. Its obligation in this respect extends much further, and may fairly include unjust and discriminating legislation, uncertain and arbitrary administration, and artificial combinations whose object it is to weaken or destroy other enterprises and industries, the healthy existence and successful conduct of which is essential to society. Nor can it be doubted that it is the province and duty of the State to interfere, if necessary, and prevent an improper exercise by associations of the powers and privileges that may be granted to them by law, and which may not be incidental to the general and ordinary avocations of life.

Such grants of power and privilege are always intended to be instruments of benefit and not of injury to the people, and when they are diverted from their proper purpose the State should not avoid the responsibility of protecting the citizen.

We cannot too highly estimate the necessity of a full and complete discharge by the government at all times and under all circumstances of its obligation to society in the matter of protection to life, liberty and property, as upon it depends the prosperity, peace and happiness of the people. To that protection every person and every character of property within our borders is equally entitled. Human life is sacred, made so by God and man, and should never be taken except as expressly permitted by law, and there can be no justification outside of the law. However severe the provocation, the welfare of society demands that the injured party should rest his case with the law and abide its judgment; and those entrusted with its enforcement are, therefore, the more strongly bound to see that the offender is brought to speedy and impartial trial, and that the penalty denounced by the law be inflicted.

When it shall be well understood by all that the criminal, whoever he may be, will be quickly and adequately punished as prescribed by law, then not only will the law be permitted to assert its right of cognizance of offenses and to take its regular and orderly course, however aggravated the circumstances, but crime also will become less frequent throughout the land. It is the uncertainty and delay that too often characterizes judicial investigation as much as the nature of the crime itself that drives the citizen to a violation of the law by visiting, with his own hands, summary punishment upon the offender—forgetting in his indignation and resentment that in so doing he weakens the authority of the law, and renders his own life less secure.

True it is that, in a certain sense, the citizen is sovereign, yet nevertheless he is subject to the law of his own creation, and he cannot break it without impeaching his own sovereignty. And more than that, in so doing he establishes a precedent, which if too often followed, will unquestionably destroy the peace and repose upon which the very life of society depends, and substitute anarchy or despotism for a government of liberty, regulated by law.

The protection of liberty—personal, religious, civil and political—comes next in order of importance, and this includes the employment of all the necessary and proper means to insure it. To pursue, without illegal interruption, such avocations as are not forbidden by law; to worship God according to the dictates of his own conscience; to stand before the law the equal of any other man, and to be judged as any other man; and to vote, under the restrictions imposed for the good of society upon the whole people, as he may deem best for his country, unawed by power and uncorrupted by bribe, and to have his ballot fairly counted, these are rights to whose protection government stands most strongly pledged; and any government that, through the imperfection of its laws or the weakness of its administration, fails to effectively maintain to the people this pledge, in all its fullness, ought to be abolished.

Scarcely, if at all, less necessary to the very existence of the social fabric than the protection of life and liberty is that of property. The fruits of industry, skill, economy and enterprise should be held by no uncertain tenure. They should be safe not only against those acts which the law declares to be felonies and misdemeanors, but also against harsh and improvident legislation. The burdens of government should be fairly and equitably distributed and imposed, and every character of property should be compelled to contribute to the public treasury according to its value. And government should go further and see to it that such property as may be favored by the law with peculiar privileges and unusual powers shall not be used to injure other pursuits that are necessary to the well being of the Commonwealth.

All legislation that directly or indirectly affects property, either as to value or as to title, should be conservative and just, and the rights of ownership, as well as the welfare of society, should be observed. To acquire and hold property lies at the very base of civilization and cannot be impaired without danger to society.

Even and exact justice, as well to the property as to the person of the citizen, should be the ruling motive and guiding principle of action in every branch of the public service, and the more strongly and the more uniformly it is maintained the more prosperous will be the State and the happier will be the people. And a similar policy of even and exact justice should be adopted towards those who may invest but not reside with us, putting and keeping them as to their investments on an equal footing with ourselves, and dealing with them as with ourselves. By so doing, confidence, both at home and abroad, will become firmly established and the best of other communities will seek homes amongst us, attracted by our genial climate, rich soil, exhaustless resources and splendid citizenship, and bringing with them wealth, thrift, energy and enterprise.

As to the laws applying to and affecting these great purposes of government, no just complaint can be urged against our State. The statute book of Texas will compare most favorably with that of the foremost American commonwealths, and as to the enforcement of the law, a comparison will be equally as creditable to ourselves. But there is room for improvement, and from the executive department, in all its branches and sub-divisions, the very best service possible should be exacted, and with less the people should not be content. There should be no condonement of inefficiency in the discharge of official duty. It is not enough that every other qualification should be possessed. The highest standard of excellence is needed for the delicate and important work of governmental administration, and, if uniformly and impartially exacted, there may be found in the great body of the citizenship those who can and will fully meet every requirement.

Having sought and accepted official responsibility, no one should be permitted to regard himself other than a public servant, and office as a public trust—to be held and administered not for the especial advantage of himself and his kin, but for the benefit of the people and of the people only. The doctrine that office is property, and endowed with property rights, may be good in law, but it is not healthful to the public service, and has sometimes led to great abuse. Nepotism is not admissible in a properly constituted government.

It should be known everywhere that in no other State is life, liberty and property so secure; in no other State are offenses against them so surely, so speedily and so sufficiently punished; and in no other State is such complete justice between all men and as to all kinds of property maintained as within the great Commonwealth of Texas.

Under our political system this is the peculiar and exclusive prerogative of the State, and it therefore becomes its imperative duty, which it cannot honorably or safely avoid, to fully and successfully discharge the responsibility thus imposed, and I doubt not that Texas will continue faithful to this important trust. In this way will she vindicate the wisdom and confidence of our fathers in their provision for home rule and local self-government, and will maintain her place among the best administered of American commonwealths.

The character of our people for peace, good order, intelligence, justice and morality, already high, will keep apace with their advancement in material prosperity, and in all lands will the fame of our State abide, each year adding lustre to her history.

An empire in extent, resources almost limitless, situation altogether favorable, and an open sea around her southern border, Texas may well aspire to a greatness and grandeur that will have no parallel in the history and experience of her sister States.

It will not, I trust, be regarded as inappropriate to this hour to invite your attention to other matters, although not directly connected with the public service.

However essential a wise and just government may be, and however efficient its administration in all respects, it must, nevertheless, be supplemented in a large degree by individual effort and enterprise in other and different directions, and having other and different ends in view. Government cannot overstep certain limits without harm to society. Its orbit, wherein it may move with wholesome effect, is restricted, and its sphere of usefulness has boundaries that are well marked. It cannot till the field, nor operate the factory, nor conduct commerce, nor follow the professions. These instrumentalities, with all their subdivisions, belong to the citizen, and should be under his exclusive control, and upon him must devolve the responsibility of their proper use.

All material development is effected upon three great lines— agriculture, commerce and manufactures. The time has been in the history of our race when a country could be prosperous, in which any of these great industries should be largely dominant, and furnish employment to the great body of its people. But not so in the present age. Conditions now are vastly different. The world is not what it was a century ago. Steam, electricity, invention, and a more extensive and accurate insight into the workings and secrets of nature have wrought marvelous changes, and the proposition has become unquestionably true that the grand divisions of labor, agriculture, commerce and manufactures, should exist and flourish within the same borders in order to insure entire independence to any people.

In this day it may be safely asserted to be an impossibility for a people to live and attain permanent prosperity by agriculture alone, or by commerce alone, or by manufactures alone. These great industries should not be envious rivals. They attain their highest development when in close proximity, and when their relations are cordial and friendly. They are mutually helpful, and when a sense of justice, or even of enlightened selfishness prevails, there will be no effort to enrich or strengthen the one to the detriment of the others. Of the full profit, when equity is recognized, the three will share in just proportion, and in so doing all will live and prosper. Depress agriculture so that it will cease to be remunerative, what then? Make manufactures unprofitable, because of the unfriendly attitude of agriculture and commerce, what will be the result? Let commerce be put under the ban, who so blind is not to foresee the end?

I submit these observations as applicable to present conditions in our State, and in the hope that we all, however engaged, may speedily awaken to a realization of what should be done in order to bring about a complete and harmonious union of these great factors in the production and distribution of material wealth, so that they may find here their best and most profitable development.

With us, agriculture—although its output is enormously large, with the certainty of becoming very much larger—has almost ceased to be remunerative beyond the extent of our own consumption. Of manufactures there are but few as compared with the quantity of raw material that is being produced, and of the vastly greater quantity that can be easily and speedily realized; while transportation—one of the instrumentalities of commerce—is exacting full compensation, notwithstanding the lack of manufactures and the very low price and greatly enlarged volume of agricultural products.

This is unfortunate, and if conditions be not soon changed for the better, they will result disastrously to every interest. I trust that wiser counsels will prevail and that a proper regard for the general welfare will characterize the future action of those upon whom the responsibility rests.

Should present conditions, however, be insisted upon, then it will become the duty of the State to exert whatever power it may possess to compel such associations as have procured from the government exceptional privileges, to deal fairly and equitably with all other interests. The exercise of such power, while firm and impartial, will, I am quite sure, be conservative, and attended with the proper consideration of every just right. The purpose will be to restrain, not to injure; to build up, not to pull down. The prosperity of every factor in our material development will be regarded as essential to the well being of the entire system. At this time there can be no policy of greater importance to the people than that which will lead to the establishment and operation of industrial enterprises of all kinds in our State. Their necessity is urgent, and it must be met if we would be prosperous.

Our cotton crop for the season just closed aggregated near four millions of bales, with a reasonable certainty of a steady increase year by year. Its price, however, is distressingly low, with no indication of improvement, unless larger and better markets be secured. Added to this embarrassment is the further necessity, so long as present conditions prevail, upon our people to send their cotton, with the exception perhaps of a few hundred bales, to other States and countries, to be sold and converted into finished products. These fabrics we buy for our own consumption at largely increased prices over that received for the raw material, thus paying transportation both ways and the cost of converting the cotton into manufactured goods, with a per cent added for profit, besides losing to our wage earners diversified and remunerative employment, and to our farmers the sale of much of their field and garden produce. A similar necessity exists as to our hides and wool, not including other kinds of raw material which are to be had in plentiful abundance.

Our store and warehouses are full to overflowing with merchandise of all kinds, the inventories of which, although long and costly, contain but few items of home manufacture. Almost everything we use and wear in city, town and country comes from distant markets. Much of our bacon, pork, corn, hay and other farm, garden and orchard products is also brought from elsewhere; and notwithstanding our wealth of timber—of many valuable kinds—we go to other workshops to procure our carriages, wagons, buggies and farming implements, and to other factories for the furniture that is used in our public buildings, churches, school houses and homes. Herein is to be found one of the prime reasons why the first of January of each recurring year finds so many of our people unable to meet their engagements, and with but small hope for the future. This condition is ruinous to our State, and unless there be a wide departure, we may expect the situation to grow worse, until poverty shall become the most distinguishing characteristic of our people.

The statement is not an exaggeration. It is unfortunately too true, and calls for an immediate remedy. Relief can be had if we will only do as other States of the Union—notably southern—are doing. That is, if we will at once direct our efforts to the promotion of such mechanical and manufacturing industries as may be appropriate to our natural resources.

We often, however, hear it said there is not sufficient home capital for the purpose, and that we must secure help from the outside before it can be accomplished. This is a fatal mistake. We must first show that we have confidence in such enterprises and in ourselves before others will risk their means in them. In Georgia, the Carolinas, Tennessee, Virginia and Alabama industrial and manufacturing enterprises were inaugurated by their own peoples, and not until their success was demonstrated were the capitalists of other States induced to invest.

In a communication to the Tradesmen's Annual, Governor Atkinson, of Georgia, illustrated the enterprising and self-reliant spirit of the people of that State by a reference which will bear quoting today. He said: "The town in which I live—Newnan, a place of about 3000 population—is a striking illustration, but not an exceptional instance. The people there, without the aid of foreign capital, have established various industrial enterprises, where twenty years ago not one existed. They manufacture wagons, buggies, acids, cotton goods, and have foundries, machine shops, etc. Not one of these enterprises have failed to pay dividends regularly, and the value of their products is nearly one million of dollars annually. Men who fifteen or twenty years ago would have hooted at the idea of their boys becoming mechanics or engineers, now send them to the shops to learn by actual experience the industrial side of life. Thus, in nearly every town in the State, old ideas give place to the new, and men have ceased to believe that their sons must engage in agriculture or enter the professions. Sons of wealthy men are preparing themselves for the management of industrial enterprises, and the vast field of opportunity is becoming more and more alluring."

These are words of encouragement and promise to the people of Texas, and their entire accuracy is more than verified by the present condition of Georgia—over whose soil immense armies, within the memory of ourselves, marched and camped and fought, carrying desolation in their pathways, and reducing almost to a wilderness a land that once was full of plenty and bright with happiness. From the ashes of her desolation—through the courage, energy, thrift, economy and enterprise of her sons and daughters—an industrial life has sprung, bringing prosperity to the present and hope for the future.

Virginia, Tennessee, the Carolinas and Alabama tell the same story.

We are of the same stock and lineage, with the best and most enterprising of other States and countries as a valuable supplement to our citizenship, and why should we hesitate to do that in which they have so well succeeded? Our situation is far more propitious for the undertaking, and we need not fear the result. The victory is won even before the battle shall be fought, and we may safely anticipate its full and substantial fruits before a single dollar has been expended. While depending upon ourselves in this emergency, yet we extend to outside capital the most cordial invitation to assist us, and we give to it the assurance of fair and just treatment at our hands. We promise, that no discrimination shall be made against it, and that the same protection will be accorded it as is given to that of our own citizens. Both will stand upon an equal footing, and special privileges will be granted to neither. Upon these terms we welcome all who desire to invest their means within our State, and express the hope to them that their investments may be profitable, and that their business connection may be pleasant. We invite them most cordially to homes with us; to assist in building up a mighty Commonwealth; to share our prosperity; to become of us; to be citizens of Texas, giving them the pledge that in all respects they will be treated as ourselves. We have room enough for all; there is opportunity for all who are industrious, temperate and frugal.

But we are fortunate in that at no other period of our history has there been so auspicious a conjunction of necessity and opportunity as now. Recent events are preparing the way for the successful inauguration of an era of industrial life, and of enlarged commercial intercourse with other nations.

Heretofore our trade relations with the East have not been satisfactory. They have been not at all commensurate with the amount, character and value of our productions. We have permitted other countries, greatly inferior to us, to outstrip us in the matter of commerce. We now have the opportunity to forge rapidly to the front. The opportunity may not come to us again within a century—perhaps never.

The construction of the canal, bringing the two oceans together, is a certainty, thereby shortening the distance between ourselves and the Orient by several thousand miles.

With our cotton fields, sheep folds and cattle ranches almost within hearing of the hum of the spindle and the whirl of machinery, and with the shortest water line to China and Japan at our command, what will stand in our way to great and permanent prosperity? Of all the States Texas will be the most benefited by these new conditions; provided her people will at once seize the occasion and avail themselves of the best opportunity by far that has ever occurred to them for achieving industrial, agricultural and commercial greatness. Every ship that leaves our shores should be laden to the guards with the products of our industry, skill and enterprise.

This, and this only is the way that will lead to permanent prosperity. If we hesitate, the fault will be with us. Hewers of wood and drawers of water we have been, and will continue to be as long as we depend altogether upon agriculture. Our ambition should be to acquire industrial independence. No less a purpose is worthy the race from which we have sprung, nor the inheritance we have received from our fathers.

Whatever the policy that may finally prevail as to territorial extension it may be considered as certain that there will be none of self-abnegation or self-imposed restriction as to commerce. Expansion of trade is not only a vital necessity but a determined fact. Our power to produce is greater than our ability to consume. The disparity will increase with the coming years, and it may be depended upon that the people of America will not surrender the commercial advantages which the victory at Manila has given to them. Other nations must accord to us a liberal share of the eastern trade. The rhetoric of the hustings, however brilliant and captivating, must yield to the logic of the situation, supported by that of an imperious necessity.

True statesmanship and a proper regard for own welfare demands that we should not sacrifice our material interests upon the altar of a political philosophy that may be very suitable for the library or the lecture room, but is not responsive to the needs of our people. The policy of today may not answer the requirements of tomorrow, and no name, however venerated for wisdom and patriotism, can be summoned from the dim past to deter us from pursuing that course which the exigencies of the present, with all its environments, point out to us as the pathway of safety, happiness and prosperity.

Texas has an easy capacity for ten millions of bales of cotton. Her possibilities in other directions are equally as certain and as great; but the best thought and greatest energy of the people must be aroused and kept in constant and vigorous action in order to reach the climax of achievement. To attain this high station will not be so difficult as would at first appear. The circumstances of the hour are propitious. The way is plain and the means at our command more than sufficient. All that will be required is united, active and earnest effort, supplemented by a lofty and patriotic ambition. We should not be satisfied with a less exalted position than that which puts us in the lead of the commonwealths of America. To upbuild the State, to promote her moral, intellectual and material advancement and to make her influence and power correspond to her domain, population and wealth of resource, should be the supreme ambition of every son and daughter.

The past is secure, the present is certain, and the future full of hope and encouragement.

I know not how to more strongly accentuate our duty than to quote from a public address by the Ex-President of the Confederacy. Speaking for the last time to those whom he loved so well, and whom he had served so faithfully, that soldier and statesman said: "Men in whose hands the destinies of our Southland lie, for love of her I break my silence to speak now a few words of respectful admonition. The past is dead. Let it bury its dead with its hopes and aspirations. Before you lies the future—a future of expanding national glory, before which the whole world shall stand amazed. Let me beseech you to lay aside all rancor, all bitter sectional feeling, and to take your place in the ranks of those who will bring a consummation devoutly to be wished—a reunited country."

Upon the verge of the grave itself, and amid the closing scenes of an eventful and honorable career, forgetting his own misfortunes and disappointments, and imbued with a lofty patriotism for the whole country and with a sincere affection for the entire people, he stood like the prophets of old—upon the mount of observation, and looking forward, as with inspired view, into the future, he foretells a "reunited country and an expanding glory, before which the whole world shall stand amazed."

Men of Texas—women of Texas—of whatever race, nationality or faith, I call upon you to lay aside all rancor, all bitterness, all differences, and to unite harmoniously in an earnest effort for the development of our State and for the promotion of her best interests, not forgetting that she is one of many great commonwealths, united in bonds that will never be broken, each moving in its own constitutional sphere and exercising every constitutional power, yet under the same flag and with a common destiny.

Second Inaugural Address *

January 15, 1901

Senators, Representatives AND FELLOW CITIZENS:

As I assume, for the second time, the duties of Chief Executive of this commonwealth, the thought occurs—how can I sufficiently requite the people for their confidence so generously renewed.

Two years ago I stood in this place with lighter heart and more buoyant spirits than now. Experience warns me against the anticipation of pleasure and ease for the two years to come.

The honor is great, indeed; the responsibility is no less.

As guaranty for the future I can only offer the record that I have made here and elsewhere in the public service.

That record, whatever it may be, I shall earnestly endeavor to improve—steadfastly relying upon the sincere and hearty co-operation of my associates in every department of the government, and in return faithfully pledging to them my own.

It is no easy task to successfully and satisfactorily administer the affairs of so great a State, yet in its infancy, with its extensive domain, its variety and abundance of resources, and its many conflicting interests; and to them upon whom the grave responsibility may fall the admonition of Israel's King applies with especial force—"Let not him who girdeth on his harness boast himself as he that putteth it off."

With a full appreciation of the importance and magnitude of the work that I again undertake, I enter upon its performance with a full determination that shall not falter, however untoward the circumstance, to do all that may be possible to advance the prosperity of the State and the welfare of its citizens. Should I so maintain myself during the term for which I have been elected, the measure of my ambition will be complete.

Journal of the House of Representatives of the Twenty-seventh Legislature of the State of Texas (1901), p. 92.

The hairs of my head have grown gray in its service, as well on the field as in the council chamber, and when my public career shall have closed I desire, above all things else, to take with me into private life the consciousness of duty well performed. If deserved, I could ask no higher encomium than that I had served the people faithfully and well. Senators and Representatives I rejoice to have you share with me the responsibilities, the duties and the honor of the hour, and upon your wisdom and your patriotism I shall most confidently rely.

XVIII

Samuel Willis Tucker

LANHAM

1903–1907

Courtesy of Archives Division, Texas State Library

SAMUEL WILLIS TUCKER LANHAM (*July 4, 1846–July 29, 1908*) was born in the Spartanburg District, South Carolina. He attended school in South Carolina. At the age of sixteen, he served in the Confederate Army and was mustered out in 1865. He studied law and was admitted to the bar in Texas in 1869. Between the years of 1866 and 1869, Lanham taught school in Red River County.

Lanham, a Democrat, served in the United States House of Representatives for ten years, from 1883 until 1893. He was returned in 1897 and served until 1903.

While in the Congress, he ran for governor in 1902 and won easily. Taking office on January 20, 1903, Lanham would be the last Confederate veteran to hold that office.

He was easily reelected in 1904 for a second term. His second inaugural address was delivered on January 17, 1905.

Inaugural Address *

January 20, 1903

GENTLEMEN OF THE LEGISLATURE AND FELLOW-CITIZENS:

The oath just administered is a solemn and comprehensive one. It has been unreservedly taken and with a "conscience void of offense," as well as with an acute sense of the obligations it imposes. So far as it relates to the future, it shall be faithfully observed; so far as it refers to the past, it gratifies him who has taken it to declare that neither in letter nor in spirit has there been the least departure in thought or conduct from any fact or purpose its terms embrace and imply. Self-respect and good conscience demand of any officer chosen by the people of our great State, a scrupulous regard for everything involved in the oath prescribed by our Constitution. He who can not accordingly qualify should never aspire to nor be permitted to hold a public trust.

I can not better describe the feelings that now possess me, than to adopt the words and breathe the spirit of the greatest political philosopher and wisest exponent of the principles of popular government the world has ever known. But little more than a hundred years ago, when the entire population of the United States was less than twice that now contained in Texas—when the Federal government was perhaps not greater in wealth and resources than is that of our State today, Thomas Jefferson made his first inaugural address. In that splendid deliverance which will live on and live forever, his opening words were: "Called upon to undertake the duties of the first Executive office of our country, I avail myself of the presence of that portion of my fellow citizens, which is here assembled, to express my grateful thanks for the favor with which they have been pleased to look toward me, to declare a sincere consciousness that the task is above my talents, and that I approach it with those anxious and awful presentiments which the

---

*Journal of the House of Representatives of the Twenty-eighth Legislature of the State of Texas (1903), pp. 105–7.

greatness of the charge and the weakness of my powers so justly inspire." You have called upon me, my countrymen, "to undertake the duties of the first executive office," not of our whole country, but of the mighty Commonwealth of Texas, and I enter upon their performance with the gravest solicitude. Mr. Jefferson further said: "I humble myself before the magnitude of the undertaking. Utterly, indeed, should I despair did not the presence of many whom I here see remind me that I shall find resources of wisdom, of virtue, and of zeal on which to rely under all difficulties. To you, then, gentlemen, who are charged with the sovereign functions of legislation, and to those associated with you, I look for encouragement for that guidance and support which may enable us to steer with safety the vessel in which we are all embarked." So declare I unto you.

In formulating "the essential principles of our government," he announced certain enduring doctrines which are as opposite today as they were in the morning of the Nineteenth century, and some of which are incorporated in our own organic law and are now and ever will be entirely applicable to the State administrations within our Union. There can be nothing more cardinal and abiding in sound civic policy and indispensable to popular institutions than "equal and exact justice to all men; a jealous care of the right of election by the people; the support of the State governments in all their rights, as the most competent administrations of our domestic concerns and the surest bulwarks against anti-republican tendencies; economy in the public expense, that labor may be lightly burdened; encouragement of agriculture and commerce its handmaid; the diffusion of information and arraignment of all abuses at the bar of public reason; the freedom of religion, freedom of the press and freedom of the person." These principles, indeed, should be "the creed of our political faith," and "the text of civic instruction," and to their maintenance, with all the fidelity and energy at his command, your chosen servant, in this mighty presence, commits and consecrates himself, imploring as did he who originally proclaimed them, the aid and blessing of the Infinite Power.

To attain equal and exact justice to all men," the law must permit equal opportunity to all men, and grant "exclusive privilege to none." The same avenues must be open to all. "Monopoly," says our Constitution, "is contrary to the genius of a free government." Competition is inseparable from free and healthy commerce. There is and must be something abnormal, pernicious and detrimental to the public, if it shall come to pass that only one man or combination of men shall buy or sell and fix the prices of the products of industry and the necessaries of human life and comfort. There is and must be something wrong if only one traffic center can be found for the sale and purchase of those commodities which enter into the daily use of all the people, or if commerce in articles required by all, can only flow through one particular channel or be governed by and through one special instrumentality, with unlimited power to determine arbitrarily the buying and the selling price. No one man can, no set of men in a corporate capacity should ever be allowed to either monopolize the commerce of Texas, control its sources of supply or the agencies through which it is conducted. Whether avaricious compassing in the individual can be legally repressed, rapacity in the corporation can be restrained, for the law creates and the law can regulate the corporation.

We shall fail in our obligations to support the Constitution, our duty to the people, obedience to the platform of the party to which we owe allegiance, and devotion to the commissions we bear, if we do not write into law, valid, operative and constitutional statutes against monopoly.

Let no honest investor hesitate to bring and employ his capital in our midst—let every such comer be cordially welcomed and duly protected—let no useful enterprise be intimidated—let industrial and legitimate development of all kinds be invited, encouraged and conserved—let prosperity along all rightful lines be hailed, stimulated and advanced, but let the world know that there is more in this State than spoilation.

The substructure of all good government is the purity and freedom of the ballot. The highest expression of our sovereignty as a people, is to participate in the exercise of political authority at the polls. That ambition is abominable that would seek official preferment by the direct or indirect purchase of votes, and that man claiming to be a citizen of Texas, is unworthy of the name and deserves the scorn of all decent men, who would sell his vote for a price. To elevate the standard of political virtue, to enlarge and dignify the estimate of honest and independent suffrage, to quicken the public mind concerning the duty and responsibility of employing in right spirit and with clean motive, whether at the primaries or at the polls, this greatest of all the attributes of true citizenship, is a charge upon all good and patriotic men. To facilitate and promote by appropriate legislation this high consummation, devolves upon the law-giver, who loves his country and desires its loftiest attainment.

It is a great thing to be a factor in the selection of the State's agents, the determination of popular issues and the inauguration and establishment of governmental policies; it is a great thing to be a citizen of Texas, with all the duties and privileges and community of interests that attach. Our people have but recently, with great emphasis, declared their opinion and purpose in this connection. We all owe something to each other, to social order, to the purification of the political methods, to public morality, to the enforcement of law, to the government of which we are each a part and the conservation, in their best vigor, of the great principles which distinguish our institutions.

It is our duty to "support our State government." Each and every citizen should "render unto the State the things that are the State's." Our Constitution now demands as a prerequisite to suffrage, some contribution to the public treasury for the common good. However small that contribution may be, he who honestly and with patriotic object makes it, can look his fellow citizen, no matter what his possessions may be, in the face without shame, and assert with pride, his equal right to choose officials and record his electoral judgment on public questions. It must not be forgotten that "of him to whom much is given much shall be required." No citizen should desire nor be permitted to withhold from the State his just and proportionate part of the revenue required for the support of the State. According to the value of his property, the extent of the protection he enjoys, and in full contemplation of the law, should his rendition and assessment be made. This is but a reasonable duty which he owes to himself as well as to his State and his fellow men. It will be but a travesty upon the equity of our system of taxation, if we take the mite from the one and let the burden rest alone upon visible possessions and otherwise permit evasions and avoidance.

There is no good reason why the rate of taxation should not be decreased and still leave ample means available for all the necessities of the public service if each and every tax payer and assessor shall do his full duty. If, added to this, we shall maintain a strict observance of "economy in the public expense," we shall not only see "labor lightly burdened," but reach the enjoyment of other attendant blessings. We should not hesitate to make reasonable appropriations for great public uses, but let it be impressed upon all the officiary of the State, that no waste, nor making individual commerce in the funds of the State to the least extent, shall ever be tolerated.

In agriculture, are to be found the store house and granary from which the world is fed. To whatever extent it can be suitably encouraged, we should be willing to go, for without its prosperity all other interests are inevitably depressed and impaired. It is something incongruous and illogical if the recompense of the farmer's toil can be fixed by artificial contrivance, before the seeds sprout in the ground, and something is wrong if there be no competition in the markets for the fruits of his labor. I but strengthen these suggestions when I quote from an illustrious predecessor who said that "all civilization begins and ends with the plow."

"The diffusion of information" in this period of our history is more demanded than it has ever been in the past. We must keep abreast with the educational progress of the times. No impediment possible to be removed should stand in the way of the inquisitive reason of the youth of our land. Our schools, from the primary to the University must reach the highest degree of efficiency—not merely in literary and scientific culture, but in all branches of practical instruction, which can be utilized in the varied occupations of our people.

We have a cosmopolitan population hailing from all over the Union and from foreign lands, and yet we are homogeneous and accordant in our aspirations for the good of the State and the well being of society. We rejoice in the fact that we are indeed a free people, free to enjoy and practice religion as our consciences dictate, free to pursue our own happiness and engage in any lawful calling, free to speak our honest convictions, free to vote as we choose, free to arraign abuses, free in person, and free to work out our own salvation and accomplish the great and beneficent purposes that lie out before us for the upbuilding of our State and the uplifting of each other. May it always be remembered that "the personal freedom of the individual citizen is the most sacred and precious inheritance of Americans."

Let us unite our hearts and hands to achieve all that the day and generation require of us, and mutually strive that "every useful, every elegant art, every exercise of the imagination, the heighth of reason, the noblest affection, the purest religion shall find their home in our institutions and right our laws for the benefit of men."

I again appropriate the language used by the great statesman on the memorable occasion to which reference has been made and thereby give voice to "the thoughts that arise in me." His concluding words were: "I repair then, fellow citizens, to the post you have assigned me * * * I shall often go wrong through defect of judgment. When right, I shall often be thought wrong by those whose positions will not command a view of the whole ground. I ask your indulgence for my own errors which will never be intentional, and your support against the errors of others who may condemn what they would not, if seen in all its parts. The approbation implied by your suffrage is a consolation to me for the past, and my future solicitude will be to retain the good opinion of those who have bestowed it in advance to conciliate that of others by doing them all the good in my power and to be instrumental to the happiness and freedom of all."

I am sure we all unite in tendering our best wishes to the retiring Governor of the State, while we cheerfully testify to his valuable service and honest administration of our affairs. He need not shrink from comparison with his worthy predecessors nor dread an impartial audit of his official conduct, for history will accord to him unstinted praise for his devotion to public duty. I know this generous audience will indulge me to say that he and I belonged to a generation now rapidly passing away. We represent and have been associated with times and scenes that are fading into tradition to those who have come after us in the later years, but they will be vivid to him and me "while memory clings to aught below." We have had a common experience in war and peace. Our friendship has been long and unbroken. We have served together in National councils, and now it happens that I am to succeed him in the highest office our people can bestow. I can only hope that when it shall come to me to turn over this exalted station to another as he now does to me, it may be to receive the approval which we sincerely extend to him, "Well done, thou good and faithful servant!"

Second Inaugural Address *
January 17, 1905

GENTLEMEN OF THE LEGISLATURE AND FELLOW CITIZENS:

For the second time I have taken the oath of office required of the Governor of the State. I am duly impressed with the obligations it imposes. From actual experience I know and appreciate their significance. It is by the will and authority of the people that I now stand officially in your presence. To them I declare abiding allegiance. For their confidence, which was so emphatically expressed at the primaries and in the final convention, and subsequently ratified at the general election, I am profoundly grateful. To merit its continuance without abatement, and, if possible, to increase and still more deserve it, shall engage whatever capacity I possess. The greatest satisfaction that can flow from filling public office, and especially the one with which I have been honored, is that which "proceeds from the consciousness of duty faithfully performed."

With supreme devotion to my State and people, and to the very best of my ability, I have endeavored to do my duty; similarly inspired, I shall continue to pursue the same course.

The magnitude of the work that lies out before the Twenty-ninth Legislature will require the utmost wisdom and persistent energy. We should promptly go about that work with earnestness, and withhold not our hands until the task is finished. The people have a right to expect results proportioned to the demands. The chief responsibility for just and useful laws devolves upon the Legislature, and it appertains not only to the aggregate body, but to the individual member, who can not afford to waive or transfer his own accountability.

I beg to assure you of my desire that cordial relations and co-operation shall be maintained between the Legislative and Executive

Journal of the House of Representatives of the Twenty-ninth Legislature of the State of Texas (1905), pp. 112–13.

departments of the government. We should not forget the relative positions they sustain to each other, and should stand ready not only to recognize their respective functions, but by concerted efforts to facilitate the objects severally committed to their care.

The Governor invokes your support and guidance; he will reciprocate to the full compass of his power. He invites your confidence in all matters pertaining to the public interest; you shall have his without reserve. He sincerely hopes that what shall be accomplished at this Legislative session will constitute an enduring monument of devotion to duty and public utility. Any assistance he can bring to such a consummation shall be readily and faithfully rendered.

XIX

Thomas Mitchell
CAMPBELL

1907–1911

Courtesy of Archives Division, Texas State Library

THOMAS MITCHELL CAMPBELL (*April 22, 1856–April 1, 1923*) was born in Rusk, Texas, and received his early education there. He attended the Rusk Masonic Institute and Trinity University at Tehuacana. In 1878, at the age of twenty-two, he was admitted to the bar in Longview, Texas. Campbell was named receiver for the International-Great Northern Railroad in 1891; from 1893 until 1897 he was general manager.

Campbell, a Democrat, won the governorship in the election of 1906 over the Republican candidate. He took office on January 15, 1907.

He won a second term in the election of 1908. Campbell was officially sworn in as governor on January 18, 1909.

Inaugural Address*

January 15, 1907

Ladies and Gentlemen, Senators and Representatives:

I am more than grateful for the words of commendation and good-will so eloquently spoken by the outgoing Governor. His exalted character, his pure life, public and private, his superb patriotism will live as an inspiration to nobler deeds on the part of those who may come after him.

He is my friend, and in retiring from the office, which he has filled with such conspicuous ability, he enjoys the confidence of the people, and wherever he may go, he carries with him my affectionate regard.

This representative assemblage, great and imposing, indeed, has with patriotic interest, and I hope and believe with friendly regard, witnessed my induction into the only public office to which I have ever aspired. I prize the great honor and am conscious of its serious responsibilities and of my duty to all the people.

In the unusually vigorous political struggle which resulted in the gratification of my cherished ambition, I undertook a discussion of governmental principles as applied to the affairs of our State, problems of interest to Texans, rather than individuals, occupied my time, and in the pride and hope of this auspicious occasion I can remember no act of mine in that campaign that I would now recall. Contesting with me for the greatest honor within the gift of the people of Texas were able and honorable gentlemen, and of them or their supporters I uttered no word that would leave a sting or that would tend to wound the most sensitive man. If in the zeal and heat of the combat, injustice was done me by anyone, it brought to me no harm, and today no suspicion or resentment or spirit of retaliation lingers in my bosom.

Public interest and the welfare of the State are of first importance to

Journal of the House of Representatives of the Thirtieth Legislature of the State of Texas (1907), pp. 110–11.

us all, and the safety of our institutions and the happiness and prosperity of all the people appeal to the patriotic official in every act of duty honestly performed.

Impelled by a sense of duty to the people whose suffrage I asked, and in justice to myself, I advocated policies which I hope to see established in Texas, and I made promises to the fulfillment of which I stand pledged and devoted.

The dominant political party in this State to which most of us claim allegiance, and to which we are indebted for the honors of official station, announced a platform of principles, adherence to which, in letter and in spirit, all members of the party hold themselves in honor bound. Party pledges to the people should be sacredly kept by its members and every platform demand faithfully redeemed. For the promotion of human happiness, to protect the weak against oppression from the strong, to secure the greatest good to the greatest number, and equal rights to all with special privileges to none, our form of government was established. In the Constitution which we have taken a solemn and binding oath to support, these essential principles of civil liberty and free government are recognized, and in every effort for their preservation this Legislature will receive my full co-operation and support.

In meeting my own obligations, I hope to have and I invite your aid and assistance for the good of the State.

Uphold the Constitution, stand by the platform demands, equalize the burdens of government, sweep from these representative halls the "shoulder clapper" and the hired lobby, strike down the corruptionist and the enemies of the people's government, by precept and example promote economy and civic righteousness and you will earn and receive the approval and the praise of a just and grateful people.

Second Inaugural Address *

January 18, 1909

GENTLEMEN OF THE LEGISLATURE AND FELLOW CITIZENS:

To be called the second time to the highest office within the gift of the people of Texas is an honor, indeed.

In acknowledging through you my debt of gratitude to the people for this evidence of their continued confidence and partiality, I renew the pledges of loyalty to their interests and to the welfare of our great commonwealth made by me when inducted into the office of Governor two years ago.

When I first stood in this place and took the oath of office, I did so with a full appreciation of the important duties and grave responsibilities before me. However, at this time I am able to appreciate more fully than I did at that time the burden assumed, and the penalties that a Governor sometimes incurs, at least temporarily, for his loyalty to that oath, for keeping his own promises, and for his fidelity to the Constitution and to the pledges of the political party to which he belongs.

The Constitution provides that the Governor shall at the commencement of each session of the Legislature, and at the close of his term of office, give to the Legislature information, by message, of the condition of the State; that he shall recommend to the Legislature such measures as he may deem expedient and that "he shall cause the laws to be faithfully executed." The powers and responsibilities imposed upon me by these manadatory provisions of the Constitution are imperative, and in respect to these and similar matters the office of Governor has not been and will not be abdicated. To the end that the laws may be enforced, the public may be protected and the best interests of the people and of the State may be conserved, I proposed to continue in the future as I have in the past to exercise in an appropriate way all the powers and as

Journal of the House of Representatives of the Thirty-first Legislature of the State of Texas (1909), pp. 115–16.

best I can to perform all the duties properly belonging to the office I hold.

In the earnest efforts that I have at all times employed to further the cause of good government, I have been often misunderstood by good men and oftener misrepresented and maligned by bad ones, but my full compensation is found in a consciousness of having faithfully performed my duty as I saw it and in the overwhelming endorsement accorded me by the great masses of the people of Texas, for whom I have been battling and in whose behalf I propose to continue the contest.

As early as March, 1908, and throughout the last campaign, I undertook to sound a note of warning to the people. I said then that it was the fixed purpose of unscrupulous combinations of selfish interests to discredit our laws and elect our officers, and that their forces were then engaged in an effort to elect a Legislature that would throttle the will of the people. I said then and I say now that I do not believe that such unholy schemes can ever succeed in Democratic Texas.

You, gentlemen of the Legislature, are the only accredited agents and representatives of all the people in the legislative branch of our State government, and I have the honor to serve them as Chief Executive. They look to you to make their laws and to the Executive Department to enforce them, and I believe that we can perform our respective duties without the assistance of corporation, literary and political bureaus, or of their organizations of self-constituted or employed legislative and executive advisers. It is certain that these outside and intruding agencies now assuming to suggest and dictate legislation are not commissioned by the people to revise their tax laws or to help you make any other laws for Texas.

The people of Texas are a just people and their own chosen representatives can be depended upon to deal fairly but firmly and justly with all concerns.

Actuated by no other motive than the welfare and prosperity of all the people and the continued progress, and the honor and glory of our State, I again enter upon the discharge of the duties of the office of Governor. Just laws, conservative policies, absolute fairness and protection to the people and to all interests, corporate and individual, economy in public expenditures, equalization of the burdens of taxation, enforcement of all the laws, adequate public school advantages, "equal rights to all and exclusive privileges to none," are principles of government to which we are nearly all committed, and these principles should guide us in our work for good government, and in securing an enlightened and unselfish development of our resources in our aspirations for a still brighter destiny for the greatest people of the greatest State in this Republic.

In performing the task laid out for me by the people and in the discharge of my duties under the Constitution, I invite your assistance and feel that I have good grounds for expecting your aid and co-operation. In the performance of your duties I hope to be of some advantage to you, and in everything looking to the public good, I pledge you my unqualified support. The Governor's office will always be open to your officers and to each and every member of this Legislature, and you will be welcome when you come.

XX

Oscar Branch

COLQUITT

1911–1915

Courtesy of Archives Division, Texas State Library

OSCAR BRANCH COLQUITT (*December 16, 1861–March 8, 1940*) was born in Camilla, Georgia. He attended public schools in Camilla and in Daingerfield, Texas. He attended Daingerfield Academy.

In 1884 Colquitt entered the newspaper business as founder and owner of the Pittsburg *Gazette*. He was publisher of the Terrell, Texas, *Time-Star* from 1890 to 1897. During the period from 1899 to 1901 he was a lobbyist. Colquitt was admitted to the bar in 1900.

Colquitt was elected to the Texas Senate and served from 1895 until 1899. In 1898 he was a state revenue agent. From 1903 until 1911 he was a Texas railroad commissioner.

Colquitt, a Democrat, ran unsuccessfully for the office of governor in 1906. He made a successful bid for the position in 1910 running as a Democratic supporter of prohibition. He took office on January 17, 1911.

Defeating the Republican candidate and several minor party candidates, Colquitt won a second term in 1912 and was inaugurated on January 20, 1913.

Inaugural Address *

January 17, 1911

GENTLEMEN OF THE LEGISLATURE,
MY FELLOW CITIZENS:

I deeply appreciate the honor and distinction that the people of Texas have conferred upon me. In taking the oath of office which has just been administered to me, I realize fully the responsibility which the obligation carries with it. I want to say that I have taken that oath of office four times before, and I challenge any citizen of Texas today to say that I have not observed faithfully its injunctions and responsibilities. I hope, my fellow citizens, that we will have a successful, restful and peaceful administration of public affairs during the next two years in this State. I promise you now to consecrate an honest and sincere heart and an honest and sincere purpose to enforce the laws and uphold its dignity and preserve the rights of persons and of property throughout the confines of the State of Texas. Without bitterness and without strife I hope I will have the co-operation of the members of the Legislature and the citizenship of Texas at large. I want the members of the Legislature to feel at home in the Governor's office; come and counsel with me and let me counsel with you, whether you agree with me on policies and upon questions that are confronting you or not. I ask that you candidly confer with me and see whether we can adjust our differences and unite upon a policy which will lead Texas to the first place in the sisterhood of States. I pledge you now every effort of mine shall be directed to the upbuilding and development of our educational institutions, our system of common schools. I want to see the hearts of the people of Texas so educated and trained that all of its citizenship can live up to the injunction of the Golden Rule, "Do unto others as you would have them do unto you." If the members of the Legislature and the citizenship of Texas will meet me half way upon this great and

---

Journal of the House of Representatives of the Thirty-second Legislature of the State of Texas (1911), pp. 137–38.

grand principle, we will not only have a season of legislative rest, but we will have an era of political peace, prosperity and development in this State that we have never had before.

Again pledging myself and every effort and all of the authority vested in the Governor of the State to enforce and uphold the law in accordance with the Constitution and beseeching the co-operation of the Legislature in this laudable undertaking, I desire now again to thank the people of Texas for the honor they have done me and I want to say to the retiring Chief Executive that I wish nothing for him but peace, happiness and prosperity.

Second Inaugural Address *

January 20, 1913

GENTLEMEN OF THE LEGISLATURE, MY FELLOW CITIZENS:

As the distinguished ex-Lieutenant Governor has just stated to you, this is one of the simplest and best forms of government ever devised by the mind of man, and I am proud to be a defender of the system of government instituted in this country under the leadership of George Washington with the assistance of men like Benjamin Franklin, Thomas Jefferson and James Madison. The government rests upon the consent of the governed; in Texas as throughout this Republic the people rule; by the will of the people their public servants are chosen. They have a system of election by which our political policies and theories can go before the people and party organization by which the public servants can go before the people and present their convictions upon public questions and leave it to the public who the public servant shall be. This is a fortunate circumstance that the American people have demonstrated better than any other people on the face of this earth, the capacity for self-government and self-control; in moments of passion in hours of prejudice when men are swept off their saner judgments and are carried away from exercising the wish of suffrage by prejudices or passion, but when the contest is over, American people have submitted to the will of the majority.

I congratulate the people of Texas today, after having passed through the fire of political strife and turmoil that they are prosperous, and happy and contented.

During the past two years as Governor of this State, without fear and without favor of any man or set of men, I have striven to perform my simple duty as Chief Executive of this State, and so help me God I

Journal of the House of Representatives of the Thirty-third Legislature of the State of Texas (1913), pp. 141–42.

will continue in that course, unafraid of any man and unafraid or dictated to by any set of men.

Today we are on the threshold of great prosperity and development in Texas, more than she has ever witnessed before.

After the campaign for Governor last summer the Democratic party met at San Antonio and adopted one of the most constructive platforms ever written by any party in Texas. If I can have the co-operation and assistance of this Legislature, and I believe I am going to have, we will put more constructive legislation on the statutes of the State than ever before which will bring neighbor closer to neighbor and build up Texas.

I want to say to you that I have felt proud of my advocacy of political peace in Texas. I believe that we are going to have it. I sincerely solicit the co-operation of the members of the House of Representatives and of the members of the State Senate and of the heads of the departments in the State Government and of all my fellow citizens in redeeming the pledges and promises to which we are committed through the party platform, the party which governs and controls the destiny of the State of Texas.

I want to say to you, my fellow citizens and members of the Legislature, that I stand ready to do, and you will find me ready to carry out the declaration which I made to you two years ago from this platform; I stand ready in matters of difference of opinion, in matters where we differ as to the correct policy of this State, to meet you half way, upon the faith of the Golden Rule, which is to do unto others as we would have others do unto us.

We may theorize, we may declaim and write platforms and legislate, but, fellow citizens, we will never legislate upon a better principle than that which is annunciated in the Golden Rule, and, as Governor of this State, I stand ready to carry out the principles therein annunciated.

Now, gentlemen of the Legislature, I want to ask each and every one of you to come to the Governor's office and discuss with me anything about which you are interested and which concerns the welfare, prosperity and the good of our great State. I stand myself for that progress which means development, for that progress which means the betterment of each individual citizen, and shall ask this Legislature to come and join with me in establishing the best system of education of any State in the American nation. I shall ask you to co-operate with me in building the best University controlled by any State. I will ask you to join hands with me in making the Agricultural and Mechanical College the best of its kind in the United States. And I will ask you to join with me in the development of the state normal schools and of the College of Industrial Arts for women; and I will ask you to put it in the powers and in each community of the State of Texas to make for themselves the best system of public schools in all the United States.

I shall ask you, gentlemen of the Legislature—not in the spirit of prejudice, but in the spirit of co-operation—to help me humanize and carry out the policy of humanity in the government of the penitentiary of Texas, and in making that penal institution what it ought to be; and I shall ask the officers throughout the State of Texas to co-operate with me in a full, fair and just enforcement of all the laws of this State; and, lastly, my friends and my fellow citizens, I renew my promise made to the people to do my whole duty as I understand it, unafraid of any man or any set of men.

XXI

James Edward

FERGUSON

1915–1917

Courtesy of Archives Division, Texas State Library

JAMES EDWARD FERGUSON (*August 31, 1871–September 21, 1944*) was born near Salado in Bell County, Texas. Although his early education was limited, he studied law and was admitted to the bar in 1897. He entered the fields of insurance, banking, and real estate. In 1907 he moved to Temple to run the Temple State Bank, which he helped to organize.

Although Ferguson had not held a political office, he had served as a campaign manager for political candidates in 1902 and 1910. In 1914 Ferguson, known as "Farmer Jim," allowed his name to be placed in nomination for the Democratic primary as an anti-prohibition candidate. He won the nomination and in the general election easily defeated the Republican and Socialist candidates. He took office on January 19, 1915.

Ferguson easily won reelection in 1916 and was inaugurated on January 16, 1917, even though he had been charged with, among other things, the misuse of state funds during his first term. These charges and his vetoing of appropriations for the University of Texas ultimately led to an indictment. Impeachment proceedings were started, but Ferguson resigned before their completion.

He left office on August 25, 1917, having served only seven months of his second term. Lieutenant Governor William Hobby was elevated to the position to complete the term.

*Inaugural Address**

January 19, 1915

LADIES, GENTLEMEN, SENATORS AND REPRESENTATIVES:

The dignity of this occasion is only exceeded by its solemn significance.

We speak of dignity because we behold here the presence of our respected judiciary, and the honored representatives of a great people ready to join hands with an humble servant in a common purpose.

This occasion is solemn because the obligation and duties here assumed carry with them grave burdens and responsibilities.

It would perhaps not be in keeping with the propriety of this event for me to enter into any extended discussion of contemplated or necessary legislation. And I shall not do so. That important duty will be performed in an official message, which I will, on the morrow, present for your respectful observance.

Suffice to say that in the exercise of the prerogative of the office which I am to fill I am not unmindful of my need of your good will and co-operation. The three departments of government which are here represented were intended to be conducted in unison and harmony. Certain checks and restrictions were placed upon each, only to prevent too much concentration of power in any one place. Each department, though supreme within itself, should strive to be in accord with the other two.

I shall earnestly respect your field of action, and I know you will respect mine.

I take it that the spirit of patriotism still throbs in your hearts, and that we are all keen and alive to the duties before us.

As we enter upon the task to carry out the people's will, I am greatly

Journal of the House of Representatives of the Thirty-fourth Legislature of the State of Texas (1915), pp. 125–26.

encouraged by the spirit of hope and optimism which seems to pervade this presence.

Let us not lightly regard our duties. Let us not forget the solemn vows we have assumed. Let us become inspired by the confidence reposed in us.

You are quite familiar with the incident in history where that restless and matchless Napoleon with his army facing a deadly foe in a foreign land upon the eve of a great battle, when pointing to the stoic face of the mighty Sphinx that stands by the mysterious pyramids of Egypt urged his devoted soldiers to go forth to battle with the inspiration that forty centuries were contemplating their actions. And the battle was won and the victory was theirs.

And so, my friends, let us also be inspired by the cause which we represent. Let us be happy in the knowledge that ours is not the conquest of war, but a labor of love in a spirit of peace.

Let us be doubly inspired by the fact that the face that looks upon us is not a face of stone. Let us be happy in the thought that the moment before which we stand is not dead.

Let us be pardoned if we shout one mighty shout that can be heard throughout the ages, as we look upon the living face of our people, and standing before the monument of our glory, we mount the summit of a glorious reward as we battle for the right.

My friends, the grand old Democratic party, State and national, must stand or fall by the developments of the next two years to come.

You and I, upon whose shoulders has fallen the mantle of the Democratic fathers, must wear the insignia of power, with credit to ourselves and with honor to the age in which we live.

That we will make mistakes is but to state that we are human.

But with a trusting faith in my people, I predict that when your labors have ended that each and every one of you can look the world in the face and challenge any mortal man to point to even one mistake of the heart.

Gentlemen of the Legislature, somehow or other, or somehow else, I know not why, there comes to me an irrepressible presentiment that I am going to like you. I hope you will like me.

"If you love me, and I love you,
Nothing can cut our love in two."

I want you to let me come to see you, and I want you to come to see me. And when you call at my office, in the language of that old familiar tune, I want you to "Just come right in, sit right down, and make yourself at home."

Second Inaugural Address *
January 16, 1917

MY FELLOW CITIZENS, GENTLEMEN OF THE HOUSE AND SENATE:

In taking the oath just administered, I have by the will and grace of a noble and generous people reassumed grave and solemn responsibilities, the degree of which I keenly and deeply realize.

And in return for the preference and generosity thus bestowed by my people with the help of God, I shall faithfully, unselfishly and with a single eye to duty, endeavor to continue a watchful and humble servant of the people who have thus honored me.

Under ordinary circumstances the taking of this solemn oath of the highest preferment within your gift would carry with it a weight of serious responsibility, but the duties of this office are greatly intensified by well known conditions which confront us. Our situation demands a clear and firm purpose, a deep measure of forbearance and the whole-souled, heartfelt co-operation of each department of our government, together with an unyielding observance of our public pledges.

In this magnificent presence may I be permitted to say that the confidence of my people is dearer to me by far than any office with its glamour of temporal power. Deeply attached to our unprecedented and marvelous history, wonderful in its infancy, glorious in later memories and attracting an amazed world in its present development, I reassume the duties of office today concerned for the advancement and wholesome progress of our people. I shall ever be watchful of our material interests and to the people of Texas I today publicly acknowledge supremacy and my respect, and rededicate my honor, my time, my energies and ability to the promotion of our well being in the work to which I have been called.

*Journal of the House of Representatives of the Thirty-fifth Legislature of the State of Texas (1917), pp. 138–39.

But far, far above all personal triumph or pleasure of pride is the distinctive and far-reaching triumph of our great Democratic party. Since our government was established for the safety and happiness of our people, the object of our laws should be to accomplish that end. The people expect much of us, as their chosen representatives. Since the great masses do and should control our government there are no better judges than the people of what is right and proper in regard to the careful performance of duty. In the masses of the people it is with pride that I express my undying confidence.

Prosperity must depend on the condition of labor and its reward. From the farm, the ranch, and the workshop come pure-hearted patriots. So every legitimate effort which tends to lighten the burdens of industry and create new life therein should receive our support and commendation. We should remember that all honest wealth is the result of labor.

I trust that all matters heretofore submitted to you will receive your careful consideration. The protection of labor and capital, the perpetuation of general education, the promotion of peace and prosperity, I am sure will be first in your minds and purposes.

The doors of my department are open to the members of this Legislature, for ours is a common work for the glory of a proud and glorious constituency.

That each one of you will act well your part I do not doubt, and I assume the duties of office today with the sincere purpose of assisting and co-operating with you in whatever may redound to the happiness and the glory of our people, their permanence, excellence and substantial welfare.

Upon this most auspicious occasion I want to express my warm appreciation of this our beautiful city. The attentions, official and personal, received during my pleasant residence here I have been glad to accept with a full sense of your kind and genuine hospitality.

With the sacred honor of my native State written deep upon my heart and with no higher object than to maintain and hold supreme her spotless record, I consecrate to her my strength, my life, and a heart of gratitude.

XXII

William Pettus

HOBBY

1917–1921

Courtesy of Archives Division, Texas State Library

WILLIAM PETTUS HOBBY (*March 26, 1878–June 7, 1964*) was born in Moscow, Texas, and attended the Houston public schools. Hobby, a newspaperman, began his career as a clerk of the Houston *Post* from 1895 until 1901. He was later a writer for the paper, then city editor, and from 1904 until 1907, he was managing editor. From 1907 until 1914 he was manager and part owner of the Beaumont *Enterprise*.

In 1915 Hobby was elected lieutenant governor and when Governor Ferguson resigned the governorship on August 25, 1917, Hobby was elevated to the position.

In 1918 he ran against and defeated ex-governor Ferguson in the Democratic primary, and in the fall general election he defeated the Republican candidate to win the governorship in his own right. He took office on January 21, 1919.

Inaugural Address *

January 21, 1919

Mr. SPEAKER, MR. PRESIDENT, MEMBERS OF THE JOINT SESSION, LADIES AND GENTLEMEN:

It is an inspiration to stand before this magnificent audience today, because not only here, but from far beyond these walls, there comes to me a voice, and the echo of that voice that speaks of peace and tells us of freedom for all mankind. The tones of victory, glorious victory—to our nation's armies gladden the sound of that voice, and that voice—the voice of the people from the plains of the Panhandle to the shores of the Gulf means more to me than I am able to express. And I am prouder still to acknowledge the command it gives, because for the first time the voice which speaks in this historic hall on this occasion is the voice of all the people, the men and women of Texas alike. (Applause.)

This formality and the words I have repeated from the learned Chief Justice impresses me more deeply with the responsibilities I now assume, and your generous favor and your hearty acclaim on this occasion, coming from the hills and the valleys, and the farms and the forests, and the plains and the prairies, and the hamlets and the towns and the cities of Texas moves me and overwhelms me almost to the point where emotion takes the place of reason.

Looking backward, my countrymen, I am sure you will agree with me, that the year has been a stormy one, and the skies of government most of the time lurid with distress, because all that war could engender; all that wrath could embitter; all that a heated political campaign could inject; all that the bitterest hatred of opposing minds in settling questions that have divided the people of this commonwealth for many years could excite; all that untoward and unsettled domestic conditions

Journal of the House of Representatives of the Thirty-sixth Legislature of the State of Texas (1919), pp. 127–29.

could evoke; all that a devastating drouth and death-dealing disease could scatter in their wake, have marked and beset the pathway of administration with thorns and thistles at every turn.

Looking forward, my countrymen, there is cause for congratulation in the brighter view that binds our nation and our State by the ties of a grander destiny. While the future, whose magnitude and whose promise could only have been dreamed of in years gone by, is now unfolding before us a living and actual reality, the silver lining beyond the war clouds is plainly visible on the horizon of Texas.

Fellow citizens, it but adds romance to history, when we recall that the spark of freedom which ignited from Plymouth Rock when the fathers landed three centuries ago, and started a small fire which after the flight of years spread into a conflagration which now envelops the world. And it seems to me that the hand of fate, which has mysterious ways its wonders to perform, was never more magnificent, and that destiny, which not only marks the sparrows fall, but shapes the ends of nations, too, was never more sublime than when in the course of human events it was given to the child of freedom over here to take back to the parent of oppression over there the rights of liberty, of equality and the laws of justice which we enjoy. And that is exactly what happened.

A few weeks ago when the Generalissimo of the allied armies, Marshal Foch, that Aurora whose name, let us hope, will be linked forever with the fame and glory of Washington and Lafayette—that is what happened a few weeks ago when Marshal Foch bade the beaten Huns come within his lines to receive the message that the victor had for the vanquished. And let me say this new chart for nations to live by and the spreading of the Declaration of Independence throughout the world, never would have occurred had it not been for the fact that Pershing and the boys in khaki were near at hand and to the tune of "Dixie" and "Yankee Doodle" were heading towards the Rhine. (Applause.)

It is but repeating what is a historic fact, when we recall that before this mighty and glorious army crossed four thousand miles of a turbulent sea to carry freedom to the Old World, the Emperor of Germany proudly and vainly boasted that he would eat his ham and eggs in the city of Paris; but after the Sammy boys landed, it is but repeating another historic fact, to recall that we soon found the Emperor of Germany boiling his sauerkraut from a delapidated old castle in Holland. (Applause.) And before the work of the Supreme Council is over in Paris it would not be surprising to find him toasting his pretzels from a frying pan in hell. (Applause.)

My countrymen, while those old and failing monarchies across the seas are tumbling towards the scrap heap, and while Democracy has been crowned with the mightiest triumph since the dawn of time because of popular government, it deserves greater vigilance than ever before. It is for those who hold a public trust to vindicate the advantages of Democracy over any and all forms of government. It is for those who hold a public trust to demonstrate that Democracy is a vibrant and animated living substance, giving life and vitality to the entire body politic from head to heel. When the system under which every person has an equal say and is given an equal show is established, members of the Joint Session, I have a more delicate and a more difficult and higher task to execute in order that Democracy may show a proud record of performance, rather than a punctured vacuum of promises. And let me, my friends, indulge the hope, that with the suffering and sorrow and the sacrifice of the war, which has brought out the best there is in mankind, with that as a foundation, that you and I together may build a structure of legislation for the common good that will lighten the burden of every citizen from the Red River to the Rio Grande—a structure of legislation and wise enactments that will stand through all the ages yet to come.

Fellow citizens, it is a glorious day for Texas. If I read the signs of the times aright, our troubles lay behind us and not before us. True, there are problems of reconstruction, but problems that concern the preservation of human life and the protection of physical property, however great they be, are small compared with those that involved the taking of life and the destruction of property. An era of joy, of achievement, of prosperity, such as the world has never known before, lies in the pathway of sacrifice and suffering and sorrow our country has trodden for these many months. My friends, with the shadow of these events cast before us, with Democracy coming into its own all over the world, with an enlarged commerce in view almost at our doors and an enlarged merchant marine to carry it on the waters of all the seas; with the triumphant march of a returning army, whose deeds of glory have encircled the globe; with our country more potential in the council of nations; with the people of all the earth turning to the "Star-Spangled Banner" with a more reverent look, in that spirit, my friends, because it was recorded in the annals of art that the Goddess of Liberty from American shores enlightened the world, and it will be recorded in the annals of war that the sons of liberty from America emancipated the world (Applause); with a vision of a better and greater opportunity for all in the light of the new day of freedom and Democracy, and industry dawning everywhere; in the spirit of these turbulent years I now assume the duties which you have so trustingly confided to me.

I realize that I will frequently fail to measure up to the expectations of my most generous and most forgiving friends; and more than that, I realize that I will frequently dispose of that which comes before me in a manner that is not even satisfactory to myself; but I promise you here in this great presence, to dedicate the best there is within me to the public service. My fondest hope will be realized if I can feel that the men and women of Texas sitting meditating in the quiet of their homes, or going about the daily pursuits of life, may feel that in the office of the Chief Executive there is a wireless station open to every citizen of this commonwealth; and beating upon the currents that come within, I can always hear the sound waves of what is in their hearts and soul and use it as a guide to what is right and what is fair and what is best for all.

Fellow citizens, if added to that relation which inspires a greater confidence among those I serve, the average citizen who passes this way can feel and look upon the rounded dome of this great edifice with a fonder gaze, conscious that Democracy's temple is dedicated to a higher cause, and with a thrill of deeper pride in the glory and honor of the grand old State that makes it possible; then, my countrymen, the ambition of my life and the highest hopes I cherish will be realized, and that is, while serving here, my countrymen, to dispose of all affairs of administration with justice and with righteousness; to contribute to the cause of honest and clean government and to add to the contentment and prosperity of that splendid people, which, by the grace of God, is permitted to perpetuate and preserve untrampled and unstained the great and glorious name of Texas.

I thank you, my friends and fellow citizens.

XXIII

Pat Morris

NEFF

1921–1925

Courtesy of Archives Division, Texas State Library

PAT MORRIS NEFF (*November 26, 1871–January 20, 1952*) was born near McGregor, Texas. He attended school in Eagle Springs and McGregor. He graduated from Baylor University in 1894. In 1897 he graduated from the University of Texas Law School. The following year, he earned an M.A. degree from Baylor.

From 1901 until 1907 he was a member of the Texas House of Representatives and served as speaker of the house from 1903 to 1905. From 1906 until 1912 he was county attorney for McLennan County.

In the elections of 1920, Neff defeated his Democratic opponents in the primary and defeated the Republican candidate in the fall general election. He took office on January 18, 1921.

Neff was reelected in 1922 and started his second term on January 16, 1923.

Inaugural Address *
January 18, 1921

GENTLEMEN OF THE LEGISLATURE, AND CITIZENS OF TEXAS:

By the authority of the splendid electorate of this State, and under the direction of this lawmaking body, the Chief Justice of the Supreme Court has, in the presence of this magnificent convocation of friends, administered to me an obligation as binding as ever linked the soul of man to the Throne Everlasting. The oath to which I have just subscribed is a comprehensive one. It is retrospective, introspective, prospective. As it relates to the past it was responded to without equivocation and without one mental reservation. Thinking of it in the light of the present, there is not a fleeting cloud to darken the clear sky of an open conscience. Looking at it in the mirror of the future, it nerves my arm and inspires my heart for the heroic. The obligation recalls my pledges to the people. The future invites me to fulfill them. Around me are the representatives of the State. My friends are gathered here. Words fail me to voice the emotions of the hour. This is no idle ceremony. It thrills; it inspires; it humbles; it is a challenge to the highest, the noblest and the best. While the solemn oath of office is fresh on my lips, I wish to plight anew my love and loyalty to my native State, and pledge to her unselfish service. Born and reared on Texas soil, educated and trained in her institutions, honored beyond measure by her people, proud that her sacred soil shall at last entomb my ashes, I am ready to give my very best to her upbuilding. With this high purpose in view I shall, within the next few days and from time to time, submit to this body of lawmakers, as it is my privilege and duty to do, suggestions as to needed legislation. This is neither the time nor the occasion to discuss the tedious details of legislative matters.

For nearly one hundred years Texas has been a potent factor in the

---

Messages of Pat M. Neff, Governor of Texas to the Thirty-seventh Legislature, Austin, Texas, (1921), pp. 3–6.

political affairs of men. During this eventful stretch of time, as emblems of sovereignty, six different flags have floated over her. Into her thrilling history of war and peace has been woven romance and heroism. Today, for the thirty-seventh time, as a State, a new legislative administration is being mobilized for service. Many are the questions awaiting solution. Texas cannot live alone. The nations of earth are interdependent. The people of the world are all neighbors. The human race is passing through a period of transition. The old foundations of civilization have been dynamited. These are testing times. Big problems confront us. We, to whom have been temporarily committed the affairs of state, must have not only the courage to meet these unsettled conditions as they are, but the ability to bridge the chasm between age-worn customs and present needs.

Under our Constitution the work of the government is intrusted to a legislative, a judicial and to an executive department. They are co-equal. While time has demonstrated the wisdom of our fathers in making these three departments as separate and as distinct as the waves of the ocean, yet it remains true that they are all one as the sea. Each must co-ordinate and co-operate with the other as the organized agencies of the State to administer public service to all. This government, so organized, represents that crystallized power which stands as a constant guarantee that every human being who lives beneath its protecting wing shall have an open field and a fair chance to life, liberty, and the pursuit of happiness. These are inalienable rights which the weakest should always enjoy, and which the strongest should never be permitted to revoke. The highest purpose of a government is to create such environments as will enable the new-born babe to grow and develop, with all the freedom possible, into a real man—clean, cultured and courageous, standing upright and fearless before the world. We do not diminish property rights by emphasizing human rights.

To strengthen this constant guarantee and to work out this laudable purpose, it is a fine thought that you and I, as the representatives of the people, have the right, unfettered, to fight wrong wherever it builds its bold and blatant bulwark. Passing bills and approving appropriations are not the only duties of those who participate in these inaugural ceremonies. Up and down the line everywhere we should fight for the things worth while. Not for what we can get, but what we can give.

I know the people of Texas. I have recently met them face to face in the fields, the forests and the factories. I have mixed and mingled with them on the roadside and at the fireside from the banks of the Red

River to the Rio Grande, from the plains of the Panhandle to the pines of East Texas, and I am here to bear witness that we will not represent the citizenship of this State if we do not feel the thrill and throb of that consciously growing pulse beat of the people for that fine, high type of civilization which countenances no dishonesty in private thinking, no camouflage in social life, and no double-dealing in public service. We are here to direct the destinies, to lift high the ideals, to make and administer the laws, to protect the weak and curb the greed of the strong, to perpetuate the liberty, to guarantee the industrial freedom of five million people. It is a clamant call and a courageous challenge to do our best.

We who serve the State cannot promote the purposes of our government unless we are true to ourselves in rendering a like service to all the people—the rich, the poor, the black, the white, the artists, the artisan, the producers, the consumers—all, from helpless childhood to feeble age. While only a part of the men and women of Texas elected me governor, yet as I took the oath of office a few moments ago, I stepped beyond the narrow and selfish confines of partisan politics and became the governor of every man, woman and child who lives within our broad borders. I am the chosen servant of all. Thus it is with you, the representatives of the people. The past is dead. No prejudice now should poison our purpose, no bias should warp our judgment, no personalities should sidetrack our endeavors, no ill-will should cloud our vision, and no petty political bickerings of the past should stifle our patriotism or divide our energies. All for all, I trust, will be the gripping thought of this administration.

Politics is not a game. It is the science of public service. It furnishes a broad field for noble endeavor. In this realm of labor is finally won the things that make a people great and good. We are not here to build political fences or to construct political machines. The work and worth of the representatives of a people is properly measured by the amount of public good that comes as a result of every public dollar they spend. To needlessly spend the people's money is a crime. The world has just emerged from a period of spending. Wicked has been the waste in both public and private life. Money no longer is cheap. Necessity now compels us to usher in an era of saving. The sane and sensible thing to do is to face financial facts as they are. We should magnify the beauties of hard work. We must take our heads out of the clouds, in public and private thinking, place our feet on the solid soil and by honest dealing, plain living, and becoming industry, give to the people of Texas the most efficient, economically administered government she has ever had in all her splendid history.

The State will always have big problems to solve. No sooner do we dispose of one question than another arises to test our moral and mental fiber. Not until all the people become angelic will the fight for liberty, and learning, and law, and freedom, and civic righteousness be finished. Let it be understood, however, that the government is not the panacea for all the evils that warp and dwarf the human race. The people must not look to the government alone, but to themselves for relief. If the people in private life will practice and proclaim the old-time, homely virtues of honesty, industry and economy, they will not then find so much fault with the government for the fallacies of social life, for the failures of the financial world, and for the frauds that line the pathways of men.

Texas furnishes an inviting field for constructive legislation. Nowhere could you find a land more conducive to the building of a high and enduring civilization than where falls the light of the Lone Star. Not only is Texas a land of opportunity, but ours is a day of opportunity. Let no one throw himself across the track to block the train of progress. Obstructionists never win battles. It is the progressive, dynamic leader that counts. You, gentlemen of the legislature, are privileged to be the spokesmen of a progressive and a forward-looking people. In the work and welfare of legislative life we can well afford to take the people of this State into our confidence. We are unworthy to represent them unless we keep ourselves in co-operative harmony with their thoughts and ideals. As we undertake to pilot the ship of state through the reefs and over the breakers and sand-bars of the legislative ocean, we shall sail without chart or compass unless we keep our thoughts in tuneful and sympathetic touch with the people by whose authority we are here. Summoned by them to serve in the highest office within their gift, I earnestly solicit the comradeship and co-operation of every Texan to join me in making this State the best place in all the world in which to live.

With courage in my heart; with fidelity to duty; with confidence in the people; with faith in the future; with malice toward none; with good-will for all, and with an abiding trust in the "Divinity that shapes our ends, rough hew them as we may," I gladly and proudly salute, as her governor, my native State, the Commonwealth of Texas.

Second Inaugural Address
January 16, 1923

Members of the Thirty-Eighth Legislature, Ladies and Gentlemen:

No one can take the oath of office of Governor and seal and sanctify it by kissing the leaves of God's Book without a deep consciousness of the responsibility that goes with it, and without an abiding realization that he plights his best for his country's good. It gives inspiration to the heart and courage to the soul. It strengthens the natural ties that bind one in patriotic love to his country. Love of country is one of the noblest attributes of human life. It has characterized the worthy citizenship of every age. In ancient days the noblest and best were ever ready to point with pride to the toga of their Roman citizenship. It was said that each Grecian loved his country so well that wherever he stood, there was the Grecian government. The Swiss love their mountains, the Norwegians their pines, the Germans their Rhine, the Frenchmen their vineyards, the Italians their clear, blue skies, the Englishmen their ivy-covered castles, the Irishmen their shamrocks, and as these people love their native heath, so do we as Texans love our broad prairies, our towering forests, our sunlit hills, our furrowed valleys, our sacred shrines and immortal history.

> "Breathes there a Texan with soul so dead
> Who never to himself hath said,
> This is my own, my native land."

HE ALONE IS GREAT WHO SERVES.

Love of country finds its highest expression in sacrificial service. In

Journal of the House of Representatives of the Thirty-eighth Legislature (1923), pp. 131–32.

song and in story, in marble and in mausoleums, in poems and in paintings, have been immortalized the lives and the labors of those who served the State.

"He who saves his country saves all things,
And all things saved, bless him;
He who lets his country die, lets all things die,
And all things, dying, curse him."

Full well do we realize and appreciate the truth of that sentiment as we stand here today beneath the portraits adorning in sacred memory these legislative halls; Stephen F. Austin, who carved from the wilderness an empire and gave it to civilization; Sam Houston, who immortalized the field of San Jacinto as he flung with martial hand into the blue sky above him the glittering star of a new Republic; Edward Burleson, an illustrious name that has enriched the annals of Texas history; Frank Lubbock, who always flashed a bright blade in humanity's name; A. W. Terrell, whose brain conceived more constructive legislation for Texas than any other citizen of his generation; last, but by no means least, that sleepless watchman on the walls who never forgot the people, James S. Hogg.

Your presence here as lawmakers is typical of the presence of all the people of Texas. You have been selected by your constituents in accordance with the provisions of our Constitution. They have deposited all their power in your hands. I commend and congratulate you that you have seen fit to lay aside for a time personal affairs and the private pursuits of life and gather here as the representatives of five million people who can only be heard and can only be represented by your voice and by your vote. What a broad and ample field you have in which to serve.

A BROAD FIELD FOR SERVICE.

You are the honored representatives of a country larger than Germany—larger than France—larger than was America when she whipped the conqueror of Napoleon. You represent a State providentially dowered with vast and varied natural resources; favored with four hundred miles of water front, an open gateway to the world; enriched with agriculture, horticulture, stock raising, mineral productions and a thousand other enterprises, all vying in a friendly rivalry for recognition as the principal industry; a commonwealth occupied by a people loyal, patriotic and true. To be the representatives of such a State and the spokesman for such a people is an opportunity for honor that comes to but a few in this world. Whether these opportunities for honor to you and me shall ripen into real honor or shrivel into dishonor depends upon whether we shall comprehend the duties that are always the correlative of opportunity, and undertake to perform them with courage, charity and humility, obliterating personal interests and rising to the heights of patriotic effort in behalf of this great State.

THE LAWMAKER.

A sacred trust is that of a lawmaker. His function is the highest known to man. He is clothed with the power and the duty to act for the people. What he commands, they must do. He gives direction to their conduct and to their activities. The people place their burdens and their problems in his hands. They look to him to protect them in life and property; they look to him to expend their money judiciously; they look to him to safeguard their interests; they look to him to strengthen their government, to lift high their ideals and to keep at all times, unsullied and untarnished, the honored commission which they with full confidence placed in his hands. Thus to serve is a noble ambition. I congratulate most heartily this lawmaking body that you selected this legislative hall as a forum in which to toil and struggle for a greater Texas. No man should consider himself too big or too busy to take an active interest in the political affairs of his country. Politics is a broad and ample field for noble endeavor. In it is won or lost at last the things worth while that touch the lives not only of the living but shape the destiny of generations yet to be. Therefore, my friends and co-workers, with mutual confidence, with enlarged vision, with quickened zeal and with lofty ideals, let us consecrate ourselves in service to the State.

A CONSTRUCTIVE LEGISLATIVE PROGRAM.

We are the trusted servants of the people. We should not forget them. We should have no ambition not in keeping with the growth and glory of the State. Nothing short of whole-hearted allegiance on our part to the people of Texas will suffice. Many grave and serious problems confront you. The educational life of the State is counting on you; the live stock interests covet your counsel; the fortunes of the farmers await your action; the barometer of business rises and falls as you vote. The eyes of Texas are upon you as you legislate for five million people. Let us not place over against the interests of Texas selfish considerations, personal animosities or immaterial issues. Let us forget discords and differences and begin our work with the one thought, that of serving faithfully and efficiently the best interests of Texas. For this high purpose I pledge to you my best efforts. I earnestly solicit your cordial co-operation. You and I together have a big, constructive legislative program. Through written messages already submitted by me to your honorable body you are familiar with my views on certain phases of legislation, and it shall be my pleasure to submit to you from time to time other recommendations for your consideration. As we work together may charity characterize our thoughts; may tolerance temper our tongues; may moderation mark our conduct; may intelligence inspire our councils, and may justice jealously guide every legislative act. All for Texas and Texas for all should be the consuming thought and the constant slogan of both you and me as we think and work together in an effort to make this commonwealth the best place in all the world to live. Members of the Thirty-eighth Legislature, as the twenty-seventh Governor of Texas, I salute you.

XXIV

Miriam Amanda

FERGUSON

1925–1927

Courtesy of Archives Division, Texas State Library

MIRIAM AMANDA FERGUSON (*June 13, 1875–June 25, 1961*) was born in Bell County, Texas. She attended Salado College and Baylor Female College in Belton, Texas.

"Ma" Ferguson, as her supporters called her, entered the gubernatorial race when her husband, former governor James Ferguson, failed to get his name on the ballot.

As a Democrat, she won her party's nomination and defeated her Republican opponent by a decisive margin in the general election in 1924. Mrs. Ferguson became the second female governor in the history of the United States and the first woman to be elected to that office in Texas. Miriam Amanda Ferguson was sworn into office and delivered her inaugural address on January 20, 1925.

She ran for reelection in 1926 but was defeated in the Democratic primary.

Inaugural Address *

January 20, 1925

YOUR HONORS OF THE SUPREME COURT, GENTLEMEN OF THE THIRTY-NINTH LEGISLATURE, LADIES AND GENTLEMEN:

I shall not at this time attempt a detail of plans and policies. But on the morrow I will in a more definite way send to the honorable Thirty-ninth legislature specific suggestions and recommendations setting forth the hopes and purposes of this administration.

While our government is divided into three distinct parts—the judicial, the legislative, the executive—yet I hope and pray that there is to be that friendly co-operation on the part of each that will inspire the confidence of the people in the administration of their business affairs. One good way to establish this relation is for each department to recognize and respect the rights and powers of the other.

GOVERNMENT OF LAW

The people have spoken. Their verdict is plain. Their edict is that this must be a government of law founded on the sacred constitution handed down to us by the fathers and mothers of the pioneer days. To this end let us reconsecrate our lives and all that we possess.

Recognizing and freely admitting my inexperience in governmental affairs, I must ask the advice and counsel of others.

I am praying for this administration to be one of the progress of matters spiritual as well as material. If the example can be set for a higher standard of morals and purity of life and conduct in public servants of the people, I shall feel that my administration has not been in vain. Let us not forget that it is more glorious to lay up treasures in heaven than upon earth.

*The Austin Statesman, January 20, 1925.

ASKS FOR GOOD WILL

As the first woman governor of our beloved state, I ask for the good will and the prayers of the women of Texas. I want to be worthy of the trust and confidence which they have reposed in me.

With love for all with malice toward none, trusting in God, I consecrate my life to my state.

XXV

Daniel J.

MOODY

1927–1931

Courtesy of Archives Division, Texas State Library

DANIEL J. MOODY (*June 1, 1893–May 22, 1966*) was born in Taylor, Texas. He attended public schools in Taylor and graduated from the University of Texas in 1914.

He served in the Texas National Guard and as a second lieutenant in the United States Army in 1918. A lawyer, Moody served as Williamson County attorney from 1920 until 1922. From 1922 until 1925 he was district attorney for the Twenty-sixth Judicial District. In the 1924 general election, Moody won the position of Texas attorney general, serving from 1925 to 1927.

While completing his term as attorney general, Moody, a Democrat, won the party's nomination for governor and defeated the Republican candidate by a large margin. He took office on January 18, 1927.

Moody won a second term in 1928 and was sworn into office on January 15, 1929.

Inaugural Address *
January 18, 1927

Mr. Chief Justice, Members of the Legislature, Ladies and Gentlemen:

The emotions of this hour beg description, and thoughts surge in my mind crying for utterance, which in the feebleness of my speech, prudence bids me not attempt to express. I accept this responsibility with gratitude and humility. Through the generosity of a gracious people I am permitted to take the oath and assume the duties of the most important office within the gift of the people of Texas. I acknowledge my gratitude for the trust thus reposed in me and acknowledge my appreciation of their confidence. It is with humility that I approach the discharge of the responsibilities of this office.

OFFICE A TRUST

I recognize that the people of Texas hold their public offices in sacred trust. And the officials of Texas, in the proper appreciation of the attitude which the people have toward public office, should feel that from the infinite spaces of this state they say to their officers what the Lord said to Moses in the wilderness on Mount Sinai, "put off thy shoes from thy feet, for the place whereon thou standest is holy ground."

The people expect much of this administration, and its success is very largely bound up in the attitude of the executive, the senate and house of representatives toward public affairs. The character of mutual responsibility which falls upon these officers and the close contact which they have, demand the largest measure of co-operation between both the executive and legislative branches of government. As for me, I promise liberal co-operation and I ask at their hands co-operation and

The Austin American, January 18, 1927.

friendly counsel. None of us lay claim or makes boast of genius. Our hope for success and for promotion of the purposes of government to protect the safety, happiness and prosperity of the people, lies in the practice of integrity and the simple virtues. We should have but one guide to direct our course, and that is the public interest.

SEEKS CONFIDENCE OF ALL MEN

The people of Texas commission us to place their government upon a plane which will restore public confidence in existing forms and receive the respect of all men. We are expected to keep our feet in the path of justice, redeem the right and by our course of official conduct, exemplify the high standards of public service which they expect and demand.

Whatever I may bring to this trust is freely and fully given to the service of this cause and the discharge of those responsibilities.

And now as we go to give ourselves to the service of the public interest, I ask as did the Hebrew of old, that God "give me now knowledge and wisdom to come in and go out before this people; for who can govern this people that is become so great."

Second Inaugural Address*

January 15, 1929

By the consent of the generous and proud citizenship of Texas, I assume the obligations of the governorship of this great state and I shall faithfully endeavor to discharge its duties.

The occasion is appropriate for an acknowledgment of my appreciation of the confidence which the people of Texas have reposed in me by continuing me in this honorable and dignified office. In return for their confidence and trust it is my purpose and desire to give unselfish service to the public interest.

I have no ambition so far as the office is concerned, except to honorably, courageously and efficiently meet its responsibilities and respond to its duties. I want to embrace every opportunity which circumstances afford me for upholding and promoting the happiness and material welfare of the people into whose service I enter for another term. I hope that you constitute the legislative department of this government, and I may join hands in a united effort to serve the interests of our citizenship.

EXISTING NEEDS PARAMOUNT

The people of Texas expect much of this administration. They are conscious of new necessities created by the ever-changing conditions of this fast-developing age. Our time is 1929. We have been chosen as their officers and entrusted with power to act for them in the present matters which concern their welfare. Therefore it is our duty to attune our thinking and our doing to their existing needs. Our attitude toward public problems should not be reactionary, but progressive and in keeping with the times of which our lives form a part.

From the legislative halls of this state and the executive office we should send forth measures of law that are written by hands and minds

*The Austin American, January 15, 1929, p. 2.

which are devoted to mankind's material and spiritual betterment and advancement. The opportunity is great and this beautiful country which thought and toil has transformed from wooded wilderness and arid plains into the home of 6,000,000 happy people demands the best of which we are capable. The people appreciate the difficulties and intricacies of the issues before us, and they will patiently but interestedly wait for our actions. Unselfish devotion upon our part to their service will earn their approval.

Throughout my life I have been the beneficiary of this state and her citizens. The people of Texas have placed me in honorable positions of trust and power; and in your presence I acknowledge my indebtedness to them and I again dedicate my thought and whatever talents I may have to the furtherance of their welfare and happiness.

XXVI

Ross S.
STERLING

1931–1933

Courtesy of Archives Division, Texas State Library

ROSS S. STERLING (*February 11, 1865–March 25, 1949*) was born in Anahuac, Texas, and attended public schools there. He was a farmer and independent oil operator. In 1910 he founded and became president of the Humble Oil and Refining Company. In 1925 he turned to real-estate development and entered the newspaper business by becoming owner of the Houston *Dispatch*. A year later he purchased the Houston *Post*.

In 1930 he served as chairman of the Texas Highway Commission. It was from this position that he entered the gubernatorial race as a Democrat and was elected in the general election of 1930. He took office on January 20, 1931.

He sought a second term in 1932 but was defeated in the Democratic primary, losing to former governor Miriam A. Ferguson.

This is a great honor that has been bestowed upon me—the supreme honor of my life. I am profoundly grateful for it and shall strive with all my power to be worthy of it, and to reflect credit upon my state and the people who entrusted this great office to me.

But I am not concerned about the honor so much as I am about the responsibility of the chief executiveship. It is a tremendous task, and I approach it with deep humility, but not with fear or trembling. A high mark of ability and service has been set for me to shoot at by our retiring governor, Dan Moody. But for the comfort of realizing that I shall have so many good friends in the legislature and in the various departments to help me and show me the way, the path ahead would look dark and rocky indeed. I crave the counsel of them all, and of the people generally.

WANTS HARMONY

I have often thought that the people's interest would be served better if their servants would work in closer harmony. There have been times, unfortunately, when some of our department heads have been antagonistic toward each other, and have regarded each other rather as competitors or rivals. Such instances are deplorable, and I sincerely trust that none will hamper the state's progress during the next two years.

I believe that the three departments of government—legislative, executive and judicial—should each be supreme in its own field. Heads of departments, elective or appointive, should be accorded their full authority. At the same time, I believe that all should bear in mind that they are working on the same job, for the same employer, and should cooperate with each other in every possible way to advance the employers interest. I don't know why the chief executive and the state department heads

*The Austin American, January 21, 1931.

should not hold regular meetings together to discuss their problems and advance the business of government, just as the directors and officers of private corporations do.

BUILD TEXAS

What is this big job of ours, this business of government, which the people have entrusted to us to carry on? Primarily, of course, it is to keep things going so that the people will have protection, schools, tribunals of justice, roads and so on, but the job means far more than that.

I think the most important function of this government is to build Texas. Build it industrially, economically, physically, mentally, socially and spiritually. If we cease building, we suffer and die; if we continue, we have prosperity, and prosperity means business. Happiness is the ultimate goal of all and the only true happiness lies in development—progress.

How, then, can we build Texas?

First, through agriculture, which we call the backbone of civilization. Farm relief by legislation seems a difficult undertaking. I think we can best relieve the Texas farmer and stockman by relieving his terrible tax burden; by encouraging him to raise his own feed and food and 'live at home;' by giving him the best possible educational advantages for his children, so that they may learn how to live and how to farm, and be contented on the farm; by promoting the conservation and reclamation of soil; and by improving in every possible way the marketing end of his industry.

DEVELOP RESOURCES

Thus can Texas be made a greater agricultural state, and thus will her vast undeveloped lands be settled and cultivated; supplying food and other commodities to the markets of the world, and wealth to her own citizenship.

Next in importance, perhaps, are the mineral resources of Texas. During the present century, the gushers of liquid gold that have been struck from the ground by the drill bits of men have provided one of the state's chief sources of wealth. Sulphur has provided millions of dollars, and there are other minerals, some of which have scarcely been touched. They should be conserved and their development encouraged; though at the same time, they should be required to contribute a fair share toward the support of the government that protects and nurtures them.

In our waterways, Texas has resources as yet undreamed of in value. Some of our seaports have been deepened and developed, and are doing a rapidly increasing business. Others may be opened in the future. The inland waterways likewise offer great possibilities—the intra-coastal canal some day will be a great artery of commerce; and the Brazos, the Colorado, the Trinity and other Texas rivers are waiting to be harnessed for power, irrigation, navigation and municipal use.

INDUSTRIAL ACTIVITY

Texas is beginning to awaken industrially and a great thing this is for Texas, for industry is the greatest factor in the upbuilding of states. Industrial development must come hand in hand with other lines of development, such as good roads, waterways, fuel and power. These advantages Texas is offering in increasing measure; plus good climate, good labor, and good raw materials of various kinds. In order to further encourage industry here, we must not so restrict its operations as to repel newcomers. Some of our laws tend to do that, as well as to discourage and keep out capital. Likewise, we should make our laws fair to labor in every way.

When I speak of not restricting industry or capital too much, I do not mean to suggest that our anti-trust laws be relaxed. They should be strengthened, if anything, and all due regulation should be maintained. But in some respects there is too much government in business, too much regulation and restriction for the state's own good.

NEED OF GOOD ROADS

I mentioned good roads as a factor in industrial development. I believe that good roads are the most potent single factor in the forward march of the state generally, and that the growth of Texas will be pretty much in proportion to the growth of the Texas highway system. North Carolina, as well as other states, has demonstrated the value of highways. By completing her road system, she has transformed herself from one of the most backward states of the union into one of the leading states in industry and wealth. Gov. Neff once said, "We shall go by way of the highway." He was right; that is the route that state progress will take, and the better the highway, the swifter will be the progress.

Building Texas requires constant development of educational advantages, adequate to attract and hold, rather than repel, settlers. The state's laws must be enforced and its justice reinforced and accelerated. We must not have a state known as one where human life is cheap, and where the safety of person and property is doubtful.

We must take care of our convicts, insane, tuberculars, and other unfortunate public charges, in such way as not to bring reproach.

We need parks, state and county, for the recreation of our people, and to attract visitors here from other states. Texas has natural scenery whose charm compares favorably with that of Colorado, California and Wyoming. It is potentially a great asset, economically as well as otherwise.

TAX AND FARM RELIEF

I mentioned tax relief as a means to farm relief. Equalization of our system of taxation would also afford sorely needed relief to others besides the farmer. As a friend declared to me recently, taxes are eating the heart out of the people. The tax burden is a serious handicap to full and wholesome state development. Home ownership is the cornerstone of good government and state progress, and the present tax load is discouraging home ownership as well as farm and ranch ownership. Some are paying more than their share of taxes while some others, usually more able to pay, are not paying their full share. Texas will suffer serious consequences if the spread is not soon made more even, and I am gratified that there seems to be such a determined demand throughout the state of equalization.

One good medicine for tax ills is economy in government. I hope it will be administered in generous doses during the next two years. Aside from the economy of frugality in state expenditures and efficiency in office, there is a very real field for economy in legislation.

In the haste and confusion of lawmaking under the old plan of a two months' regular session and emergency special sessions, it was natural and inevitable that a bill would be passed now and then without full consideration of all its consequences. Some of these measures have proved costly to the state and its people in dollars and cents and otherwise. Several have been called to my attention recently.

LEGISLATURE'S OPPORTUNITY

With one full month in which to introduce bills, a month to take them up in committee, and two full months for action on passage, the 42nd legislature has an unprecedented opportunity to deliberate upon bills from every angle. I anticipate that the laws to be brought forth by this assembly will save money rather than lose it, strengthen the government rather than weaken and confuse it, and advance the welfare of the state rather than retard it.

I have recited these directions and landmarks of the route that leads to a greater and better Texas, so that we might remind ourselves of them and get our bearings anew as we start out upon this two-year journey of government. Texas has a glorious past, and a more glorious future.

TO WORK WITH SOLONS

When the fathers founded Texas, a century ago it was a diamond in the rough. They hewed out its shape, performing a magnificent feat, considering their crude, meager tools. Now, with our modern instruments, we have the task of polishing the facets and finishing the gem. It will never be entirely finished, but every constructive stroke we apply brings it nearer to perfection.

Let me say in conclusion that I welcome the opportunity to work hand in hand with each and every member of this joint assembly for the advancement of good government, for the building up of the Lone Star State for the fulfillment of her great destiny, and for the increased happiness of her people.

XXVII

Miriam Amanda

FERGUSON

1933–1935

Courtesy of Archives Division, Texas State Library

MIRIAM AMANDA FERGUSON (*June 13, 1875–June 25, 1961*) served as governor for one term (1925–1927) and was defeated for reelection in a runoff Democratic primary. She ran again in 1930 but was defeated by Ross Sterling.

The financial hardships created by the Great Depression brought about a resurgence of Mrs. Ferguson's popularity, and she was elected by a five to three margin over her Republican counterpart.

Mrs. Ferguson, in addition to being the first woman governor of Texas, now became the first Texas governor to win a nonconsecutive second term.

Her second term began on January 17, 1933.

Inaugural Address *

January 17, 1933

Ladies and Gentlemen of the Texas Legislature, Friends and Fellow-Citizens:

In again taking the oath of office, I fully appreciate the duties which I have assumed and the obligations which I agree to perform. Having been declared by your speaker with your sanction to have received the highest number of votes I am constitutionally eligible, I fully realize that I again become a co-laborer with the Texas legislature in the service of the people.

While I shall not at this time enter into a long discussion of facts and figures dealing in detail with the state's condition, in inform you that on the morrow I will do so and in accordance with the law made and provided will fully present for your consideration such information and suggestion as will in my opinion aid in some degree at least in the disposition of the problems which confront us, in so doing I hope to be as specific as the law requires and as plain as my duty requires.

But on this occasion I want to emphasize my conception of the relation that should exist between the legislative and executive departments of the government. While the constitution draws the line clearly and distinctly as to our respective powers and jurisdictions, yet a clear study of its provisions plainly reveals the intention of the framers of the constitution to make as plain just what you and I can do as it does as to what we cannot do.

HARMONY URGED

While I lay no claims to powers of legal interpretation, yet with a common-sense construction of the English language, I dare to say that

**The Austin American,* January 18, 1933.

there is nothing in our constitution that prevents you and me from being at all times on the most cordial and friendly terms. In fact, I find nothing in the constitution that authorizes you and me to be on unfriendly terms.

Any cause or condition that would lead to unkindliness or unfriendliness must ultimately lead to confusion. So you and I are going to be friendly because we both want to do right.

While most of us are a little too old to carry on a fan and handkerchief flirtation, yet I am going to quote that old verse we used to write each other on Valentine day as my sentiments and intentions:

"If you love me as I love you,
Nothing can cut our love into."

I crave the opportunity to co-operate with you, the members of this legislature, in solving the troubles that now afflict the people who have sent us here to bring relief. My great hope and prayer is that your office and my office may find wisdom and inspiration from "on High" that will blend and direct us in a common campaign and purpose for the common good.

The door of the governor's office is open to every member of this legislature, whether you voted for me or not. You are cordially invited to call for social or official discussion and you will be welcome. I want to know you better and I want you to know me better. Maybe if we get a little better acquainted we will do more for the people. At least the people will have a little more hope as long as they know that you and I are working together in the spirit of harmony and good will.

LET'S PUT HAND TO PLOW

You and I take up the most serious and desperate task that ever confronted the people of our state. On every hand there is want, and need, and hunger that has already led to despair and desperation. Hope is nearly gone. The burdens of government are falling heavily on the masses. Reduction of taxes must come and come quickly or the government will fall and fall quickly.

Imbued with the full solemnity of these conditions I trust that you and I may be of signal service to our day and generation.

Impelled with the pride that we represent the greatest people that ever lived, let us put our hand to the plow and prove ourselves worthy of the confidence that has been in us reposed.

Inspired with the hope that some way, and somehow, we can bring needed relief to our suffering masses, let us get a little closer together and reconsecrate our time and talent to the cause of duty well performed and victory justly earned.

XXVIII

James V.
ALLRED

1935–1939

Courtesy of Archives Division, Texas State Library

JAMES V. ALLRED (*March 29, 1889–September 24, 1959*) was born in Bowie, Texas, where he attended public school. He attended Rice Institute and in 1921 was awarded the LL.B. degree from Cumberland University.

During World War I, Allred served as a seaman in the United States Navy. Following his military service he practiced law and engaged in business. From 1923 until 1926 he was district attorney for the Thirtieth Judicial District. In 1930 he was elected attorney general of Texas and served one term.

In 1934 Allred won the Democratic nomination for governor and was elected without opposition. He took office on January 15, 1935.

In 1936 he won his party's nomination and easily defeated the Republican candidate in the general election. He took office on January 19, 1937.

Inaugural Address *

January 15, 1935

Mr. PRESIDENT OF THE SENATE, MR. SPEAKER OF THE HOUSE, MEMBERS OF THE FORTY-FOURTH LEGISLATURE, REPRESENTATIVES OF SIX MILLION TEXANS, AND MY FRIENDS:

Within itself, the constitutional oath of office just administered is sufficient to inspire the highest resolves and noblest impulses of the human heart. To assume that obligation, even in ordinary times, immeasurably thrills and stirs the souls of men. To take this time-honored oath, as I am privileged, amidst these historic surroundings, upon the centennial eve of our Lone Star State, is to me not only an honor beyond expression but a challenge to action.

To our great commonwealth of citizens, I shall ever be grateful for the honors bestowed upon me. May my every private and official act be acceptable in their sight and evidence that their faith has been well-founded.

In talking to the Nation on March 4, some two years ago, President Roosevelt spoke at a time of great crisis. His inaugural address, a model of brevity and frankness, will last as a pattern of inspiration for generations to come. He gave us a new deal in words and speech as well as in ideals and statecraft.

It was another great President, Woodrow Wilson, who first used the expression, "open covenants, openly arrived at."

I trust that we may be able to inaugurate here today the forthright policy in Texas of "open covenants, openly arrived at" between the people, the Legislature, and the Executive Department.

I thank God I am not standing before you in times as distressful as

Journal of the House of Representatives of the Forty-fourth Legislature of the State of Texas (1935), pp. 93–95.

those under which the President came into National power. Under his leadership, this Union of states has steadily gone forward. Our own Lone Star State has played its part and we Texans may properly say that no other State has ever more intelligently followed two such great leaders as Wilson and Roosevelt. Texas stood united behind the great War President and now stands behind the great Recovery President. I pledge you that this administration will continue to go forward with President Roosevelt whenever our State rights and duties may harmonize with the objectives of the National administration.

Our immediate Texas problems are recovery problems. They are not the problems of your Governor alone; they are not the problems of the Legislature alone. They are the problems of Texas. But, to a great extent, their solution depends upon a sane, intelligent and, above all, a patriotic approach by this Legislature and your humble servant.

Each generation, no doubt, feels that its problems most seriously threaten the stability of government. This new day in Texas is no exception. As we seek to revise our government to meet transition from old to new circumstances of life, grave doubts assail us. Too many of our citizens are on relief rolls; and fear clutches at the hearts of even those fortunate enough to be employed. The welfare of all our people seems to us at stake. Looking back a hundred years, however, to a State then forming with little material wealth and a total population of only a few thousands, with its then perplexing problems, we must say that the genius of Texas has gone a long way.

Truly then, our six million people with billions of wealth in oil, cotton, timber, cattle, and natural resources should have nothing to fear today. We are ready for a new cycle of progress. It shall be my concern that that progress may be directed primarily in the interest of Texas' six millions. This great State, with its unbounded resources and a citizenship in whose veins still flows the achieving blood of pioneers, can lead the Nation in its recovery march.

We can, we must, restore opportunity, vitality, and hope to our distressed people. It can be done! If we can be but furnished with the type of patriotic leadership Texas needs, if the natural resources and the wealth of Texas are properly developed and distributed, if greedy privilege is kept out of government and legislative halls—in short, if Texas is properly governed by all of us who have been honored by the people— then the task so boldly begun by our great National leader can be completed.

The program of the Federal Government now recognizes that "charity is a poor substitute for justice." Too many of our fine citizens now upon relief do not belong there, did not want to be there, and were placed there by circumstances utterly beyond their control. So far as it is within the power of Texas to do so, we must dedicate ourselves to the task of restoring them to their normal walks of life. The New Deal in Texas must be no mere phrase-making. For these worthwhile but unfortunate citizens, it must be also a "Fair Deal."

As a Texan, I am proud of the fact that the "new order" program of the National Government, proposing to substitute work for direct relief, follows almost verbatim the State Democratic platform adopted in Galveston last September. As pointed out in that progressive document, in order to secure the maximum benefits possible under a recovery program, the State should co-ordinate its efforts with those of the National Government. This I propose, in public works projects, in old age pensions, in soil erosion prevention, and in every other worthwhile manner.

My friends, there is another field of public welfare in which we must stage a big recovery. No citizenship can be happy, no benefits in government can be worthwhile in a State where that government is not respected. Perhaps the saddest feature of the past few years in Texas, even sadder than that of relief rolls, is the wholesale flaunting of the law by a dangerous minority which does not typify Texas. The reports of the Senate Investigating Committee contain startling revelations of conditions in some communities which brings shame to every true Texan.

Almost fifty years ago when the great Jim Hogg relinquished the Governor's office to Charles A. Culberson, he closed with this admonition:

"Legal science, political philosophy, and experience teach us that the greatest imperfections of human government can be traced to the failure to impartially and faithfully enforce the laws. Completeness of the law must not be expected, for the perfection of civilization can never be reached; but the tranquility, safety, and happiness of the people may be assured by strict obedience to their will in the faithful execution of such laws as their duly constituted representatives shall adopt. The germ of discontent lying in the hearts of Americans was placed there by treacherous official hands thrust above duty to confer on the favored few immunity from all law. Texans will not participate in the crime."

My friends, these principles are eternal and everlasting. They fit changing conditions of life and are fully as applicable today as when they were uttered.

One of our leading newspapers in a recent editorial said:

"Texas is essentially a community of virtuous people. They do not want the grosser liberalism of a New York, a Chicago, or a New Orleans!"

My friends, a vast majority of the people in Texas are not going to be overrun by a vicious minority. Gangsters, bandits, thugs, and thieves, and their pardon-peddling accomplices higher up, have no place in the clean life that Texas needs.

Primarily, it is the duty of local officers to enforce the law. As Governor of Texas it is my duty under the Constitution to "cause the laws to be faithfully executed." I am going to perform that duty and I want you, my friends, to call upon your local officers to enforce the law. If they fail to do so, I want you and your representatives and senators to back me up in the performance of my duty. I pledge the good officers and decent citizenship of Texas that once these law violators are behind prison doors they will receive clemency only when entitled to it, based on merit, and merit alone.

The people have a right to change any law by a majority vote. I have no fear of any change the people of Texas may so make or approve. But, so long as laws are on our statute books, they must be enforced.

The problems of Texas are too many, too varied, and too complex for further discussion here.

In considering these, or any other subjects, I expect to be guided and controlled by the enunciated principles and platform demands of our Party, in the light of my oath of office. In any matters wherein it may be my duty as Governor to advise with the Legislature, I will at all times act in the interest of the "Fair Deal" for six million Texans.

Every problem of government has been intensified by economic conditions prevailing throughout the country. My friends of the Forty-fourth Legislature, this unparalleled flow of events has brought us together today with a common responsibility. We must have a maximum of cooperation and forbearance by the various departments of government.

It is my constitutional duty to advise and consult with the Legislature from time to time. I so shall do, submitting timely questions as fast as the Legislature is ready to act. The custom is old-fashioned, but I believe inaccurate, whereby the Governor places before the Legislature at one time a complete program for a session in an undigested and cumbersome manner. As I counsel with the Legislature from time to time, I pledge you that six million stockholders in Texas shall be taken into our confidence.

The day of the political trickster, the day of "closed-door" logrolling, the day of patronage trading, the day of political sniping, the day of political sabotage—these days, all of them, should pass out with the fogs of yesteryear. The sunshine of truth should come through open doors so all may see just how this government is carried on.

To the Legislature I propose a working partnership between the executive and legislative branches of this government in the interests of the people. At all times I shall welcome suggestions from members of the Legislature. The doors of the Governor's office are open to this splendid body of senators and representatives. I need your help and Texas needs the devoted, consecrated services of all of us. If we will work together, then truly Texas may go forward.

My fellow citizens, humbly invoking, as did our fathers a hundred years ago, the blessings of the Almighty, I pledge all I have of physical and mental strength in your service.

Second Inaugural Address *

January 19, 1937

Mr. SPEAKER OF THE HOUSE, MR. PRESIDENT OF THE SENATE, MEMBERS OF THE FORTY-FIFTH LEGISLATURE, MY FELLOW CITIZENS:

It is impossible to visualize a more soul-stirring circumstance or ceremony than the one decreed by Constitution and custom which has just been enacted. To take the oath of office and kiss this Holy Bible at the very beginning of our *second* century of progress is not even surpassed by the unutterable joy which was mine at the time of my inauguration two years ago. At the request of my splendid little partner in marriage, I have today added to that custom and made it, if possible, more sacred, by also kissing a marked verse in our own family Bible, one to be handed down to our children.

Under a custom inaugurated by Governor Pat M. Neff, who presented a Bible to his successors in office, each outgoing Governor marks a passage for his successor in office. Since, by the grace of the people, I am to succeed myself, Mrs. Allred has selected the passage which, for the ensuing two years, shall be my constant prayer. It is echoed and repeated throughout the Psalms.

"Give me now wisdom and knowledge, that I may go out and come in before this people."—2. Chronicles 1:10.

As I stated two years ago, the constitutional oath of office just administered is sufficient, within itself, to inspire the highest resolves and noblest impulses of the human heart; but to take that oath as I am

Legislative Messages of Hon. James V. Allred, Governor of Texas, 1935–1939, pp. 110–12.

322

privileged, amidst these historic surroundings, after the marvelous vote of confidence given me by the people, is more than an inspiration. It is a definite, a challenging call to service!

Upon this platform, within the shadows of the Capitol dome, surrounded by public officials and loving friends, upon this anniversary of the birth of Robert E. Lee, and 40 years to a day and hour since the second inauguration of Governor Charles A. Culberson, the very air itself seems charged with inspiration from the past.

It is beyond my power to express in words my appreciation to loyal friends and to the general citizenship of Texas who have honored me beyond boyhood's fondest dreams. To all of you I can only say that today I am reconsecrated and rededicated, in all humility, to the tasks that lie ahead.

These tasks are easy by comparison with those which confronted us two years ago. Due to the beneficence of the Almighty and to our own efforts, the prospect, as we face forward, is far brighter now than then. I thank God we have crossed through the valleys and already climbed to where the peaks of hope are now vivid realities.

We still have, however, our pressing problems. They are chiefly financial. With the right kind of leadership, with the right kind of statesmanship, with the right kind of patriotism, we can make the government of Texas a real, a vital force.

Without hesitation I declare my firm conviction that ours is the most glorious history, the grandest record of achievement, ever to mark a century's development of any state or nation. The presence on this platform here today of two of those immortals who, more than sixty years ago, by force of arms threw tyranny from out the halls of our Texas government, brings to my mind the peculiar wording of Section 2, Article 1, of the Bill of Rights of our State Constitution:

> "The faith of the people of Texas stands pledged to the preservation of a republican form of government and subject to this limitation only they have at all times the inalienable right to alter, reform or abolish their government in such way as they may think expedient."

This limitation, providing that the people, in any change they make, stand pledged to the preservation of a republican form of government, was first placed in the Constitution in 1876.

Today you and I still stand pledged by the faith of the people to the preservation of our form of government. The aim of that government should be to secure the maximum of human happiness for six million people.

Real principles of government are eternal and everlasting; but with time new problems arise, testing our ability to apply those principles to the people's needs. More and more, demands are made upon the State Government to quickly minister to present needs and provide greater security for the future. Today the stability of our form of government is being tested, the strength of its principles weighed in the balance, by problems perhaps never conceived or visioned by our forefathers.

Whether that government is to be preserved, whether that government is to secure the happiness to which the people are entitled, depends largely upon you and upon me. We are the chosen, the charged representatives of Texas' six million people. Through us, and through us alone, can they express their needs. Through us, and through us only, can their problems be solved.

My friends, I firmly believe in the sufficiency of our form of government to meet all our needs. I believe it is the best form of government ever instituted by men. I am firmly convinced that, if the will of the people is carried out in the manner designed and, indeed, provided in our State Constitution, we can settle all our problems and lay the foundations for an even greater Texas of tomorrow than that of yesterday or today.

It is good, it is ennobling, to reflect upon our matchless history, to refresh ourselves anew at the springs of inspiration and ideals which motivated Texans of fifty and a hundred years ago; but it is not enough for us to rest upon their laurels or to mark time upon the fancied security of the present. We must "go forward." We must justify the faith of our fathers, demonstrate the wisdom of the form of government to which they pledged us.

To do that, the hand of privilege must be kept from the halls of government. Its influence must never find lodgment in our official actions. The people, not the interests, must be kept continuously "in the saddle." If we are to carry out our pledges, if we want to really serve the people, we must be patriots. At times it will be under pressure and will call for courage.

To prove our love of country in this day of peace, we are not required to defend our land with guns or shell an enemy's fortification with cannon. These trials and tribulations, these testing times of government, present to you and me the only opportunity we have to be patriots. No man was ever a patriot except in times of pressure. That pressure is upon us now—the pressure of human needs, the pressure of social security, the pressure of the demand for better, cleaner, more efficient government.

But this very pressure, this very need presents at once the gravest duty and the most golden opportunity to us all. Texas never needed more toilers, more statesmen or greater patriots than today. If we are to intelligently settle the questions confronting us, we must plant our feet upon the firm ground of principle, distinguish that which is important and disregard the trivial, and, irrespective of personal preferences or private influence, drive straight ahead.

Members of the Forty-fifth Legislature, I propose to you a continuation of our working partnership together. To that end I pledge you and all our public officials my constant cooperation, the open doors of my office and the hospitality of my home, my readiness and availability at all times to discuss the measures introduced, the needs of our people.

Sustained by the faith of our fathers, let's work together! By every word and action let's send this word to Texas people: that we are "on the job"; that we can and will meet our responsibilities by making taxation equal and uniform, by amply providing for greater social security, by carrying out the platform demands of our Party; and, in every particular, giving effect to the will of the people. Let's publish to the world that Texas *is* sound, and, with a confidence born of conviction, tell our people to "be of good cheer."

"And the eyes of them that see shall not be dim, and the ears of them that hear shall hearken."—Isaiah 32:3.

XXIX

Wilbert Lee

O'DANIEL

1939–1941

WILBERT LEE O'DANIEL (*March 11, 1890–May 11, 1969*) was born in Malta, Ohio. He was educated in the public schools of Arlington, Kansas, and a business college in Hutchinson, Kansas.

O'Daniel became well known in Texas as a song writer, singer, and radio entertainer. He directed the "Light Crust Doughboys" and authored the song, "Beautiful Texas."

An unknown political quantity, "Pappy" O'Daniel entered the 1938 Democratic primary race for the governorship and won the general election the following November. He took office on January 17, 1939.

He was reelected in 1940 and became the first candidate for governor to receive more than one million votes.

His second term began on January 21, 1941; however, he resigned in August of that year having won election to the vacated seat in the United States Senate. In both 1956 and 1958, he attempted to recapture the governorship but without success.

Inaugural Address[*]

January 17, 1939

"FELLOW CITIZENS, SENATORS, AND REPRESENTATIVES:

In taking the oath, I have, by the grace of a generous people, assumed grave responsibilities, the obligations of which bear heavily upon me. In return for the confidence bestowed, I hope, faithful service will be rendered by a grateful officer.

On this occasion, I must eschew a discussion of State politics and of measures meriting legislation attention, for, by message Wednesday, I shall present to the Legislature my views on many important subjects with confidence that they will be duly considered, to the advantage of public interests.

This government was instituted for the safety and happiness of the people and the object of all laws should be to accomplish those ends. The splendid body of Senators and Representatives now in session, with those objects alone in view, will receive my hearty and earnest assistance in accomplishing the work that lies before them. While the people expect much of this administration, they can be trusted to wait for results, in which they will not be disappointed. Honest, faithful efforts on the part of their servants can not fail of their approbation. There are no better judges of what is proper, or of the efficient performance of duty than the great masses, who of right do, and should forever, control this government. In them it is with pride that I confess my confidence. To them before this imposing welcome assemblage here to witness the beginning of my official service, I publicly acknowledge unfeigned gratitude. From penury in boyhood, all along life's rugged way, they have liberally shown me favors; and now, from the summit of my political ambition, I acknowledge their supremacy and dedicate

[*]*Journal of the Senate of the Forty-sixth Legislature of the State of Texas (1939)*, pp. 82–83.

331

my honor, my time, and my abilities to the protection and promotion of their sacred rights and material interests.

In conclusion, I beg to tender to the Senators and Representatives the freedom of the department over which I am to preside, and to assure them that on no occasion will the doors be closed to their coming, for with them I join in a common work for the good of a proud and confiding constituency, whose pride centers in the glory, the honor and the advancement of a great State."

Ladies and gentlemen, the words I have just uttered are the exact words spoken by Governor James Stephen Hogg during his first inaugural address delivered before the Twenty-second Legislature January 1, 1891. Pray tell me what words could be more properly chosen to express the needs of our people today. Pray tell me who could read those words with more sincerity than I. And what could better prove that history repeats itself in the perpetuation of the rights of the common citizens than for those immortal words of Governor James Stephen Hogg to be on this Tuesday heard by millions who now listen here, and on these numerous radio networks, as they were repeated by one who was born in the same year that Governor James Stephen Hogg was elected.

Possibly I may fall far short of the humanitarian achievements of my ideal Governor, but his glorious accomplishments certainly provide a goal for which any governor might proudly strive to reach. If full and complete self-sacrificing devotion to duty, determination to achieve happiness and prosperity for others, contribution of every ounce of my ability, and supplications to Him on high for guidance, will lead me on and on in the same path trod by Governor James Stephen Hogg, I shall be happy. Anything short of that accomplishment will leave me sad.

No man could be more void of selfish motives or political ambitions than I. I come to you untarnished politically, and by the grace of God, I hope to remain forever in that category. In my opinion, democratic government is intended to serve but one main purpose and that is to establish correct rules of conduct and enforce those rules, to the end that the citizens, individually, may equally have the opportunity to enjoy happiness and prosperity in accordance with their own talent and ability, and to properly care for those of our citizens who become helpless and are unable to obtain assistance from their relatives and friends. Other functions of government may become temporarily necessary from time to time during emergencies.

Texas is rich in soil, climate and natural resources. Those things are the gift of God. The touch of man is necessary to develop these great gifts. After we have untangled some of our legislative mistakes of the past and placed our government on a sound, constructive, economic business basis, so that the pangs of hunger and poverty of our helpless citizens are appeased, and the minds of our business men eased, we shall then be ready to enter a new era of industrial and agricultural development which should bring to every man, woman and child in Texas, happiness and prosperity. All this is within our easy reach, but we must all earn it by the sweat of our brow, because it is a basic fact that happiness and prosperity can not be legislated into existence. We need to tackle the problem and work harmoniously in a cooperative spirit to bring about its realization. It is not a one-man job, but it is the job of more than 6,000,000 citizens of this great State of Texas. Each of us must do our part, and the laurels gained shall be sufficient to crown all who take part.

To study and determine these needs and requirements and transmit his recommendations to the Legislature is the duty of the Governor. To formulate the rules by which we shall be governed in carrying out our plans is the duty of the Legislature. I am determined to do my duty. I am fully convinced that the Legislature will do its duty. I pray that glamor and color will be eliminated from our session, and that seriousness and dignity will reign supreme. I pray that the poisonous pens of selfish interests and their hirelings which have, since the primary elections, dipped into the well of venom for the purpose of embarrassing and humiliating some of us folks chosen by the people, shall run dry for the duration of our administration in order that those of us who have been chosen, and who have a burning desire to serve honestly and well, may not be handicapped or our work imperiled. I pray that the good, clean, honest, common citizens of Texas, during the term of our administration, go daily on bended knees in the silent sanctuary of their homes and ask the blessings of God to rest upon your legislators and your Governor. No government ever long survived without resting on a firm foundation of religion.

Today I take my seat in a little office on the second floor of the State Capitol Building. On one corner of my desk is a book containing the Constitution of the State of Texas and of the United States, and another book containing the laws of the State. On the opposite corner of that desk is the Holy Bible given to me by my mother containing the Ten Commandments and the Golden Rule, which constituted my platform, plus the brief pledge printed and distributed during the campaign reading as follows: "If and when I am elected Governor of Texas I shall honestly and faithfully perform the duties of that office with fairness to all and special privileges to none." These are my chart and compass with which I intend to guide the Ship of State over turbulent seas into the harbor of happiness and prosperity for all passengers who are aboard.

It was the teachings of my hardworking, religious mother that prepared me for a happy life of service based on faith in God, compassion for the poor, respect for the rich, praise for the right, and forgiveness for the wrong, all of which tenets are essential to the job I am now commencing.

In a little country churchyard near Arlington, Kansas, now rests the body of that saintly mother. At this very moment there are gathered around her grave some of my relatives who were unable to come to this ceremony and for me, in her memory, they are tenderly laying upon her grave a cross of fresh flowers. By that act, and with trust in God, allegiance to all the citizens of Texas and devotion to duty, I now pledge my all to help perpetuate government of the people, by the people and for the people.

MR. PRESIDENT, MR. SPEAKER, LIEUTENANT GOVERNOR STEVENSON, MEMBERS OF THE JUDICIARY AND OF THE TEXAS LEGISLATURE; LADIES AND GENTLEMEN:

Through the process which they have established for their self-government, the citizens of Texas have decreed that I shall serve them in a position of leadership for another term. I accept that mandate with gratitude for their confidence, with enthusiasm for the task ahead, and with the fervent hope that I shall be worthy of the trust reposed in me.

History records that—throughout all ages—in times of great stress and strain, men have abandoned their individual selfish purposes and people of all classes and of all walks of life have united in support of the common cause, for the preservation of their organized society, and the perpetuation of their civilization.

The world today is disturbed as never before. In my judgment, we face a situation which demands that every private citizen and every public official—that all men and women throughout this Nation—devote their time, their energy, their every effort to the protection of those fundamental principles of democracy upon which depend the happiness and well-being of our people.

There is demand today, as never before, that we, as a people, proceed with a unity of purpose; that each and every one of us, in the field in which we are called to serve, give our best thought and our devoted attention to the task assigned; that those who occupy places of public responsibility lay aside every selfish thought, avoid bickering and

---

**Journal of the House of Representatives of the Forty-seventh Legislature of the State of Texas* (1941), pp. 150–55.

criticism of each other, and seek to advance those principles and those activities which will make our commonwealth strong and effective, and which will redound to the benefit of this and future generations.

When I say that we should work with unity of purpose and without personal criticism, I do not mean that the time has come when open discussion of public questions must cease. I believe that all of those who occupy positions of trust in a democratic government have the obligation of contending vigorously for those things which we believe will best serve the welfare of our State. There come times, however, in the experience of every government, when problems are so grave and peril so imminent that consideration of inconsequential details must be abandoned and attention directed to the basic phases of our condition. Let us, then, present our opinions on the important aspects of our public questions, and let us all be actuated in our discussion by the same motive, that motive being the advancement of the common good.

I believe in the majesty of the law. I believe in respecting the law because it is the law. I think that is one of the sound principles of the system of government which we enjoy. I have never thought that I had the authority to distinguish between laws which I liked and those which I disliked; nor do I believe that any citizen of Texas has a right to select the laws he will obey and the laws he will disobey. There can be but one end to the course of choosing the laws which we will respect, and that is the utter disregard of all law. I believe it is especially important under the conditions which exist today that we lose no opportunity to impress upon the people of this State the fact that our liberty, our personal rights, and our property rights, are all dependent upon a respect for law—and I mean a respect for the entire body of the law.

There may be enactments on the statute books of this State which should not be there. If so, they should be repealed—they should not be ignored.

If part of our people disobey the traffic laws, if others disobey the game laws, others the usury laws, still others the laws which to them are distasteful, we shall come, finally, to be a citizenry of law violators, each excusing himself because he thinks the particular law he violates is undesirable. Some of our statutes may be unimportant and obsolete, but let us change them, instead of disobeying them.

The sound, fundamental principles of obedience to the law should not be tampered with.

I, for one, am a great believer, also, in the basic concepts of democratic government as laid down in the Constitution of the United States and in the Constitution of the State of Texas. And today as I assume the responsibilities of the office of Governor for another two years, I should like to rededicate myself and to rededicate the office which I hold to the task of protecting and defending the Constitution of this State against any and all who may seek to ignore or pervert its sacred principles.

Let it be said of all of us that we stand for the whole Constitution of the State of Texas, not just part of it. Let it be said that we stand not only for the letter of the Constitution, but for the great principles outlined in that great document. Let it be said of all of us that we will stand for and fight for those provisions of the Constitution which promise to place the protecting arm of the State around the unfortunate with the same vigor that we will stand for those sections of the Constitution which protect the property of the more fortunate. There is no place in a democracy, and there is no place in the Constitution of Texas to classify the patriotism or the statesmanship of our people on the basis of "haves" and the "have-nots." Let us who are charged with the responsibility of leadership in this State, seek to secure unity of thought and unity of action. Let us recognize that Texas needs the devotion and the support of all its people whether they live in modest homes or in the most stately mansions.

I want to emphasize the fact that the Constitution very wisely divides the authority of government and delegates its powers to three departments—the executive, the legislative, and the judicial. I believe that no emergency warrants an attempt to destroy or to modify that essential plan of government, which provides for the separation of the responsibility of government into these three major branches.

As Governor of this State, I have sought carefully at all times to avoid infringing, in any sense, upon the rights of the legislative branch of the government or upon the rights of the courts of this State, and it is my opinion that the future welfare of the commonwealth will be best served if the Governor respects the rights of the Legislature to act within its sphere and the Legislature respects the rights of the Chief Executive to act within his field of authority, and they both accept, with full respect, the decisions of the Judiciary. That is the system which is specifically provided in the Constitution of this State.

During recent years, there has grown up in Texas a tendency to delegate to bureaus and departments authority which formerly was exercised by either the executive, the legislative, or the judicial branch of the government, and I think the tendency is bad. Such organization of bureaus and departments, as a rule, violates the principles of democratic government. A bureau or department is created by law; it is then authorized to legislate by the issuance of its own regulations; then frequently it sits as the judge on its own legislation and sometimes serves as the prosecuting attorney. I maintain that it is a dangerous process of government which concentrates power to function as prosecutor, legislator, judge, and jury in the hands of one bureau or department of government, and it is my opinion that until this violation of the tenets of good government is discontinued or corrected, you cannot have a rule OF the people, BY the people, and FOR the people.

Little by little, through the years, these principles of true democracy have been violated or abandoned, until today, in my judgment, the whole system of government in Texas is in a critical condition.

More than a million voters went to the polls in Texas last November and voted for your Governor—voted for him, it is to be presumed, because they had faith in him, voted for him with the belief, I imagine, that the Governor of Texas had much authority to direct the executive branch of this State Government. I am sorry to say that most of that executive power has—in recent years—been stripped from the Governor's office, until today your Chief Executive has about as much power and authority in guiding this Ship of State as an honest and experienced captain who attempts to cross the ocean in a vessel which has neither rudder, nor engine, nor sail.

It is, naturally, embarrassing for a Governor to stand before his people and make this statement, but I must deal in facts. I have told the people of Texas about this situation before. I proclaimed it far and wide during the campaign, explaining that the election of Governor was of secondary importance to that of members of the Senate and of the House of Representatives. It is gratifying to me to know that the people listened to that statement and that they gave particular attention to the selection of members of the legislative body. The Legislature, I am glad to say, is still all-powerful, and it has full authority to transform this faulty system into a true democratic form of government, a form which our forefathers envisioned and established.

I have made recommendations to the Legislature, which, if enacted into law, will go far toward taking the control of this Texas government from the hands of self-seeking, influential cliques and restoring it to the great rank and file of our common citizens, to the six and a half million people who reside in this noble State.

I hope this Forty-seventh Legislature does this for you.

I am glad that I have had the opportunity of calling this condition of affairs to the attention of my people. That is one power which could not be denied the Chief Executive—the power of communicating with the citizenship and giving them the picture of the affairs of this State.

If I were motivated by the desire for personal gain, if I sought political power and private profit, I would not be insisting upon the things which I have called to the attention of the Legislature and which I emphasize here today. It would be to my material benefit to allow this system to remain undisturbed, to appoint members of boards and commissions for long terms, and seek favors from their hands when my term shall have expired. But last week, I recommended to the Legislature that they amend the law so that, along with the power of appointment, the Governor will have also the right to discharge those who have been appointed to office. Of course, as far as I am personally concerned, I will have a majority of my appointees on all of these boards by the end of this term, so this authority to dispense with the services of certain officials will accrue to the next Governor of Texas who can dismiss all of my appointees if he sees fit.

Your Chief Executive should have this authority. You elect a Governor in whom you have confidence; you place upon his shoulders certain grave responsibilities. How can he perform these duties unless he has authority to surround himself with those who will assist him in carrying out the mandate given him by the people?

In a representative democracy, it is imperative that someone be entrusted with executive authority, so in my judgment it is best for the people to give that right to the Governor whom they can remove in two years if he abuses the privilege. This plan is to be preferred, I say, to our present system whereby power is given to a group of individuals whom the people do not elect and whom they cannot remove in two years, or four years, or six years, as is the case with members of these boards and commissions which are set up with six-year overlapping terms of office.

My friends, it is my considered opinion that—working together—we can give Texas a system of public administration which will place it in the front rank of governmental units of the world if the Legislature will correct the abuses that have been suggested and turn the government back to the people.

All of our trouble is man-made.

God has done more than His share.

He has bountifully blessed us. He has made abundant provision in this commonwealth for our support and for our delight. Here is a fruitful soil; here mighty rivers make their way to the sea, enriching our land and furnishing power to move our machines. Here the good earth yields its wealth of minerals and great treasure. Here are vast range lands where graze the herds which help to feed and to clothe a people. Here are trees from which houses and furniture and paper and ships are made. Here are stones of amazing beauty which will adorn the buildings of tomorrow.

A coastline stretches for three hundred miles and more, providing harbor for ships in the commerce of the world. Against those shores break the waves of the sea from the waters of which men of science are extracting chemicals to enrich our lives and advance our well-being.

Here is fuel in quantities to challenge the comprehension of man. (Yet the climate of our State makes fuel for heat unnecessary during most of the year.)

Here are wide-open spaces—fields of cotton, and plains with flowing grain. Here are valleys with amazing yields of fruit, and vegetables in vast supply.

Tall mountains rise in majestic splendor, providing scenic beauty which cannot be surpassed.

Here the wheels of industry turn with ever-increasing speed.

Here miles of highways, rails, and airlines serve six and a half million people and give them access to markets near and far.

Woods and streams and mountain trails; resorts by the sea and camps high in the hills, abound for the delight of mankind.

Here are ALL those things which man requires—food for his sustenance; shelter for his comfort; things to be shaped into other things by his handiwork and skill or to be molded and fashioned by mighty machines; resources of energy at his every command. Here are playgrounds for his pleasure; scenes of beauty for his inspiration; and empire for his conquest.

People who are abundantly blessed often become complacent in the enjoyment of Nature's beneficence. For many years in this land of ours, it was traditional for us to harvest our crops, tend our herds, take that which we needed of God's good gifts of timber, water, minerals, and fuel, and leave the rest—unused. We lived in a land of abundance; we lived comfortably and well; we were self-sufficient; we dwelt in peace and contentment; we thought not of the morrow.

But it could not be forever so. The processes of civilization changed. Distance was telescoped. Close contact was provided with other regions of our Nation. International trade increased, presenting a maze of complications which mingled the destinies of Nations throughout the length and breadth of the world. We could no longer live as one apart. Competition grew strong. The organization of society became vastly more complex, and attention to the conservation and development of our own natural wealth infinitely more important.

In an orderly and scientific manner, with the world picture before us, now must we organize the resources which are ours, chart the direction of our course, prepare the plan for our destiny.

We must supplement our traditional industries of agriculture and mining with an industrial economy to utilize the products which Nature yields, to furnish more employment for our own people and for the increasing numbers who are coming to share our wonderland, and to create more wealth that will improve individual prosperity and provide those essential services of government and of civilization which our society requires.

We must provide adequately for the health and the education of our people; for their rest and recreation when labor is through.

An environment conducive to growth and strength in mind, body, and heart must be maintained for the youth of our land, and well earned comfort in declining years assured to those whose work is done.

The unfortunate among us must be attended with kindness and compassion.

The grandeur of our physical state must be matched by the nobility of our character.

And we cannot go about our development in the mean and selfish way. We are today a part of a Nation—a Nation with glorious heritage, the promised land of the world. We must give that Nation, in full measure, the physical support and moral encouragement which it requires in this day of tragic trial. All the facilities at our disposal, the resources at our command, the strength of our bodies, the skill of our minds, the prayers of our hearts must be laid at the altar of America as we join our hundred and thirty million countrymen in dedicating our all to the firm resolve that this shall remain the home of the brave and the land of the free.

The President of the United States of America, the commander in chief of the Army and the Navy, addressed the Congress on January the sixth, presenting to that body and to the people of this Nation a message of unparalleled solemnity.

From his exalted position, where he can view the world situation with a horizon unobstructed by false rumor or by unwarranted complacency, he dispatched to his people a warning of direst danger ahead.

Performing his constitutional duty to give to the Congress information on the state of the Union, he found it necessary to report "that the future and safety of our country and of our democracy are overwhelmingly involved in events far beyond our borders." He assailed the new order which has plunged four continents into a maelstrom of confusion, conquest and despair. He voiced the moral indignation with which Americans have seen Nations once as free as ours trampled into the dust of disaster for no greater crime than that they stood in the path of the despot's desire.

"This Nation," he said, "has placed its destiny in the hands and heads and hearts of the millions of free men and women; and its faith in freedom under the guidance of God. Freedom means the supremacy of human rights everywhere. Our support goes to those who struggle to gain those rights or keep them. Our strength is in our unity of purpose. To that high concept there can be no end save victory."

In the name of the people of Texas, and I know in accordance with the dictates of their desires, I have pledged to the President of the United States, our leader in this grave crisis, the unbounded support of this State and all that it has and all that it can give. I have told him, in your behalf, that we shall work hard, employing the talents which God has given us to the task at hand.

I have told him that our factories would place their facilities at the Nation's command; that labor in our State would not fail in the essential function which it must perform if our duty is to be done.

I have told the President that—with a sense of the deepest responsibility—we shall receive within the borders of our State, within the life of our communities, within the embrace of our hearts, the thousands upon thousands of young men whom the Army and the Navy will send here for their training; that we shall welcome them, guard zealously their health and their physical well-being, place at their disposal without restriction the facilities which may be required for their development, their training, their contentment of mind; and that we shall do our part to see that they return to the circle of their loved ones as clean, and fine, and as good as they were before.

I have told the authorities of our Federal Government upon whom the responsibility rests for the protection of this country, that we will strengthen every part of our State structure, improve to the utmost every phase of our social organization, rise to every situation which this extraordinary occasion demands.

This I have done, as the Chief Executive of this State, in the name of each and every one of my people. I made these promises for you, my fellow-citizens, with calm assurance and complete confidence born of the knowledge of our historic past and of the belief that that same spirit of patriotic zeal abides in the hearts of those who tread this hallowed soil today.

This is indeed a day of dedication—a dedication of our energy and our every effort, a dedication of our will and of our zeal, a dedication of our hopes and of our prayers—to the cause of commonwealth and country.

Only God, in His infinite wisdom, knows what trials the next two years will bring to you, to me, to us all. But come what may, I join you in the solemn pact that we, with our fellow-countrymen and with the friends of freedom wherever they may be, will give every ounce of strength and skill which we possess for the perpetuation of the democratic way of life.

It was that way which led our forefathers from oppression to freedom. It was that way which guided those brave men and women who found here a wilderness and made of it a garden.

It was that way—the American way—which characterized the lives and the works of those who gave us this proud and noble land of Texas. It was the courage and enterprise, the self-sacrifice and common concern, the unity of spirit and the solidarity of purpose, which stood out in such bold relief in their lives and in their living—it was that which gave us Texas, with all that it has meant in a glorious past, with the vital significance of its thrilling present, with the inspiring prospect of its future hope.

And today of all days, now as never before since Goliad, the Alamo and San Jacinto's time, are we called upon to defend those sacred traditions and to emulate those high resolves which brought the achievements of years gone by.

Somewhat more than a century ago, a hundred and fifty-four men—our men—stood beside Travis in the crumbling dust of a mission's walls. It was, as Sidney Lanier has said, one of the most pathetic days of time. All hope was gone. The garrison was outnumbered forty to one. To the people of Texas and to "All Americans in the world," Colonel Travis had sent his heroic message:

"I shall never surrender or retreat . . . I call upon you in the name of liberty, of patriotism, and every thing dear to the American character, to come to our aid with all dispatch. . . . If this call is neglected, I am determined to sustain myself as long as possible and die like a soldier who never forgets what is due his own honor and that of his country. Victory or Death."

On the fateful date of the final assault, Travis and his men advanced to their positions behind the walls of the Alamo— advanced to the doom of that particular day, but to the immortality of all future time.

In that heroic moment of history, there was set for us a standard of valor, of comradeship, of unselfish devotion, that must be maintained as long as patriotism is deemed a virtue and love of native land a noble attribute of man.

To the challenge of the new day and of the new danger, I have no doubt that Texas and Texans—in the continuing spirit of the Alamo— will make answer just as bold, just as unselfish, just as heroic as that of William Barrett Travis and his brave men, and that we, too, will give all of the strength, all of the power, all of the courage with which God has endowed us to preserve the sacred heritage of the past, to protect our noble land, and to defend the rights of men everywhere to be free. May God bless us and guide us in our noble aspirations.

XXX

Coke R.
STEVENSON

1941–1947

Courtesy of Archives Division, Texas State Library

COKE R. STEVENSON (*March 20, 1888–June 28, 1975*) was born in Mason County, Texas. He was self-educated and became an attorney, banker, businessman, and rancher.

From 1914 to 1918 he was county attorney of Kimble County and from 1919 to 1921 he was county judge. He was a member of the Texas House of Representatives from 1929 until 1939 and served as speaker of the House from 1933 to 1937. He was elected lieutenant governor in 1939.

When Governor O'Daniel resigned the governorship to take his seat in the United States Senate on August 4, 1941, Stevenson became governor.

In 1942 Stevenson sought the governorship in his own right. He was unopposed in the general election and took office on January 19, 1943.

He was reelected in 1944 and joined O'Daniel in having received over one million votes. Stevenson was sworn in as governor on January 16, 1945. Upon completion of his second term he had served as governor longer than anyone else to date.

*Inaugural Address**

January 19, 1943

Mr. PRESIDENT, MR. SPEAKER, LIEUTENANT GOVERNOR SMITH, JUDGE ALEXANDER, MEMBERS OF THE TEXAS LEGISLATURE, LADIES AND GENTLEMEN:

Several times on this rostrum and several times in other places I have subscribed to the oath which you have just heard the Chief Justice administer to me. What import and meaning is pictured in these impressive words—to preserve, protect, and defend the Constitution and laws of the United States and of this State! These immortal documents contain the best thought of the old masters on the subject of government. They are the handiwork of the lovers of freedom in both State and Nation. How sincerely we cherish those we love, whether it be members of the family or close and dear friends. A devoted husband will gladly give his life for his wife and will gladly sacrifice any material thing to promote her happiness. In lesser degree, the sacrifices we make for other loved ones are cheerfully sustained.

And who can estimate the value of a true friend? I am in debt today to a multitude of friends who have made sacrifices of time and convenience to assist me in all my undertakings. Perhaps no man ever occupied the executive office who was blessed with as many personal friendships both in the Legislature and out of it as it is my privilege to enjoy. It is never necessary to examine the credentials of true and tried friends. To do so occasionally, however, may increase the value of the friendship.

In similar manner our appreciation of our charters of government may be increased by an occasional examination. When we think of the

Journal of the House of Representatives of the Forty-eighth Legislature of the State of Texas (1943), pp. 83–85.

purposes of government, of its functions, of its objectives and its efforts to attain those objectives, we have a renewed sense of obligation to support it. When we think along these lines we are grateful for the blessings we enjoy, and we are conscious of our responsibility to the next generation.

We are passing through a critical period, and we would be less than human if we were not deeply concerned with current problems. The friendships we enjoy give us greater confidence in our mutual efforts to solve these problems. A friendship for, and consideration of, the benefits of liberty which we enjoy inspire us to the supreme effort to maintain them. This is evidenced by our willingness to fight for freedom and to place our lives, our fortunes, and our sacred honor upon battlefields around the globe.

This nation and the world are in the midst of a gigantic war effort. The result of this struggle will determine whether the peoples of the world are to be subjected to slavery, or whether they will emerge with the banner of liberty, supported by the bayonets of freedom. The aims of the United Nations in this raging conflict are now undoubtedly clear to most of the peoples of the world. The war lords of Germany, Italy, and Japan, and the situations which brought them to prominence, must be thoroughly destroyed. To this end our armed forces are fighting, and to this end they will persevere until the task is finished.

Is this an idle boast, or could it be wishful thinking? I think neither. I consider it only as an expression of that determination which is the heritage of unfettered races. Our thinking about conditions as we want them to be after the war is concluded can be effective only when we accept the assumption that victory will be ours, and that our aims will be accomplished. Most of us believe in the gift of prophecy. Generally we associate it with interpretation of the Scriptures. The Scriptures teach us that where there is no vision the people perish, and history affords the evidence of men who have had a vision in the affairs of state. Thomas Gray is chiefly remembered for his "Elegy Written In A Country Churchyard." Every school child is familiar with it. One of the stanzas was made more famous by the English General, Wolfe, as he proceeded to the assault on Quebec and repeated:

"The boast of heraldry, the pomp of power,
   And all that beauty, all the wealth e'er gave,
Await alike the inevitable hour:
   The paths of glory lead but to the grave."

Wolfe was probably influenced by the certainty that there is a time, we know not when, a power we know not where, that marks the destiny of men to glory or despair. Within a few short hours Wolfe's experience led him through the emotions depicted by Gray as his footsteps marched the path of glory which wandered through the grave. He became immortal to the lovers of heroism as he died responding to his sense of duty. These lines of Thomas Gray may have comforted Wolfe as he made the supreme sacrifice in his country's service.

The same Thomas Gray wrote other lines which should be inspiring to us today, a free translation of which reads:

"The time will come when thou shall lift thine eyes
To watch a long-drawn battle in the skies;
While aged peasants, too amazed for words,
Stare at the flying feet of wondrous birds.

"England, so long the mistress of the sea,
Where winds and waves confess her sovereignty,
Her ancient triumphs yet shall bow on high
And reign the sovereign of the conquered sky."

Thomas Gray had a vision—a vision of a long drawn battle in the skies; a vision of aged peasants, too amazed for words, watching the giants of the air as they engaged in mortal combat! These lines were written more than two centuries ago. That part of the vision embracing aviation has been fulfilled. Every newspaper carries the account of fleets of bombers and fighters engaging in long-drawn battles in the skies. We marvel at the remarkable foresight and the prophetic instinct evidenced by Gray's vision. But even more than astonishment greets us when we consider the second stanza. We are comforted and thrilled to know that:

"England, so long the mistress of the sea,
Where winds and waves confess her sovereignty,
Her ancient triumphs yet shall bow on high
And reign the sovereign of the conquered sky."

The pictures of battles in the air is a forecast of remarkable accuracy. The forecast of England's ultimate triumph may be as uncanny but we accept it with unmeasured confidence. The name, England, in his vision may be considered emblematic of all the united nations in the present struggle. Two centuries ago America was a part of England, and Gray's designation was fitting as including all of the Anglo-Saxon race. It is a prediction of victory which coincides with the marvelous effort of America in common with the United Nations. The fight may be long and hard. Many vacant places may be in our homes when the struggle has ended. Many sacrifices of material things will be demanded and will be given. Our resources, both natural and human, may be severely strained, but the ultimate end is victory for the ideals of democracy.

What are these ideals? For the average man it means the right to live, to work, to worship according to the lights before him; the right to engage in the vocation of his choice, and the opportunity to be successful in that vocation; to reap the reward of his efforts; to be secure in his personal possessions; to be protected against his fellowmen who have criminal instincts.

Our government holds the world's record for success in fostering such ideals. A nation that has produced so much in mechanical achievement, in inventive genius, in industrial leadership, must be founded on correct principles.

A nation which has produced so many brilliant men and women, scholars, scientists, and public servants, undoubtedly has the mental strength to determine its destiny. A nation which has developed the highest standards of living known to history should be careful when considering views of government which come from other parts of the world.

The American citizen enjoys more automobiles, telephones, radios, picture shows, bathtubs, and beauty parlors than all the rest of the world. These things have flourished under the stability of Constitutional government which was designed to preserve, protect, and defend the home, the church, the school, and the business or vocation in which each of us is engaged. It is the American way.

We will change methods from time to time, and very likely following the war we will adopt plans which are more workable and more equitable. We will discontinue things that changing conditions have outmoded, but we should never change the form of our government to fit the nebulous dreams and theories of the advocates or regimentation.

In democracy the very word means voice of the people. We are not slothful in statecraft when we keep government close to the people. But the voter in Precinct 2 in Kimble County or the voter in Precinct 3B in

Travis County cannot make his voice heard when his county seat is moved to the desk of a bureau chief in Washington, D.C., or to the desk of a bureau chief in any other city. Government is not an exact science. The economics of a country is not an exact science. The fundamentals of our government imply an elastic administration based in large part upon local conditions. Upon us rests the duty and responsibility of applying correct principles of government to the problems of State, county, and municipality. This calls for courage, faith, and understanding; courage to meet the issues as they arrive, faith in the sufficiency of our democratic processes, and an understanding of fundamental principles which will promote progress fast enough to meet the needs of the times, and slowly enough to permit adjustments without chaos and change without disruption.

Today we celebrate the anniversary of the birth of that great American soldier, General Robert E. Lee. When the conflict was over, he at once turned his attention to the building of a better civilization in strict conformity with the law of the land. When the present conflict ceases, when victory comes and peace returns, let us emulate his example.

Second Inaugural Address *

January 16, 1945

MR. PRESIDENT OF THE SENATE, MR. SPEAKER OF THE HOUSE, MEMBERS OF THE LEGISLATURE IN JOINT SESSION, LADIES AND GENTLEMEN:

I deeply appreciate the introduction by my long-time personal friend, Claud Gilmer. If it reflects a bias in my favor, it is the result of that type of affection found in the hill country where the faith of men in each other is founded upon the strongest ties of confidence and performance.

It is that type of affection between persons which ought to prevail between individuals and their government. Such affection will prevail if the individual has faith in the integrity, stability and justice of government and if government has confidence in its citizens—confidence in the character and the ability of the individual to manage the affairs of household and vocation with true concern for the welfare of his fellowman.

The conduct of each must be based on correct foundations. The importance of substantial foundations has been emphasized repeatedly in the development of the human race. The Biblical illustration makes the comparison between a man who built his house upon the sand and one who built his house upon a rock. The house built upon the sand could not withstand the terrors of the elements and it fell and great was the fall of it. The house built upon a rock withstood every assault made upon it and continued to render the service for which it was intended. This illustration was used by the Master of men in His effort to teach us the correct principles of life.

Its application is beneficial in every human activity. The architect of this magnificent Capitol building designed a sure foundation. The builders followed the design and the result is a building of great service

---

Journal of the House of Representatives of the Forty-ninth Legislature of the State of Texas (1945), pp. 56–58.

to the people of this State. The same principles of architecture apply with equal force to the humblest home in the land. It will last longer and give better service if it is built upon a good foundation.

The structure of government is no less important. Government is the result of the desire of individuals for an authority which will serve the whole of society. Its origin is of great antiquity. In the earliest periods of recorded history, the desire seems to have been for some strong individual who could exercise authority. This is reflected by the number of kings, emperors and other types of the despotic ruler who controlled the activities of his subjects with an iron hand.

The destiny of the nation was almost determined by the character of the ruling monarch. The Bible says that when the wicked ruled, the people mourned. Under beneficent despots, the people made some progress and under profligate tyranny, the social gains were largely destroyed, though not entirely. That group of men who had faith in God and in themselves made gradual progress. This progress disclosed the weaknesses of despotism and the injustice of control by one man or by a set of men whose decrees were absolute. The desire of the individual for equal rights to all and special privileges to none continued to assert itself. It finally culminated in two revolutions which were closely related in point of time. The first was the American Revolution of 1775 and the second was the French Revolution a few years later. Both of these revolutions asserted the supremacy of personal rights over the despotism of government. Both asserted the principles of equal rights and equal chances to the individuals. Together they constituted a period of Democratic revolution in behalf of the liberties of mankind.

The American people utilized the success of their revolution to build a government upon a solid foundation which recognized the Fatherhood of God and the brotherhood of man. They established a government of law, not the authority of one man, but the authority of the citizen, exercised by representatives chosen by the people. This government has given us the greatest benefits ever provided for the individual in any nation in any period of the world's history.

This government recognized that a man's home is his castle agreeable to the Divine precepts embodied in the Biblical commandments. The prohibition against theft and against covetousness of our neighbor's property is a recognition of the individual's rights in the premises. At the same time, it recognized the philosophy embraced in the teaching that I am my brother's keeper, under which the greatest social gains have been registered.

The desire of certain individuals for one-man control, however, has never been entirely eliminated. Selfish groups, actuated by totalitarian philosophy, have endeavored to obtain control of government at various times. Even when the communistic movement succeeded in Russia in 1917, it merely substituted a government of one man for the government of the Czar which it abolished.

When state socialism triumphed in Germany, it evolved as the government of one man. When fascism triumphed in Italy, it emerged as the government of one man. In our struggle for independence, we accepted the aid and assistance of governments of men, but we did not adopt any of their ideologies. In the present struggle for the preservation of Democracy, we have the assistance of one government run by a strong man. We are not lacking in appreciation of such support, however, to say to all the world that we do not now accept the ideology of that government or of any government which is not a government of the people, for the people, and by the people.

We do not want the socialism of Germany, the fascism of Italy, or the communism of Russia. We want a continuation of the Americanism of our forefathers in these United States. It was built upon the solid foundations which enabled the American farmer, the American laborer, the American businessman, and the American professional man to pool their efforts in the advancement of civilization. Each of these great divisions of our society has had faith and confidence in the integrity and the willingness of the others to support the government—a government which will act as an umpire and not a dictator—a government in which the people, through representatives like you, and under the direction of Divine Providence, decide their own destiny.

My statement today may be commonplace. But, I regard it as standing up in prayer meeting to be counted. It shows which side we are on, and we repeat the performance frequently as an expression of our faith and allegiance. The oath which I have just taken is the same as before and the same one subscribed to by all public officials. It is repeated with every term of office and is a pledge of faith in and allegiance to our government. It means that we will do the best we can for the next two years.

Tomorrow is a challenge to us. It may be as great as that which confronted a little group of men on the banks of the Brazos River in 1836. They projected a government for a free people and fought a war to sustain it. We are in another war today and the sons and daughters of Texas are fighting everywhere. They fight with different weapons—

modern equipment. But, the will and determination to win are the same.

The problems of tomorrow will be different, but demands for faith in our ability to meet them remain the same. The Brazos River men knew their task was enormous, but they faced it cheerfully. Theirs was a task of conquering raw land, but they had no necessity for concern about the dignity of the individual. That dignity had been established by their forefathers for generations, and no force of regimentation had come forward to challenge it. Our task in producing from the land is no less than theirs, but we have the added responsibility of maintaining the dignity and self-respect of the individual. We can solve our problems and meet every challenge of tomorrow if we rededicate ourselves to our work and pray—not for easy jobs and the bounty of the government, but for strength equal to the tasks which are before us. May we prove worthy of the blessings we enjoy and the heritage which has been bequeathed to us.

Thank you.

XXXI

Beauford Halbert

JESTER

1947–1949

Courtesy of Archives Division, Texas State Library

BEAUFORD HALBERT JESTER (*January 12, 1893–July 11, 1949*) was born in Corsicana, Texas, where he also attended public school. He graduated from the University of Texas in 1916. Jester attended Harvard Law School in 1917. During World War I he was captain in the 90th Division. Following his military service, he returned to his law studies at the University of Texas and was awarded his law degree in 1920. He practiced law in Corsicana.

From 1929 to 1946 he was a regent of the University of Texas and chaired the Board of Regents from 1933 to 1935. During World War II, he was a member of the Texas Railroad Commission.

Jester, a Democrat, was elected governor in the general election of 1946 and took office on January 21, 1947.

He easily won reelection in 1948 and began his second term on January 18, 1949. A week after the legislature adjourned in the summer of 1949, Governor Jester died while traveling to Galveston. He was the first governor of Texas to die while in office.

Inaugural Address*

January 21, 1947

MY FELLOW TEXANS:

As I stand before this great assemblage gathered in front of this historic Capitol of Texas, I assure you, and those who participate in this ceremony throughout the land, that the emotions which overwhelm me at this moment are gratitude and humility.

Being elected and having taken the oath of office as Governor of Texas is a great responsibility. It is the greatest honor my native State could bestow upon me. My fellow Texans, my gratitude for your expression of confidence and trust is surpassed only by my awareness of the great responsibility entrusted to me and my humility in undertaking it.

In this challenging hour, it gives me heartening and inspiring assurance to be encompassed by this vast assemblage of fellow Texans both here and in the invisible audience. I am happy and grateful to have present with me my nigh onto sainted mother, my family, relatives, lifelong friends, and neighbors. Here with me are brave and loyal men with whom I served in combat in World War I. Here also are fine men and women with whom I have been associated in various activities and endeavors. Flanking this platform are the members of the Senate and House of Representatives of our Legislature—the men and women who are our lawmakers. With them are Judges of our highest courts and the heads of our departments of State government.

Before all of you, with the oath of office and the touch of this historic and Holy Bible fresh upon my lips, I here and now dedicate myself and such talents and ability as I possess to the service of all the people of this State.

Every inauguration of a Governor of Texas is an historic event. This ceremony today is distinctly historic in that it is the first inauguration

**Journal of the House of Representatives of the Fiftieth Legislature of the State of Texas* (1947), pp. 60–63.

of a Texas Governor officially attended by high officials of the national government of the Republic of Mexico, Governors of Mexican States, representatives of the Panamanian Government and various others, all bringing official greetings from our Latin-American governments and neighbors beyond the Rio Grande and bordering upon the Gulf of Mexico. Because of the friendship of President Aleman, the Band of the Mexican Navy is here for these ceremonies and the Republic's Minister of Finance, Ramon Beteta, who married a Texas girl, is the official representative of President Aleman. In behalf of the State of Texas, I greet you and express sincere appreciation of your presence and cordial felicitations on this occasion. To and through you, as Governor of Texas, I want to assure you, your governments, and your people of the desire of the government and the people of Texas to know you better, to be helpful, friendly neighbors who are bound to you with strong ties of friendship, mutual helpfulness, trade, commerce, travel and good will.

Our State is also honored today by the presence of General Wainwright, Lieutenant General Stratemeyer, our Country's internationally known heroic leaders in World War II, and other distinguished officers and men of our armed forces too numerous to name in my allotted time. The people of Texas salute you. Likewise we welcome and express our appreciation to the many citizens of our neighboring and sister states who have come to participate in these inaugural events.

As the Chief Executive of this commonwealth I ask the counsel and assistance of the people of Texas and those who represent them in every branch of our State government in all things looking to the advancement of the well-being of Texas and its people. I shall need your prayers—to be added to mine and to those of my loved ones—to the God of us all, that He give me as Governor of Texas the wisdom and strength sufficient unto the need of the daily demands of my trust and responsibility.

Texas has entered its second century of statehood shortly after its participation in the victorious military conclusion of World War II. There is much unrest throughout the world, in the United States and even in our own great State. Such unrest is ever the by-product of war. In some instances, new theories of government have evolved in other countries—theories strange and antagonistic to the democratic principles of government upon which our Nation and State have built their greatness.

In my campaign for the Governorship of this State, I made it clear to Texans in my proposal that the path our Government should take and follow was the one taken by the pioneers who builded this State. That was the path and pattern of democratic principles of government. These principles establish government of the people, for the people, by the people—that government must be subservient to the will of the majority; — that government must stem from the bottom up, and not from the top down; — that those who are governed least are governed best.

The key to this kind of government is the will of the people. But the will of the people has been and still is in danger of frustration because of two conflicting theories thrust upon us, with no alternate choice. One extremely far to the right, would imperil labor. The other equally far to the left, would subjugate capital and management and destroy free enterprise in the conduct of Texas business. The great masses of the people of Texas are given scant consideration in either of these strongly pressed political programs. And yet, it is the great masses of our people who pay the cost and are squeezed between labor and management in their disputes and strikes and are the victims of the delays, inconveniences, and threats to their health and workaday tasks.

In the program I presented to the people of Texas for the building of a greater Texas,—presented as Texas stands on the threshold of great industrial and agricultural development,—I charted a path between the extremes of the left and the right. This path would give first consideration to the great masses of the people of this State. It was built upon the principle that the people of Texas are entitled to first consideration in all public matters. This path includes the importance of capital and labor, both of equal dignity and responsibility, with both supported by and answerable to the people. Since the sovereign democracy by their impressive vote chose this path and approved my program for our State government, I take their vote and my election as a mandate to proceed upon this path and to consummate that program. I have every reason to believe that members of the 50th Legislature who were elected in the same elections will likewise consider this mandate of the people of Texas.

Our charge from the voters of Texas, whose will has been decisively expressed, calls for a progressive and a solvent State government. It calls for a government that will keep pace with the great possibilities of this State, foresee and shape its marvelous destiny. In so doing, our government must be possessed of Christian heart and brain. It must always be mindful that the Home, the Church, and the School are the very foundations of our well-being and ever strive to strengthen these foundations.

Our Legislative and Executive branches aided by the Judicial and other agencies of government must furnish direction and leadership as, at this very moment, we are entering a new period of great industrial and agricultural development. Texas will have a great increase in population during the coming years. We cannot grow without money and work, capital and labor. There must be leadership in government that will bring about harmonious relations between capital and labor. It is government's duty to encourage men and women and money to work and receive just returns in Texas.

We must discharge the duties of our public trust in meeting the needs of public education, health, social welfare, law enforcement, safety, and the conservation of our national resources. Adequate provisions must be made for our war veterans, State employees, eleemosynary and penal institutions, and National Guard. These broad and general terms include the detail of many specific subjects and measures which, as Governor, under the law and in keeping faith with the people of Texas, I will submit and recommend for the consideration and approval of the Legislature.

As we of the Legislative and Executive Departments of our government work hand in hand for the public good, let us be ever mindful of our tradition and heritage as Texans. Texans are a race of people because of the impress of the history of Texas upon them.

In the concluding paragraph of William Ransom Hogan's recent book, "The Texas Republic," is this summation:

"So there arose a Texan way of life that still exists, even in the face of all the mass promotion and standardization of machine civilization. Stamina, individualism, 'go-ahead' initiative, pride in everything Texan—these were and still are, in varying degrees, among the ingredients of the Texas spirit. Better courage, wry or raucous laughter and kindliness stood out amidst the drabness and coarseness of frontier life. An astonishing number of urbane and intelligent men found a satisfying freedom from compulsion. Indeed, the Republic of Texas worked a curious alchemy with its citizenry, educated and untutored alike. It took the sons and daughters of Tennessee, the Carolinas, Georgia, Mississippi, New York, France, and Germany, and set its own ineffaceable stamp on their souls. The same process is still working in Texas today."

I deem it our duty in government to effectuate the spirit of Texas and Texans into the greatest State and finest civilization under Heaven. In our planning to do so, we may well follow the safe and sound pattern of government of those Texans whose public service has contributed to building the State and government that is ours today.

In 1895, as Governor James Stephen Hogg concluded his term at the inauguration of Governor Chas. A. Culberson, the third speaker on that occasion, my revered father, Lieutenant Governor George T. Jester, closed his speech with this admonition:

"In our deliberations let us adhere to the doctrine taught by all true apostles of American liberty, that the sole end of legislation should be the greatest good for the greatest number; that the government should do nothing for the citizen which the citizen is able to do for himself; that the people shall support the government, not the government the people . . . ."

"In this day and time when all forms of paternalism are invading the politics of the State and Nation, let us stand close to the Constitution, and contending as our fathers did of old, for its strict construction; administer economically and on a cash basis, the affairs of the government, with a revenue sufficient to maintain the different institutions of the State commensurate with its growth and development."

This concept of our public duty is as sound today as it was a half century and two years ago.

My fellow Texans, this is neither the time nor the place for details pertaining to governmental problems of our State. I am neither unmindful nor forgetful of my advocacy last summer of definite proposals for the improvement of State government. These subjects, from time to time, will be recommended in general and special messages for necessary action, which I hope the Legislature in its wisdom may see fit to adopt—thus preserving the check and balance control so necessary to our Democratic form of government.

In conclusion, I pledge my efforts to serve my State and all its people during my term as Governor. I shall serve no master save my God and the people of Texas. I ask the pastors of every church in Texas to have their congregations next Sunday sing that great hymn of responsibility, "A Charge to Keep I Have." For I would like to have the God-trusting people of Texas to sing this hymn and then remember me in their prayers after they have sung it, remembering as they do, that the second verse is my desire as Governor of Texas:

"To serve the present age,
My calling to fulfill;
O may it all my powers engage
To do my Master's will."

Second Inaugural Address *

January 18, 1949

MY FELLOW TEXANS AND
DISTINGUISHED GUESTS:

In this historic granite Capitol of our beloved State, with the oath of office as Governor of Texas and the touch of this historic Bible fresh upon my lips, I extend heartfelt, cordial greetings to this goodly assemblage before me and to you of the invisible audience.

It is heartening and inspirational to take the oath of this office, which is the highest gift of the people of Texas, surrounded as I am by you who are present at this historic event.

Here are my fellow-workers in the public service of Texas. Here are my Mother, members of my family and friends whose loyalty and devotion have sustained me through the years. Here are my comrades in arms of World War I.

Here have come representatives of our friends and neighbors to the South—the magnificent Republic of Mexican States. Here is the personal representative of His Excellency, the President of Mexico and others of high place and distinction from the Mexican States.

Here are officials of the Government of the United States and visitors from other States—and here have come thousands of my fellow Texans from every part of Texas.

I am profoundly moved and grateful for your interest and your presence here today. I cherish and shall, to the best of my ability, endeavor to merit the confidence of the people of Texas who, for the second time, have elected me as their Governor.

As one of those selected to serve the people of Texas, I stand in humility at the threshold of my second administration as your Governor.

Journal of the House of Representatives of the Fifty-first Legislature of the State of Texas (1949), pp. 44–46.

In the presence of these Members of the Senate and House of Representatives of our Legislature, the judges of our highest courts, the heads of our departments of our State Government and those who by appointment are serving on the Boards and Commissions of our State, I am, and I feel sure, with them, here and now rededicating myself and such talents and ability as I possess to the service of all the people of Texas.

I am grateful to the Members of the 50th Legislature, the heads of the various departments of our State Government, and to all of my fellow workers in the service of the State, as well as to the people of Texas for their cooperation and helpfulness during my first term as Governor.

We can view with satisfaction the success which by cooperative thought and effort we have been able to achieve during the past two years.

We are paying our public school teachers today the highest salaries in the history of the State. We have built more roads during the past two years than any other State in the Union. We have doubled our appropriations for public health and have attained new all-time low records in deaths from communicable diseases.

We have reorganized our Prison System and have increased by 100 per cent our appropriations for State hospitals and schools of special instruction for the handicapped and unfortunate among us.

We have provided funds for assistance to the aged, the needy blind, and dependent children to the full limit allowed by our Constitution.

We have given the most substantial support to higher education in the record of our State. We have built a new institution—the Texas State University for Negroes—and have devoted our attention to the task of making it worthy of Texas and the equivalent of any educational institution of the State.

We have given the closest study to proper measures for the conservation and scientific utilization of our resources-agricultural, industrial, and mineral.

We have launched larger programs in the fields of water and soil conservation and flood control.

We have sought to provide more adequately for the safety and well-being of our people in every walk of life.

All of these things have been done without imposing new taxes, and at the beginning of this second administration we have in the surplus fund of the State's general revenue the largest amount in the history of Texas and more than twice as much money as was there two years ago.

We have strengthened our friendship, cooperation and good relations with our good neighbors beyond the Rio Grande.

These accomplishments are recounted as indicative of what Texans working together—for Texas—can in truth achieve.

Our opportunity for the future and further betterment of the well-being of Texas and its people is great with possibility. I have indicated to the 51st Legislature during the first week of the session my idea of some of the opportunities which lie ahead. As the session progresses, I shall have the privilege of suggesting still other directions for our steady march toward the destiny which so surely is ours.

I have consistently adhered to the philosophy that government must stem from the bottom up, and not from the top down; that those who are governed least are governed best; that government must always be subservient to the will of the majority; that we must strive unceasingly and to the utmost of our capacity and ability to see that ours is indeed a government "of the people, by the people, for the people."

If we are to have strong State government and local government, State and local governments must perform their functions of government. States cannot preserve their rights unless they exercise their duties. Every yielding or surrender of government duties and functions to higher government weakens the government closest to the people.

Texas and other States of the Union must exert every effort to stem the tide of centralization of governmental power, authority, regulation, taxes, and property in the hands of the Federal government. The signs and trends of this tide are ominous. Texas is now faced with the danger of the taking of its tidelands and submerged lands by the Federal government in the face of its Republic and State ownership which was expressly acknowledged and was a part of the annexation agreement when Texas entered the Union.

I believe that Texas and other States can almost write their own program in the setting up and meeting the responsibilities and activities of their local governments. Meeting local government responsibilities and demanding that the Federal government meet only Federal government responsibilities is the only sure way of keeping in adjustment the Federal and States' balance of responsibilities, services, rights, and powers.

In every department of government, in every sphere of public activity, we must eliminate waste, inefficiency and questionable practice. We must develop character in our institutions of government as well as in the lives of our people.

Government should face up to and endeavor to alleviate the sins of modern society which Canon Frederick Lewis Donaldson, of Westminster Abbey, enumerates as "policies without principles, wealth without work, pleasure without conscience, knowledge without character, industry without morality, science without humanity, worship (and I shall add, public service) without sacrifice."

In all areas of governmental activity, we must choose the high road and the middle path between extremes.

God and nature have richly endowed us. Here in Texas are all the elements of material greatness. Here is climate and terrain and power; here are natural resources which in many respects are unequalled elsewhere in all the world. From the utilization of these things can come products of which mankind is greatly in need. From this potential there will come more remunerative employment for our people, increased revenues for our cities, our counties, our State—improvement of our entire economy.

The things material are here. Do we have the skill, the ingenuity, the wisdom and spiritual qualities to use them for the advancement of the well-being of our people?

I think we Texans have.

I think the spirit of a heroic past abides with us still. The courage of men who pioneered this empire, the bravery of those who have defended it against many foes, the strength of those who have tilled its soil and ridden its ranges, the vision of men who have harnessed its rivers, and mined the riches of its good earth, the devotion of those who have died that the greater Texas of tomorrow might live—all of these things are our heritage.

How can we fail our heritage? How dare we go forward with less courage, with less vision, with less abiding faith?

We must draw our plans for the future to a comprehensive scale. We must proceed with determination, to achieve a great purpose.

In our planning and in our work may we always place our reliance upon God. Let us seek His aid and try to do His will.

We who have been chosen to administer the government of our people must ever know

"A mighty fortress is our God
"A bulwark never failing;
"Our helper He, amid the flood,
"Of mortal ills prevailing."

In conclusion, I ask the ministers of every church in Texas to have this four-century-old hymn sung in their churches next Sunday, and that they pray for God's guidance of those of us who are serving the people of Texas.

XXXII

Allan

SHIVERS

1949–1957

ALLAN SHIVERS (*October 5, 1907–*) was born in Lufkin, Texas. He graduated from the University of Texas in 1931 and from the University's Law School in 1933. He was a practicing attorney and businessman and was general manager of the John H. Shary Enterprises and owner of Mission *Times*.

Shivers served in the Texas Senate from 1935 until 1946 when he ran successfully for lieutenant governor. He won a second term in 1948. Upon the death of Governor Jester on July 11, 1949, Shivers moved into the governor's office to complete Jester's term

Governor Shivers sought and won the governorship in his own right in the general election of 1950. His first inaugural address was delivered on January 16, 1951. He won a second elected term in 1952 and his candidacy was endorsed by both the Democrats and Republicans. His second inaugural address was presented on January 20, 1953.

In 1954, running for a third elected term, Shivers had Republican opposition but won by an overwhelming majority. Shivers was the first Texas governor to be elected three times. His final inaugural address was delivered on January 19, 1955.

Inaugural Address *

January 16, 1951

M R. PRESIDENT OF THE SENATE . . .
MR. SPEAKER OF THE HOUSE . . .
MEMBERS OF THE 52ND LEGISLATURE . . .
DISTINGUISHED OFFICIALS AND GUESTS . . .
MY FELLOW TEXANS:

The feeling of humble gratitude with which I assume this, the highest office of my beloved State, is too deep to be translated into words. Rather, I shall try to express my appreciation, not with empty phrases, but by dedicating all my strength and my every effort to the upbuilding of this great commonwealth and for the well-being of all its people.

To my family, to my fellow workers in the public service of Texas, to my friends who have come here today, and to all those who are following this ceremony by radio, I can only say: "Thank you for your presence, your loyalty and your prayers. Your interest is inspiring. Your confidence renews my courage to face whatever task the future may bring.

As we stand here today and try to look ahead, there are clouds on the horizon whose somber hue is unmistakable. Before the wreckage of one vast conflict has been cleared away, the world is threatened with another war more terrible than the last. The godless flag of Communism unfurling its dishonest hate, greed and lust would consume a free people.

We have all hoped and prayed that some near-miracle of international diplomacy, or some real miracle of brotherly love, will yet save us from World War III. We shall continue to pray in that vein, asking the Almighty to grant great strength and great wisdom to our leaders in this crisis. "Blood, sweat and tears" may not be enough this time. We need enlightened and intelligent leadership in a united effort and purpose.

**Journal of the House of Representatives of the Fifty-second Legislature of the State of Texas (1951)*, pp. 61–62.

We must face the possibility that the evil forces now rampant over two continents will not listen to any message that is not written in blood—the blood of brave democratic peoples who would rather die for liberty than survive in slavery.

The fighting goes on today many thousands of miles away, but the sound of the guns carries around the world. In nearly every home in Texas they can be distinctly heard, even now.

The newspaper and the radio bring us word of the national emergency, total mobilization, universal draft, mounting costs of defense, higher taxes, the threat of controls and regimentation. We face the danger that spiraling prices, accelerated by vastly increased expenditures for defense, will bring on a depreciation of the American dollar so disastrous as to turn inflation into a real money panic.

The prospect for the American people is one of austerity and self-sacrifice. At no time in the history of our great state and nation has it been more imperative to put first things first—to place the welfare of the whole country above the demands of individuals and groups.

The task before us is made more difficult by the necessity of maintaining our essential institutions and services here at home. As we eliminate the non-essential in this national emergency, we must not let democracy default in its obligations.

In our zeal to save the world, we must not enslave our own people. The principles of democracy will become fragile bulwarks of freedom if, in protecting them abroad, we devalue our own heritage.

Even in time of war and sacrifice, the more fortunate must continue to interest themselves in the lot of the less fortunate.

Our state hospitals must be operated. Public welfare must be continued. Roads must be built and maintained. The public health and public safety must not be neglected. Our natural resources of soil, water and minerals must be conserved—now as never before.

Continued progress must be made in our school and youth development programs, remembering that "there is but one thing more expensive than education, and that is ignorance."

Our democratic processes must be preserved and strengthened. Today is not a time for "business as usual"—certainly not a time for "politics as usual." But let us be sure that there is always time for democracy as usual.

We must be prepared to pay the price, in money and service for the things that make democracy worth fighting for.

Four years ago, upon my inauguration as Lieutenant Governor, I stated: ". . . The energetic exercise of its powers by a revitalized state government is destiny's call to us today."

That responsibility still exists. The obligations of state government have not been cancelled by the national emergency; they have merely been made more difficult to fulfill.

But Texas has solved grave problems before. At San Felipe and San Jacinto, at Gonzales and Goliad, the broad shoulders of stalwart Texans have pushed the wheels of progress and freedom. We search the pages of history in vain for evidence of indecision, despair or wavering courage on part of Texans who have gone this way before.

In some parts of America today there is too much evidence of a defeatist attitude. Texans can play no nobler part in this grave hour in our nation's history than to take the lead in generating confidence, courage and self-sacrifice to meet the perils that lie ahead.

We will go on with our work—we will take our cue from an early American statesman who in a great emergency said, "If the day of judgment approaches, I choose to be found in my place doing my duty."

We would be unworthy of our trust as public servants if in this critical hour we did not humbly invoke the blessings and the guidance of a power that is greater than all of our councils and our armies. May God bless our labors together, to the end that we may be equal to the demands upon us.

Four years ago I stood here and said: ". . . To the great people of Texas, I pledge that during my term of office, with malice toward none and justice for all, I will do the right, as God gives me to see the right, from the first day to the last."

With all my heart, I renew that promise today.

Second Inaugural Address *
January 20, 1953

MR. SPEAKER OF THE HOUSE ...
MR. PRESIDENT OF THE SENATE ...
MEMBERS OF THE 53RD LEGISLATURE ...
DISTINGUISHED GUESTS ...
MY FELLOW TEXANS EVERYWHERE:

This is an occasion that belongs not to the individuals who are assuming office today, but to all the people of Texas. As the word itself is defined, this inauguration is the formal beginning of another administration. The fact that the new administration is more or less a continuation of the old does not detract from the opportunity—or the responsibility—of starting anew, with a determined and dedicated spirit, to find ways of serving better the people who have elected us.

For myself, and I believe for all those who are a part of this administration, I accept this challenge in humility, in sincerity and with a deep sense of gratitude—to the electorate, to the Legislature, to the other officials and employees of state government, and to all the others who have cooperated and will continue to cooperate in our efforts to build a greater Texas.

This is a day for the broad view of our state government. It represents one of the milestones of our march through history, where we pause in retrospect and look toward the East to remember whence we came and speculate as to where we are going.

It is a day to remember, amid pomp and pageantry honoring the Governor and Lieutenant Governor of Texas, that these tributes are for the position and not the individual. Ours is a government of laws and not of men—and may God grant that it will always remain so.

---

*Journal of the House of Representatives of the Fifty-third Legislature of the State of Texas (1953), pp. 60–61.

This being true, it is important to remember today that the Constitution and the statutes are the repositories of our basic rights and the sources of our civic duties. The structure of our government is controlling over the ideas or whims of individuals who happen to be occupying that structure at any given moment.

Ineptness or corruption in the administration of a democratic government can and will be corrected by the people, if they are given the facts and the opportunity to act upon them. The important thing is to preserve that opportunity.

This is a responsibility we all must share, and it should be paramount even to our duty, as citizens and officials, of rendering the greatest public service possible within the extreme limits of our wisdom, our energy and our courage.

I mention this obligation as a fundamental qualification and reservation upon any and all proposals to change the basic structure of our state government.

Once that consideration is met, however, we are ready to face the fact that it is desirable, and often essential, from time to time to revamp and modernize our governmental structure to meet the changing and growing demands upon it.

Just as we would not send out an army carrying muzzle-loaders to face the terrible weapons of the atomic age, we should not expect the governmental structure of 1876 to serve us fully in 1953.

Reorganization of our state government is a subject that has intrigued many minds down through the years. It has been the subject of more discussion than accomplishment. The dream of a completely reordered and revitalized government, perfect in every detail, has always ended with a rude awakening to political and human realities. The value of democracy often lies in its slowness of action.

This is not to say that the dream has no value, and the perfectionist no place in our plan of improvement. We need a goal toward which to set our faces—a pattern to follow in general outline, so that each small accomplishment will contribute to the whole. In addition to individual suggestions, we have had surveys and research projects that, to say the least, excited interest and concentrated attention upon the problems of state government.

Let us have more ideas, more information, more research—yes, more dreams of a better day in state government. We must not allow the practical difficulties of full-scale reorganization to discourage the continued search for the ultimate solution.

At the same time, we should not let the distant goal of perfection blind us to the task near at hand.

That is the task of accomplishing what we can, in however small degree, toward a stronger, more efficient and more responsive state government.

There is a great deal to be said, in fact, for the piecemeal approach to governmental reorganization. The history and experience of generations should not be delivered over to reformers with enthusiasm for the moment, but possibly lacking in respect for the past and without due consideration for the future.

In recent years the Texas Legislature has shown the vision and the courage to make changes—not just for the sake of change, but in response to the meritorious needs of an increasing population, an expanding economy and a growing sense of moral obligation upon the part of our citizens.

Some of these changes have been highly significant: the Gilmer-Aikin program for improvement of the public school system; the State Hospital program; the Ellis Plan for prison reform; the Youth Development Council as a modern approach to an age-old problem—these are a few examples.

The 53rd Legislature has an opportunity to accomplish much in equally important fields. I will mention these few:

The writing and implementing of a sound state water conservation policy.

Coordination of our programs of higher education.

Improvement in our methods and policies of public school financing.

Reorganization of certain departments upon sound administrative lines, with proper attention to our experience that the most efficient formula we have yet developed is that of a small policy-making board functioning through a strong executive director.

Standardization of personnel policies, both as to qualifications and salary, in the various agencies of the government.

An orderly approach to the growing problem of governmental housing, and an intelligent application of existing revenues toward a business-like solution.

These are merely some general suggestions. There are opportunities before us of saving money—and of spending money more wisely. Few of them offer a chance for spectacular reforms, but rather for increased economy and efficiency in our government.

The opportunity is not so much to make headlines as to make history.

The near task is not always the most attractive one. But its accomplishment becomes part of the general pattern of development toward our goal of a more responsive and responsible state government.

In an era of vast and even frightening scientific progress, in an atmosphere of international danger and a time of grave domestic decision, we would be neither children of man nor of God if we failed to put first in our thoughts and prayers the hope for peace and the preservation of our way of life.

At the same time, let us not forget that in the poet's words, "the task we must do is the near."

That we will have the wisdom to see our duty, the willingness to undertake its accomplishment and the energy to carry it through, is my hope for all of us. With divine guidance and sufficient human courage, all tasks can and will be done.

Third Inaugural Address *
January 19, 1955

Fellow texans:

"So teach us to number our days, that we may apply our hearts unto wisdom."—90 Psalms 12.

Under the Providence of God and by action of the people of Texas, I have again taken the oath as Governor of Texas. During the five and one-half years that have elapsed since I first took that oath in front of our old family farm home near Woodville, Texans have fought and won many bitter battles. The high stakes have been our tidelands, our sovereign rights in state and local self-government, the true principles of traditional Texas democracy, and the future place of Texas in the national sun. It has been our great privilege to prove again that it is never idle to fight for principle.

In an era of unparalleled industrial growth and tremendous increase in population, we have worked together to attain progressive state government within the ancient landmarks of the faith of our fathers. For the most part our labors have been richly blessed.

With this brief, grateful glance together at the past, let us now look ahead.

On this day of dedication, we honor the system of government which has so successfully served us. In all humility, we unite to answer the challenges placed before us by residence in this State and citizenship in this Nation.

Under our federal Constitution, the liberty of the individual is most effectively protected by the reservation of all undelegated powers to the states and to the people. This limitation upon the powers of the central government has served freedom well in America, throughout this century while so many of the earth's governments have fallen into the totalitarian tyranny of an all-powerful central government.

---

*Journal of the House of Representatives of the Fifty-fourth Legislature of the State of Texas (1955), pp. 70–71.

If our nation is to be strong, and if our liberties are to be secure, we must establish on the state level an exacting new standard of effectiveness for the operation of state government.

Today our state governments are being blunted as effective instruments of public service by failure to modernize their structures and organization to permit proper functioning in these demanding times.

The task is neither easy nor can it be quickly accomplished. Although the work will take years to complete, it is our clear and compelling duty to begin.

In the humble faith born of long experience in the service of our State, I offer these recommendations for strengthening the government of Texas.

Over the years, the duties of the executive branch of our state government have multiplied manifold; but where the responsibility has been concentrated the authority has been diffused. New functions, new boards and new agencies have been added to the executive arm to serve new needs; but, in far too many instances, the line of authority and accountability has become dim and obscure. This is neither sound policy nor good government.

I believe we should begin giving serious thought to reorganizing the executive branch. If the Governor is to be held accountable for the conduct of the executive branch, future Governors should have direct authority over—as well as responsibility for—the performance of administrative functions which are not policy-making in character. Those offices which are, in effect, a part of each Governor's administration should be subject to his appointment and removal. These changes would not lessen the burdens of the office of Governor, but they would increase the obligation for faithful and responsible service.

If we give the executive more authority and a higher degree of accountability, we should also follow the example of most other states by giving the executive a longer term. This principle has been endorsed by the recent constitutional amendment extending the term of county officials to four years. The same principle should apply to elective state offices—with proper prohibitions against officials seeking one office while holding another.

Attention should also be given to maintaining full legislative and executive responsibility in fiscal matters. Today we separate our state income into many special segregated funds and give varying degrees of preference and priority to these special purpose commitments. Proper and realistic authority over the use of state revenue is rapidly vanishing.

Last week, I submitted to the Legislature a program calling for expenditures of $209 million during the next two years. This is larger than ever before; and yet it represents, on an annual basis, only about one-seventh of the more than $700 million which the State of Texas will spend. The cause of good government demands that we place control over the expenditure of all state income on a current basis under a central budgeting authority.

These are changes for the future—changes which would enable the public officials who follow after us to render more effective, more beneficial service to our State. We must not allow our preoccupation with current needs to turn our eyes away from a long look ahead.

We must, with vision and with courage, strive to make our own state government a respected example of good, responsive, and progressive government. If we should fail, our victories for principle would be hollow and our fights for our rights would be in vain.

We can keep faith with our obligations as Americans and as Texans only to the extent that we exercise fully the rights which are ours. We neither divide our loyalty nor weaken our purpose when we serve faithfully both our Nation and our State, for good citizens must not serve one and neglect the other.

Our challenge is to build an example of state government at its finest.

On these and all other issues in the days ahead, may the Wise and Merciful Father of us all—who can go with you and stay with me—bind us one to another in this great commonwealth and so direct and rule our hearts and minds that we may render unto our country, our fellow man, our beloved Texas, and unto Him, our last full measure of devotion.

XXXIII

Price

DANIEL

1957–1963

Courtesy of Archives Division, Texas State Library

PRICE DANIEL (*October 10, 1910–*) was born in Dayton, Texas, and attended public school in Dayton. At the age of sixteen Daniel was a newspaper reporter, first for the Fort Worth *Star-Telegram* and later for the Waco *News Tribune*. He graduated from Baylor University in 1931 and a year later graduated from Baylor Law School. He practiced law in Liberty, Texas, until 1943.

Daniel was a member of the Texas State Democratic Committee from 1939 until 1941 and a member of the Texas House of Representatives from 1939 until 1943. In 1943 he served as Speaker of the House.

Daniel served in the army during World War II from 1943 until 1946. He returned to his political career in 1946 and was elected attorney general, a post he held until 1953. He won a U.S. Senate seat in 1952. In the elections of 1956, he made a successful bid for the governorship, defeating his Republican opponent by a commanding margin. He assumed office on January 15, 1957.

Governor Daniel was reelected in 1958 and in 1960. He sought an unprecedented fourth term in 1962 but was defeated.

*Inaugural Address**

January 15, 1957

The official oath which I have just taken, as prescribed by the Constitution of Texas, ends with the words, "So help me God." With this supplication I have sealed my solemn pledge to you. With this same prayer for Divine Guidance, I now accept the sacred trust bestowed upon me by the people of Texas.

This is not a day of triumph. It is a day of dedication. With that in mind, we began this day with emphasis upon the importance of spiritual guidance in the lives of men and the affairs of government. I appreciate the inspiring message brought earlier today by Billy Graham and thank him sincerely for being with us.

It is with a grateful heart and a spirit of humility that I express my appreciation and my sincere thanks to those of you here and throughout Texas who made possible this high honor and great responsibility.

I pray that with God's help I may be worthy of your confidence and friendship.

I am conscious of the fact that all Texans did not agree with your choice. Be that as it may, I have just pledged myself to perform the duties of this office for the benefit of our entire citizenship. I shall do my best to be a faithful Governor for all of the people, regardless of personal or partisan differences of the past. In that same spirit, I earnestly solicit the cooperation, counsel and prayers of all the people of Texas.

Always with us there will be a few extremists who prefer discord and thrive upon conflict, regardless of the consequences. It is not to them but to the overwhelming majority of our citizens who truly love Texas that I offer, as I seek, cooperation, unity and good will. Our people have had enough division. It is time for Texans to pull together for the future progress and glory of our beloved State.

Never misjudge this desire for patience, reason, and good will. There

*Journal of the House of Representatives of the Fifty-fifth Legislature of the State of Texas (1957), pp. 64–67.

are some of us who are warm at heart and humble in spirit who still know when and how to fight—and fight we will when there are battles to be waged for our State and our people.

I offer my wholehearted cooperation to you, Governor Ramsey, and to you, Mr. Speaker, to the members of the Legislature, with many of whom it has been my honor to serve, and to the other officials of our State. We have subscribed to the same oath of duty. Together we must work for a free and noble people who govern themselves through those of us who act as their chosen representatives.

With proper support from the people, I predict that this administration and this Legislature will mark the beginning of a greater era of progress, integrity, and good government for Texas. When the record is finally written, I hope above all that it may be said that together we considered each office a public trust and that we conducted a government truly of, by and for the people of our State.

Ten times before, I have taken official oath similar to the one repeated today; thrice as a member of the Legislature, once as Speaker of the Texas House of Representatives; once as a private in the United States Army, then as an officer; thrice as Attorney General of Texas; and finally, as a member of the United States Senate. Each time I have done my best to discharge with diligence and honor my sacred obligation. Each time, as again today, my heart has been moved by a renewed pledge of allegiance to uphold and defend government by law rather than by men.

In this oath I have pledged myself to "preserve, protect and defend" both the Constitution and laws of the United States and the Constitution and laws of the State of Texas. This I shall do to the best of my ability. There is no real conflict in this obligation to dual sovereignties. Each is supreme in its respective sphere of action. Conflicts arise when there are strained interpretations which cause one of the sovereigns to encroach upon the powers and rights of the other.

In modern times, this encroachment most usually has been on the part of Federal officials who have sought to centralize and expand their powers at the expense of the States and the people. I shall uphold and defend the Constitution of the United States in all of its parts, but I shall emphasize and fight for one portion of that immortal document which has suffered from disuse and disregard, especially at the hands of the Nation's highest court. I refer to the Tenth Amendment, without the certainty of which there would have been no agreement to the original Constitution. By that amendment, all "powers not delegated to the

United States by the Constitution * * * and reserved to the States * * * or to the people."

The writers of the Constitution and its first ten amendments had lived under the tyranny of a king. They never wanted the power of government to be centered again in the hands of one man or a few men at the top. They believed decentralization of power and local self-government to be the best safeguards of liberty and freedom. Because I believe this is in accordance with the Constitutions of the United States and our own State, I shall continue to fight with all the vigor at my command against further encroachments by the Federal government upon the rights of our State and our people.

As you well know, I have devoted many of the years of my life to this fight to preserve the rights and property of our State. Today I dedicate the rest of my life to this cause. In so doing, I am convinced that this is best for both the Nation and the State.

The real strength of America lies not in Washington nor in centralized power nor in military might or weapons of defense. The enduring power of this country lies in the faith and strength of our people and in the strength of our States and our local units of self-government.

The surest way to protect and preserve the rights of the State of Texas is for us to have a dynamic and constructive exercise of the responsibilities which accompany these rights. This week I shall present such a program to our Legislature.

My first and most important recommendation shall be that we take action here which will justify the faith and confidence of our own people in the honesty and integrity of our State government. The cornerstone of my program will be simple honesty and moral integrity in the halls of government. That is the way to have public confidence, and without it we shall have little success in attaining our other important objectives.

I shall recommend as emergency legislation a strict lobby control and registration law, a code of conduct for State officials and employees, and a State Law Enforcement Commission with power to make complete investigations of alleged official misconduct and recommendations for improved law enforcement.

Good government requires clean government. An overwhelming majority of our State officials and employees have been faithful in the discharge of their duties, but if there is one blemish or hidden act of misconduct it must be exposed and eliminated, with proper punishment of anyone who has violated his public trust.

As far as material things are concerned, the most important need for proper exercise of our State responsibility is the enactment of a Statewide program for conservation and development of our water resources. This is necessary for the future growth of our municipalities and industries and for the relief of our drought-stricken farmers and ranchers. I shall submit as emergency matters the proposals of the Water Resources Committee and other recommendations which will aid in the solution of this important problem. The future growth and prosperity of our State depends upon prompt and effective action, and I hope there will be no timidity or delay in our action.

Other recommendations will include improvements in our public schools—from the primary grades to the ultimate reach of higher education, with salary increases sufficient to retain and recruit adequately trained teachers for our boys and girls. We should make our public schools and institutions of higher learning the finest in the land, and it should be done with Texas money. A state as wealthy as ours has no reason to seek Federal aid and thereby invite Federal control.

Coupled with the biggest highway building program in the history of our State, we must have an expanded program of highway safety to reduce the ever-increasing toll of death and destruction on our highways and streets.

We must strengthen our laws and enforcement against the vicious narcotics traffic, and provide stronger measures to combat other crimes and juvenile delinquency.

Other important fields for action are groundwork for revision of our State Constitution, attraction of new industry to our State, good relations between labor and industry, industrial safety, further improvement in our insurance and election laws, continued improvements in our State hospitals and special schools, additions to the prison system, an adequate system of probation and parole, and cost-of-living increases for employees of the State and for old age pensioners.

Whatever the price may be for progress and good government in the future—for exercising the responsibilities which will best preserve our State's rights—it will be worth the cost to Texas and our people. As you know from past service, I abhor waste and extravagance in the use of public funds, and will do everything possible toward keeping the essential services at a minimum cost. I shall work for a balanced budget under the "pay-as-you go" amendment to the Texas Constitution.

With this brief outline of the work ahead, you can see more clearly why we shall need the advice and counsel of the people whom we serve.

And let us be thankful that in this land we are not dependent alone upon man's advice but, as indicated in the closing words of our official oath, we depend also upon Divine Guidance in the discharge of our duties.

May He who guides the destinies of nations as well as the destinies of men be with us in our endeavors. May we, with humility and courage, act boldly and wisely, knowing that there is a Hand above which will help us on.

Second Inaugural Address*
January 20, 1959

It is with sincere gratitude and deep humility that I again accept the public trust and sacred duty bestowed upon me by the people of Texas.

Twice the people have given me this, the greatest honor and highest responsibility at their command. I express to all the people of Texas my heartfelt appreciation, and my special thanks go to all my family, friends, and associates who have made this possible. With God's help I will do my best to be worthy of your confidence and trust.

I thank all of you who are present for this occasion, especially the distinguished representatives of all four of the adjoining States of the Republic of Mexico, as well as the special representative of our Ambassador to Mexico and representatives of other countries of the free world. We welcome you to Texas and appreciate your joining with us in another demonstration of the friendship and good will which exists between our people and your people. May our ties be strengthened and our efforts ever united for the type of understanding and good will which brings peace and happiness to mankind.

It is ever significant to me that the official oath which I have just taken ends with the words, "So help me God." As stated in my first inaugural message, I shall take seriously this plea for Divine Guidance with which I have sealed my pledge to "preserve, protect, and defend" both the Constitution and laws of the United States and the Constitution and the laws of the State of Texas. I shall uphold and defend the Constitutions of our dual sovereignties in all of their parts, but as pledged two years ago, I shall continue to emphasize and fight for those neglected portions of both State and Federal Constitutions which recognize that "powers not delegated to the United States by constitution . . . are reserved to the States . . . or to the people."

As Governor, I pledge you to keep the Lone Star of Texas in the

*Journal of the House of Representatives of the Fifty-sixth Legislature of the State of Texas (1959), pp. 54–57.

forefront of the constant battle to preserve the property and rights of State and local governments. Already there has been too much centralization of power and money in Federal bureaus far away from observation and control of the people.

The real strength of America lies not in Washington nor in centralized power, military might, or missiles to the moon. The enduring power of this country lies in the faith and strength of our people and in the strength of our States and our local units of self-government.

I shall continue to fight with all vigor against further encroachments by the Federal government upon the rights of our State and our people, but to be successful we must properly discharge the State responsibilities which accompany these rights. We must have as much talk and action on State responsibilities as we have on State rights. This has been my philosophy since I entered public service as a member of the House twenty years ago, and it shall be my guiding principle throughout this administration.

The State government is faced today with many challenges—in finances, in law enforcement, in maintaining the integrity of public office, and in building for the future of the greatest State in the Union. However, I have looked through the pages of history and have found, especially from the messages of the Presidents of the Republic of Texas and the Governors of our State, that no chief executive has taken this oath of office in a time free of stresses and crises. In many instances, they were stated to be the "greatest emergency" or the "worst financial crisis" the State has ever known.

Perhaps the most urgent was Governor Sam Houston's report in his message to the Legislature in 1861 that "not a dollar has been in his command for months," and his warning that Comanche Indians were threatening within 50 miles of the Capitol building. Some of the finest chapters in Texas history were written by Governors and Legislatures which faced and met problems and challenges that demanded the full measure of public service and leadership. The Texas we know today was built by men and women with the courage to overcome hardships and fight for their convictions.

Two years ago on inauguration day, we faced our full share of crises in Texas. We had been through seven years of drought, and we were in dire need of State-wide water conservation and planning. There were critical problems of restoring more public confidence in the State government. We needed improvements in law enforcement and a program to stop the slaughter on our streets and highways. Our public schools and institutions of higher learning needed more resources to keep pace with the demands of the times.

Your Governor and the 55th Legislature struggled to solve these problems through the regular session and two called sessions. At times some of them seemed insurmountable, but the record shows final enactment in whole or in substance of all the 52 recommendations which I made to the Legislature.

For the first time in our history, we now have a State-wide water and soil conservation program and the facilities to plan for present and future development. We enacted a lobby registration bill, a code of conduct for State officials and an insurance reorganization bill. We took broad steps to fight crime and to improve law enforcement in our State. A Law Enforcement Study Commission has just delivered its recommendations for further improvements. We provided much-needed salary increases for school teachers and college faculties and took measures to maintain local control and operation of our public schools.

We have the biggest highway construction program in the history of the State. Equally important is the new State-wide highway safety program which has helped to save at least 200 lives by reducing our traffic fatalities last year more than any other State. This program involves the lives of human beings needlessly slaughtered on our streets and highways, and I am as proud of it as any accomplishment of this administration.

We put into operation a program to attract new industries through the State Industrial Commission; established the Texas Youth Council and a system of paid parole supervision for adult parolees; increased old-age pensions; provided for higher workmen's compensation benefits; and laid the groundwork for a revision of the State Constitution.

Because the last Legislature enacted this extensive program for progress and good government, the 56th Legislature will not face anything like this number of major legislative proposals. Our task this year will be to make further improvements in the programs already enacted and to provide finances for commitments already made. This task, of course, is equally as important and more difficult than the origination of the programs in the first instance.

Yes, every Governor and every Legislature have problems of the day which appear greater than those of yesterday. However, seldom has any administration faced a brighter future for the State and its people. Our population is growing at a rate much faster than the national average. Nearly 100,000 school children enter our schools each year. Personal income and bank deposits are at an all-time high. New industries are flocking to Texas. The drought is ended and farmers and ranchers are enjoying better times; corporation income is up and employment continues to grow. And Texas is still the biggest State in the Union, without a glacier.

All of this phenomenal growth plus the corresponding increase in the cost of governmental services has contributed to the anticipated deficit and the need for more State revenues for the next biennium.

In this situation I shall recommend to the Legislature tomorrow that we place first and foremost the retirement of the anticipated deficit before the end of the fiscal year, and I shall submit this as an emergency matter. Secondly, I shall propose means for providing new revenues for the next biennium with an annual new tax bill smaller than the last one enacted in 1955.

Finally, I shall propose that we enact measures which will give greater respect to the General Fund and the "pay-as-you-go" amendment so as to keep our budget balanced as intended by the Constitution.

This third proposal includes the need for a complete study and reorganization of the State's administrative and fiscal policies.

Texas today has over 175 separate departments, agencies, and boards, and many of them have overlapping functions.

We have 213 separate funds in the State Treasury and 30 separate funds deposited in banks without ever entering the Treasury. There is a need for certain special and permanent trust funds such as our Public School, University, and other constitutional funds, but I am positive that more efficiency and economy can be obtained by eliminating and combining many of the separate State agencies and special funds.

There is something wrong with a system that allows its housekeeping fund, the General Fund, to receive nothing but the crumbs left over after statutory transfers are made to other funds, most of which remain in excellent condition. Every bank in Texas would have a cash deficit if it had to keep each depositor's money in a separate safety deposit box rather than merely have it credited for withdrawal when called for.

So, it shall be the aim of this administration not only to balance the budget this year and provide for the needs of the next biennium, but also to maintain the pay-as-you-go program intended by our Constitution and lay the groundwork for a permanent and more efficient reorganization of State government and revision of our fiscal procedures.

To you, Mr. Lieutenant Governor, Mr. Speaker, and Members of the Legislature, I pledge my cooperation, and I earnestly solicit the cooperation, counsel, and prayers of all the people of Texas.

In the same manner that I closed my first inaugural message, I pray that, with humility and courage, we may act boldly and wisely, knowing that there is a Hand above which will help us on. May He who guides the destiny of nations as well as the destiny of men be with us in our endeavors.

Third Inaugural Address*
January 17, 1961

For the third time the people of Texas have entrusted with me this, the greatest honor and highest office within their power. With sincere humility and deep gratitude I again accept the office of Governor and express to all the people of Texas my heartfelt appreciation. My special thanks go to all my family, associates, and friends whose constant assistance have made this possible. I pray that my actions will be worthy of your faith and confidence.

I thank all of you who are present for this occasion. Especially do I welcome the distinguished representatives of the adjoining States of the Republic of Mexico. We appreciate your joining with us in another demonstration of the friendship and good will which exist between our people and your people. You honor us by your presence.

As stated in my previous inaugurations, it is ever significant to me that the official oath of office which I have just taken ends with the words, "So help me God." I shall continue to take seriously this plea for Divine guidance with which I have sealed my pledge to "preserve, protect, and defend" the Constitution and laws of the United States and of this State.

For the third time this morning, we began an inaugural day by stressing the importance of spiritual guidance in the lives of men and the affairs of government at a prayer breakfast for State officials and members of the Legislature. I appreciate the inspiring message which Dr. W. R. White, President of Baylor University, delivered on that occasion.

I offer my wholehearted cooperation to you, Governor Ramsey, and to you, Mr. Speaker, to the members of the Legislature, and to the other officials of our State. We have subscribed to the same oath of duty. Together, we must work for a free and noble people who govern

*Journal of the House of Representatives of the Fifty-seventh Legislature of the State of Texas (1961), pp. 58–60.

themselves through those of us who act as their chosen representatives. May we strive always to make our government truly of, by, and for the people.

Today marks the thirteenth time that I have taken an official oath similar to the one repeated here; three times as a member of the Texas Legislature, once as Speaker of the Texas House of Representatives, once as a private in the United States Army, then as an officer; three times as Attorney General of Texas; once as a member of the United States Senate; and now three times as Governor. Each time, as again today, my heart has been moved by a renewed pledge of allegiance to uphold and defend government by law rather than by men.

In accordance with this oath, I shall uphold and defend the Constitutions of our dual sovereignties in all of their parts. However, as pledged two years ago, I shall continue to emphasize and fight for those neglected portions of both State and Federal Constitutions which recognize that "powers not delegated to the United States by constitution . . . are reserved to the States . . . or to the people."

The real strength of America lies not in Washington nor in concentrated power or centralized authority. The enduring power of this nation lies in the faith and strength of our people and in the strength of our States and our local units of self-government.

As Governor, I shall continue the fight against further encroachments by the central government upon the rights of our State and our people. To be successful in this fight, we must properly discharge the State responsibilities which accompany these rights. We must have as much talk and action on State responsibilities as we have on State rights. This has been my philosophy since I entered public service as a member of the Texas House twenty-two years ago, and it shall continue as the guiding principle of this administration.

Today we face many responsibilities which must be exercised for continued growth, prosperity, and sound government in our State. By properly meeting these State responsibilities, we will contribute not only to the future of our State, but to the preservation of constitutional government and the original concept of State-Federal relations which gave birth and strength to our Nation.

I am proud of the progress of this administration and the State responsibilities which have been exercised during the past four years. Through legislative and administrative action, we have restored honesty, integrity, and public confidence in our State government.

For the first time, we have a statewide planning program for water conservation and development. We have had the State's largest highway construction program, and along with it we inaugurated the first statewide highway safety program, which has appreciably reduced the slaughter on our streets and highways. We have established the Texas Industrial Commission and the first State program for attracting new industries, tourists, and new residents. We have made improvements in public education, including salary increases for public school and college teachers.

Other enactments during this administration included creation of the Texas Youth Council, the first paid parole system for adults, increased pensions for the aged, and improvements in our State hospitals, special schools, correctional institutions, and law enforcement programs.

Indeed, these have been significant accomplishments during the past four years. They have been important exercises of State responsibility. However, in a growing State like Texas, we hardly have time to look back with pride before it is necessary to look forward with action for new accomplishments and continued expansion.

In practically every field, which I have mentioned, the passage of time, our rapid population increase, and the need to meet competition of other States have placed upon us the need for further improvements and additional revenue. If we are to pay for present services and make the improvements necessary to keep pace with the rapid growth of our State, we have the further responsibility of raising sufficient revenue to retire the present deficit and operate this State on a balanced budget.

This is not the first time that a Texas Legislature has faced a deficit, and Texas is not the only State which has the problem of raising new taxes. Throughout the history of this State, Texas Legislatures have been faced with deficits more often than with balanced budgets, and now and during the past two years most of the other States have been confronted with needs for new taxes—some of them greater than ours.

None of this lessens in any degree the magnitude of the fiscal problem which faces the 57th Legislature. It is greater in total dollars than any before in our history. I shall present the reasons, the details, and recommended solutions in my first message to the Legislature. This much I shall say now:

I shall recommend to the Legislature that we place first and foremost the retirement of the deficit, and I shall submit this as an emergency matter. I feel strongly that we should arrange to pay for past commitments and present debts before undertaking new programs and new expenditures.

In the meantime, it is my sincere hope that those citizens and business groups who believe in State rights and State responsibilities will lend their cooperation and support to the Legislature in its effort to adequately finance State government. All too often some who proclaim the loudest about State rights are in the forefront against State taxes, even with State taxes being deductible from the Federal income tax. Those who thus contribute toward higher Federal tax collections and lower State revenue simply weaken the power of the States in our system of State-Federal relations. So often the same taxpayers end up financing Federal programs which the States could have operated at far less expense and with far more efficiency and success.

I am convinced that the people of Texas realize that the phenomenal growth of our State requires additional taxes. I believe they will welcome prompt action, and that friction, dispute, and delays will result in far more disappointment and criticism than whatever solution might be finally adopted. It is my hope that all of us in State government will look upon our task not only as a serious problem but as a great challenge. Some of the finest chapters of Texas history have been written by Governors and legislators who faced problems and met challenges that demanded a full measure of courage and statesmanship. Texas, as we know it today, was built by men and women who had the courage to overcome hardships, to withstand selfish interests, and to fight for what they believed to be right. As they met the challenges of the past, I have faith that we shall meet the challenges of today.

Again, to you, Governor Ramsey, Mr. Speaker, and members of the Legislature, I pledge my full cooperation, and I earnestly solicit for all of us the understanding, counsel, and support of all the people whom we are honored to serve.

XXXIV

John Bowden

CONNALLY

1963–1969

Courtesy of Archives Division, Texas State Library

JOHN BOWDEN CONNALLY (*February 27, 1917–*) was born in Floresville, Texas. He graduated from the University of Texas in 1941. A practicing attorney, Connally was president and general manager of radio station KVET in Austin from 1946 until 1949.

In 1949 he served as administrative assistant to Senator Lyndon B. Johnson and was a member of the law firm of Powell, Wirtz and Rahout in Austin from 1949 until 1952. For the next nine years he practiced law in Fort Worth. In 1961 he was appointed Secretary of the Navy.

John Connally won the governorship in 1962 and took office on January 15, 1963. Wounded in the assassination of President John F. Kennedy in Dallas on November 22, 1963, Connally's popularity heightened, and he was easily reelected to a second term in 1964. In 1966 he won a third term as governor of Texas.

Inaugural Address *

January 15, 1963

The oath I have taken is mine to uphold, but the trust assumed at this hour is yours and mine—to honor and fulfill together.

On this day, a new voice speaks in Texas—not the voice of one man alone, but the voice of all Texans united. For we bring our differences to the steps of this Capitol to leave them, not to carry them inside.

We are all Americans. We are all Texans. Wearing these labels—and none other—let us be unified in our common purpose as we are united by our common heritage.

We in Texas are inheritors of great riches from a long history. Twenty-seven years after Columbus—one hundred one years before Plymouth Rock—explorers from the Old World first came to Texas. The story of the intervening years is one of the noble chapters in the annals of man. But the duty which falls to us is not to read our own history—but to write our own future.

Today—five hundred years after its discovery—the world of Texas is still a new world: a land still awaiting fulfillment, a promise still awaiting realization. Seeing what we see, knowing what we know, believing what we believe, we come to this day recognizing that the time of fulfillment for Texas has come—and the realization of its promise has passed to our hands.

In our world—and in our nation—great new forces are beginning to work their will upon the destiny of man. For the world, this is the beginning of a new age of exploration. For America, this is the beginning of a new age of growth and expansion and migration. Here in Texas, we stand at a point on the globe—and at a point of history— where these two great forces will converge.

In man's last great age of exploration, five hundred years ago, Texas was only a point of destination for the explorers—but in this new age, Texas will be a point of their departure. The Columbus and Magellan,

**Journal of the House of Representatives of the Fifty-eighth Legislature of the State of Texas* (1963), pp. 60–62.

the Coronado and Cabeza de Vaca of the Age of Space will be men who call Texas home as they explore among the stars.

As young pioneers among us begin to reach to the stars, it is an event of no less importance that many more Americans are beginning to follow the sun, moving Westward and Southward where the land is bright—to build new homes and start a new life. While this is a movement of tens of thousands today, we cannot stand on this platform and stop our ears to the foot-treads of the hundreds of thousands coming tomorrow if we prove worthy of our opportunity.

The challenge and change of the next fifty years will far exceed all that we have experienced in the last five hundred years. On the land where we live—the lands of the great American West—will be built the greatest cities of our continent, the most important industries of our economy, and the richest opportunities of our world for the individual.

What has gone before will find its meaning—or lose its purpose—by how we respond to the trust of these moments of opportunity which begin for us today.

We can succeed greatly or greatly fail, but we cannot ride at anchor and wait for smoother seas. The destiny of Texas will not be fulfilled at dockside in the harbors of yesterday—but out on the open waters of the Twentieth Century.

Great challenges are presented to us. Great opportunities are entrusted to our care. On this day of dedication—and at this solemn hour of consecration—let us in humility and with courage commit ourselves to the goal of guiding our State to a time of new greatness.

Greatness is not an attribute of governments but of the people who create them and are their masters. If this era is to be remembered as a time of greatness in Texas, it must be because the people stood taller, rather than because their State government grew larger. To those in whom the public's trust is vested, let the purpose of our joint efforts be to make the Government of this State the people's greater blessing rather than the people's greater burden.

To serve the people at all, we must serve all the people alike, making no distinctions among them, for the governments which the people have created are not wiser than the God who created the people free and equal in His sight. As we strive to realize the fullest use of our natural resources in Texas, let us strive with greater purpose to realize the highest use of all our human resources.

In this great enterprise, on which we join together, the tasks we face are many. We must maintain the vigor of our farms and assure the vitality of our cities. We must preserve the strength of the industry which is here and add the strength of new industry which can be built here.

But above all, these things must be done within the concept that neither farms, nor buildings, nor plants is the final objective.

They are but material things to be used to provide opportunities for people—to insure greater personal freedom from want—to encourage more individual enterprise—and to enrich the lives of all our citizens.

If the chapter of history we write is to be honored, we must bring to our public affairs that rare quality which won honor for the founders of Texas a century ago. That is the rare quality of vision. We must invest our talents, our capabilities, our efforts in those things which will long live rather than soon pass. We must, above all else, invest in our youth.

The riches in Texas today are in large measure a return on such an investment made in the youth of Texas by those men of vision long ago. They wisely committed the resources of this State to the support of education of the first class in their time. We must renew that commitment and re-endow the future with greater investments today. If Texas is to stand first in the eyes of the nation, our own youth must stand first in the eyes of Texas.

The greater support of education—at all levels for all our people— will be the first and greatest work of the effort on which we today begin.

This is a time of trial and test for our Federal system and for the role of states within that system. The question is not alone whether the states can stand against encroachment of the central government but whether the central government can continue to stand under burdens of responsibility defaulted by the states.

It is an essential truth—born in difficulty and certified by history— that all the power and all the strength of the central government is drawn from the people. We will not accept the proposition that in a time when the central government must be strong, the state government must be weak. Power flows in when responsibility ebbs away. And I say to you that the strength of our system—and the order of our system— urgently demands a renaissance of responsibility among the states. We would propose to begin that renaissance here in Texas, by our own efforts, by our acceptance of our responsibility.

A free society is the greatest achievement of a free people. Freedom untended is freedom lost. Our supreme task is to insure a future that guarantees the highest personal achievements and the greatest individual happiness. This is a job for each of us as individuals. No government can be more enlightened than the enlightenment of its people. Nor stronger in its basic concepts than the will and the dedication of a free people who sustain it. Government can guarantee us nothing. But each of us can provide the future we want through a government responsive to our will.

As I carry the greatest trust that can be bestowed by the people of Texas, I am fully conscious of the magnitude of the burden. In meeting the great responsibilities of government, your chief executive should supply vision without being visionary, should meet challenges without cowardice, should lead without arrogance, should reflect humility without weakness and humanity without gullibility. He should encourage every citizen to aspire to a higher sense of individual worth and accomplishment, and in his every action, he should lend strength to the firm belief that service to mankind through service in government is the highest calling in a society of free people.

And so let us begin our work.

Let it be heard wherever there are men of purpose and goodwill, that here, on this day, Texas reaches for greatness.

To those of you who want more for your children than you had for yourself, we offer hope.

To those of you who pray for achievement that endures, we pledge hard work.

To those of you who believe that tomorrow is a challenge to be won we set forth our resolution.

There are no magic formulas, no easy directions. But nothing great was ever gained easily.

To this task of tomorrow, I dedicate myself with a solemn determination and a humble spirit. As you hand to me the sacred trust of public office, I pledge to you to point the way always to the high road of responsibility, morality and integrity. And as I assume this task in the administration of the laws of men, I reverently hold as my guide the greatest laws of the ages . . . the Ten Commandments.

To this I pledge my all this day, with the help and strength of Almighty God.

Second Inaugural Address *

January 26, 1965

My FELLOW TEXANS:

I accept with gratitude, with humility and with firm resolve the honor and trust bestowed by the oath I have taken.

This morning we closed a chapter of Texas history. This afternoon we begin another.

It is ours to write, but our children's to judge.

How well we succeed, or how badly we fail, rests with the breadth of our own vision, the length of our own imagination, the strength of our own character.

As Texans and Americans, we start our quest with advantages undreamed by peoples of other lands. The heritage of freedom is a golden thread unbroken for 180 years of our national life. We were molded not by kings and conquerors, but by the courage and toil of pioneers who saw the wilderness as a challenge, never a barrier.

Winston Churchill said: "Every nation or group of nations has its own tale to tell. Knowledge of the trials and struggle is necessary to all who would comprehend the problems, perils, challenges and opportunities which confront us today."

The trials and struggles of Texans of the past are known and remembered by each of us. Let their legacy comfort us when a burden grows too heavy, sustain us when peril confronts us, and inspire us to fulfill the opportunities which freedom and initiative have offered us.

Traditions are worthwhile only when they guide us more effectively in the present and direct us more intelligently in the future.

Our most cherished tradition is a free society where man can learn, can work, can go as far as his own capacity carries him and seek the goals of his own choosing.

In a free society, knowledge cannot be decreed; it must be sought.

Journal of the House of Representatives of the Fifty-ninth Legislature of the State of Texas (1965), pp. 63–66.

Opportunity cannot be assured; it must be cultivated. Security cannot be given; it must be earned.

In this climate of freedom we have built a system of government necessary to the growth of the nation and the progress of the people. Civilized men create government to meet their needs, and its very role demands responsiveness to change. But when that government becomes so unwieldy, so inflexible that it fails to serve those who created it for their common good, it becomes a burdensome and negative force.

We live our lives sometimes haphazardly, sometimes by plan. While we live inevitably in the present, deep within us we have a purpose, and even more a faith, in the hereafter.

So it is in government. It continues day to day, sometimes by plan, sometimes by happenstance. But always in the mind of each of us there is a hope and there is a faith that this government will endure beyond us. All too often, however, we live governmentally day by day, limiting our vision scarcely beyond tomorrow and rarely if ever beyond the next election.

We do not do justice to our sacred trust if we as the momentary custodians of our precious government yield to these tendencies of our time.

Our dedication must transcend personal desire. Our determination must rise above personal ambition and fleeting popularity of the hour.

The highest order of public service demands vision unhampered by the narrow blindness of personal gain, strength to sustain in the face of partisan or unenlightened opposition, and faith that permits dreams of what might be, not what is.

Beyond that, it demands the courage to translate that vision into action: advocate and seek the changes which anticipate the needs and aspirations of a restless, surging, hopeful people enmeshed in an age and surrounded by circumstances from which only the most intelligent, the most daring and the most resolute will survive.

This philosophy must inspire our directions and give stimulus to our actions now and in the future.

Responsibilities must be reviewed in the light of what exists today, not what existed 40 or 50 years ago.

We have learned this truth in the foreign affairs of the nation. A generation ago we were secure in the knowledge that the British navy ruled the seas and would keep the peace. We need not be involved. Today it is we Americans who are committed to the defense of freedom, from the DEW line in the Arctic wastes to the jungles of Vietnam.

By no logic must we assume that any government—national, state or local—can stand aloof from the turbulence and excitement and responsibility of a world transformed by spectacular change.

As we commit ourselves to the immense duties of world leadership, so must we commit ourselves to the compelling duties before us in our communities and in our state.

There are only two ways in which people have banded together to devise systems of self-government: by revolution or by evolution.

I am no revolutionist, but in the context of the time in which we live, evolution cannot mean centuries of time, because we live in a world compressed in time. We live in a day when man can outrace the sun and live in perpetual daylight. We live in a generation that has accumulated a greater wealth of scientific knowledge in its brief span than all previously obtained in the thousands of years of civilization behind us.

We want change for our personal happiness and enrichment. We expect changes in the industrial society in which we live. But in our system of government, which is a partner for better or for worse in whatever progress is made, we have had few changes—either in our concepts or our practices. This we cannot long abide. If government is to be a servant of the people, its institutions and its concepts and its practices most assuredly must change.

If we want strong and effective local government, we must exercise local responsibility.

If we want strong and effective state government, we must exercise state responsibility.

At no point in the 130 years of Texas history have we faced a sterner test of our integrity as a people. In one generation we have seen a new Texas imposed on the face of the old. It is a Texas which bursts with vitality—growing, exploring, seeking its place in the sun. It demands much, but it yields much more in return.

We are a people in transition, and in migration. The distance from the farm to the city grows shorter. Machines are replacing human hands. Industry pleads for skilled workers while the unskilled go jobless in an era of plenty.

Knowing all of this, and anticipating that the old way of life will never return, we come to an hour of decision.

Do we have the integrity to act as we know we must act, or will we postpone the inevitable?

Do we respond to change as we know we must, or leave to our children the more difficult task of correcting our errors?

The oath I have taken today would be a mockery if I, as Governor of Texas, were satisfied to leave things as they are.

I did not seek this office to be custodian of outdated concepts.

If we who are the elected representatives of the people are afraid to innovate, afraid to open our minds, afraid to examine new ideas—then we will be suffocated by our own fears while the world moves on without us.

This administration and this Legislature have before us avenues of leadership which can bring untold riches to the life of our state.

We can create an educational system worthy of our greatness and second to none in America.

We can use education, the progenitor of change, to foster the minds and the skills for a more prosperous economy.

We can use our knowledge to alleviate the suffering of the ill and infirm.

We can, at last, devise the plans to assure water for our teeming cities, growing industries, and the farms and ranches which produce our food and fiber.

We can give new meaning to self-government and local solutions to local problems.

All of this, and more, will be ours if we have the courage to seek it.

Progress demands criticism. It demands dissatisfaction. It demands an inquisitive mind and a restless, relentless spirit.

On tomorrow I shall recommend many changes, and if I have apology to make to those I serve, it is only that in the retrospect of future generations I may not have reached far enough.

The only fear I have is not of the changes I shall recommend, but of what I may fail to recommend.

If you and I are to be harshly judged, it will be because we inherited so much, planned so poorly, and left so little.

As we begin again, let our doctrine be the doctrine of faith—faith in our institutions, faith in our heritage, faith in the power of an Almighty God who rules nations as well as men, faith in our own resolve to seek the greater destiny for Texas.

Third Inaugural Address*
January 17, 1967

My fellow Texans: Once again, I assume with pride and humility the sacred trust you have bestowed on me. I shall uphold that trust with all the strength I can muster.

As we gather here in the shadow of this historic landmark, I cannot help but reflect for a moment.

No man can wear the mantle of high office that has been my honor without being touched, and indeed sobered by the experience.

There have been during these years moments of defeat and disappointment.

And there have been the moments warm with the glow of achievement.

There has been the loneliness of decision . . . and the drain of human strength it exacts. And occasionally, there has been the pride in judgment vindicated by the flow of events.

As it must on all men, time has exercised its tyranny on me.

But the faith of millions of Texans . . . has provided sustenance for my endeavor.

And if one indelible mark eclipses all others, it is my deep and growing respect for the precious legacy that transcends all governors—something born of men but more than human—the institution of government itself. I cannot help stand in awe of its durability, of its capacity to shield us from our folly, to protect us from our incapacity, to inspire and retain our admiration even when it falls, as occasionally it must, into unworthy hands.

As we set out to write another chapter in our state's proud history, I think our cause would be served if we considered for a moment this miracle in our lives—government, and its relationship to the people who are its masters.

You have entrusted to my hands and to the hands of the distinguished

*Journal of the House of Representatives of the Sixtieth Legislature of the State of Texas (1967), pp. 108–10.

Texans who share this rostrum the machinery which must maintain order in our society, and must be relied on to protect from contamination the institutions which we have defended in blood.

By shaping and altering these institutions, we shall influence and direct every single man, woman, and child in Texas. I am confident that we shall exercise this prerogative wisely, to add new richness to a good life, to extend by some margin a greater wealth of opportunity to all, to protect our heritage from false prophets and spoilers.

But as we gather here today with high sense of purpose, it seems to me we face a compelling concern of our time: the urgent need to preserve the precious balance between responsive government and the bold, free spirit of man which produced this most advanced civilization in history.

There pervades our land today a growing and disturbing doctrine of universality. A relentless cloud of conformity threatens to envelop us. Conformity is urged upon us everywhere, in the name of social order and justice. We are told we must immerse ourselves in the aggregate, must abandon individuality by immersion in the whole. Some have become preoccupied with averages and norms, and some have become obsessed with managing people's lives.

Order and social progress are the worthy aims of all of us in public service. But while we are motivated by humanitarian instincts, we must not press down on the brow of the individual a system which imposes order at the precious price of mediocrity, and results in a society of orderly and uncomplaining, but senseless and mindless mass.

We all aspire to progress. We all want greater states and greater cities, higher standards of living for more and more people, the ultimate in tangible achievements in every form.

But we are not now . . . nor shall we ever be . . . perfect. Whatever our aspirations, and however great our dedication, we are but men.

And in our well-intentioned zeal to improve the quality of life, we must at all costs avoid imposed conformity.

Rather, we must keep the door open to human adventure, and reinforce the daring of the individual.

Within the wide confines of our splendid institutions, we must be free to experiment. We shall seek with all the resources of human ingenuity for the quality of life. We shall never quite find it, for our reach will always exceed our grasp. But this is the essence of the meaning of being free men—to be free to experiment. We must be free to develop our own style and to reach for the moon so long as we do not tread on our neighbor's lawn. We must be free to travel our own road whatever destiny may lie in wait for us. For our birthright is the infinite variety of humankind.

When experimentation and aspiration are stultified by the heavy hand of government, the very vitality of our people is destroyed. We have robbed the individual of a climate where imagination and ingenuity can have free play. And we do grave injustice to an unbounded faith in people themselves.

In one of our nation's most trying hours, a great president once enunciated four great freedoms.

In our age of growing complexity, surely man is entitled to other compelling freedoms: Freedom to dream. Freedom to venture. Freedom to work. Freedom to think. Freedom to be an individual.

A man should have the freedom to seek great riches. He should have the freedom to espouse great teachings. He should have the freedom from group oppression. And he should have the freedom to live in modest means with tranquility and serenity, if that be his choice. He should not be reduced to a common denominator, to an average. For the truth is, there is no average of ambition, no average of determination, no average of faith.

We recognize no average man. They were not mediocre men, shackled to conformity and drained of their daring and spirit, who carved this state and this nation out of the wilderness.

They were uncommon men who wrote and then boldly signed the Declaration of Independence in Philadelphia in 1776.

They were uncommon men who ventured, despite crushing hardships and fear and disaster, to subdue the limitless vastness of the American West.

They were uncommon men who dared dream of a new life on the Texas frontier more than a century ago, and then died at the Alamo, and at Goliad, and at San Jacinto for that dream.

They were uncommon men who settled this community on the banks of the Colorado, and who built this magnificent seat of government.

They were uncommon men who built the great cattle and oil industries of Texas and left behind a legacy of wealth and power for all of us.

And they were uncommon men too who dreamed and failed before us. The lonely sod-busters of the high plains who struggled with nature against cruel odds. Poor, fractious, quarrelsome, often ungovernable, they were nonetheless self reliant and determined. They lived hard, unsentimental lives and asked nothing. They left us not material wealth, but a Texan spine of flint to sustain adversity.

Here on these hallowed grounds, we are in the shadow of glories of strong men of another day. All around us stand majestically the tributes to the courage and dreams of Texans before us.

But there are no monuments here to mediocrity.

They are monuments to the will of man to shape his own destiny, to dream his own dreams . . . to reach for his own stars.

As we resume the journey here together today, they stand as inspiration to us in our own undertakings. Let us resolve as we begin our work once again to measure up to the daring and to the vision of these great Texans before us. Let us dream the dreams and attempt the deeds of uncommon men.

For with all the resources that are ours, none is so precious as the indomitable spirit of Texans. It, and it alone, can provide us the strength to meet the challenges to come.

Regardless of our other endeavors, we must preserve and nurture that spirit . . . for that spirit is the very essence of the opportunity of free men.

And we will preserve that spirit . . . to keep faith with our heritage, and to keep faith with the future.

XXXV

Preston

SMITH

1969–1973

Courtesy of Archives Division, Texas State Library

PRESTON SMITH (*March 8, 1912–*   ) was born in Williamson County, Texas. He graduated from Texas Technological College in 1934. He engaged in the motion picture theater business.

Smith served in the Texas House of Representatives for three terms, from 1945 until 1951. He served in the state senate from 1957 until 1963. In 1962, while in the Senate, he ran successfully for the position of lieutenant governor, a post he held until 1969.

A Democrat, Preston Smith was elected governor in 1968 in a campaign marked by a show of competitive strength by the Republican party. Smith's margin of victory was just over 400,000 out of a total vote of over 2,900,000. He took office on January 21, 1969.

Despite rumors of Governor Smith's involvement in a stock fraud scandal, he was elected to a second term in 1970 in a repeat contest against his 1968 Republican opponent, Paul Eggers. His second term started on January 19, 1971.

Inaugural Address*

January 21, 1969

By taking the constitutional oath of office, I have assumed the Governorship of Texas—a land of 270,000 square miles and 11 million people.

One who was not impressed with the magnitude of this responsibility would be asleep to reality.

I am impressed.

One who did not consider this the highest political honor the people of Texas could bestow would be ungrateful for their favor.

I am grateful.

But being Governor of Texas is not alone a personal experience. It is an experience in which 11 million Texans must share, for it is their office.

More than most chief executives, the Governor of Texas must rely upon the people for his strength and for his inspiration.

"All political power is inherent in the people, and all free governments are founded on their authority, and instituted for their benefit."

The earliest Texans wrote that into the Constitution of the Republic in 1836, and into the first State Constitution in 1845. It remains in the Texas Constitution today.

In accepting the office of Governor, I accept that principle with all its implications. There is no question in my mind for whose benefit this office exists.

I accept also, as your Governor of this State, the responsibility of executing the duties of this high office.

Those duties are both general and specific, and the means of executing them are not always clearly available. The fact remains that the Governor is the chief of state, the symbol of state leadership and the person to whom Texans look for answers.

I pledge again that, to the fullest extent of my capacities, I shall ". . .

---

*Journal of the House of Representatives of the Sixty-first Legislature of the State of Texas (1969), pp. 99–101.

faithfully execute the duties of this office, and will to the best of my ability preserve, protect and defend the Constitution and laws of the United States and of this State . . ."

One duty of this office is set out in Section 10, Article 4, of the Constitution of Texas, which begins:

"He shall cause the laws to be faithfully executed . . ."

We think first of laws to preserve public order.

The maintenance of domestic tranquility and the protection of persons and property from criminal acts and deeds of violence will carry a high priority in this administration.

Just as this constitutional responsibility must be carried out, the constitutional guarantees of fairness and justice must be maintained.

We will not tolerate violence, either in breaking or enforcing the law.

The responsibility for law observance is not the Governor's alone, nor the Legislature's, nor that of the peacekeeping agents, state and local, nor of the courts—but ultimately of every citizen. We must all want to see the laws enforced. We must countenance no other course.

We will say to the law violator with one voice: "You may break the law, that's your choice, but you are going to face consequences. You are going to face the bar of justice."

As your Governor, I will seek not punishment or leniency but justice for all.

There are a multitude of laws, certainly, without reference to public order. Here, too, the Governor is pledged to "cause" faithful execution.

Here, too, the rules of fairness and justice are pertinent. Here, too, the constitutional guarantees must prevail.

All Texans, both men and women, are guaranteed equal rights. This is not an idle phrase. It must not be casually interpreted.

This is another guarantee.

"Every person shall be at liberty to speak, write or publish his opinions on any subject, being responsible for the abuse of that privilege . . ."

The Constitution says every person.

Although the Bill of Rights applies to individuals, there is an inherent implication in our Constitution that corporate "persons" and all other groups are entitled to equal protection under the laws of Texas.

Any realistic and understanding approach to our future must start with a promise of fairness and one of justice.

I find it possible and plausible to apply this principle to the Governor's duties stated in another section of Article 4:

"The Governor shall . . . recommend to the Legislature such measures as he may deem expedient . . . And at the commencement of each regular session, he shall present estimates of the amount of money required to be raised by taxation for all purposes."

"Fairness and justice" are not inappropriate terms to apply to legislative programs or the levying of taxes.

For one example: There are a great many reasons for us to be continually concerned about the quantity and quality of public education in Texas. At the base we find what we are seeking is fairness.

We seek fairness to the youth of Texas, individually and collectively, because it is not fair to deny them the education demanded in this amazing industrial and scientific age.

We seek fairness for one child as compared to another, so that one will not suffer unduly because of his economic, racial, cultural or social background, or his remediable physical or mental handicaps.

We seek fairness for one school as compared to another, so one will neither be deprived of equal support nor allowed to shirk its obligations to the community and the system.

And we seek fairness to the business, industrial and professional interests, which cannot compete without access to trained and educated personnel—and which must be willing in return to pay their fair share of the cost, on a fair basis.

The elements of fairness and justice also must figure in the eventual answer to another major challenge in our future, and that is the development of a water supply for the years ahead.

This is a grave and subtle challenge—to provide water for our soaring population; water that is fresh, water that is clean, and water that will nurture our crops and provide the food and fiber necessary to our well-being . . . and to start preparing now.

In fairness, the Texas water plan must distribute equitably both the water and the cost of providing it.

In justice to the future of Texas and to future Texans—and even many who are living today—we cannot fail to provide it.

Fairness and justice are entitlements of individuals and groups that have not necessarily received them in the past. We have not always had the money, the incentive or the will to deal adequately with human problems—problems of the young, of the old, of racial minorities, of disadvantaged economic groups, problems of the sick, the afflicted and the mentally ill.

Promises made for political purposes and then forgotten have added to the dilemma. It is cruel and irresponsible to foster an illusion that solutions are coming cheap or easy. I will only say, in frankness as well as fairness, that the money is still a problem—but I am aware of injustice and willing to confront it with the weapons at my disposal.

Students of government say the Governor of Texas must fight with a limited arsenal—and they are right. In some ways his lack of legal authority to enforce the laws and install his programs is a handicap and, at worst, can make a mockery of his efforts.

It is true that the Governor of Texas cannot succeed without the active cooperation of the Legislature, of his fellow officials, of business and industry, and—most importantly—of the people of Texas at large.

To paraphrase a popular expression of the day, the Governor of Texas has to replace legal power with people power.

This is not necessarily a bad trade!

It may be a source of ultimate strength for this office.

Someone has said "Cowardice asks, Is it safe? Expediency asks, Is it politic? Vanity asks, Is it popular? But Conscience asks, Is it right?"

I intend to heed my conscience in the weeks and months ahead.

Let me say that I sought this office in full knowledge of what it is and what it is not—and I accept the necessity and the privilege of holding it and administering it with public support and broad-based cooperation.

And I realize full well that the Governor of Texas must earn and re-earn that support and cooperation, not only at the election but from day-to-day.

The prospect of serving as Governor of this great state is so awesome that no one could undertake it lightly. It is the most serious and challenging opportunity I have ever faced.

But I face it cheerfully and without dread; certainly without fear. Dr. Norman Vincent Peale once wrote:

". . . Fear is only the second most powerful force in personality. The more powerful force is faith."

I have a powerful faith in the future of Texas, and in the spirit of Texas. I have a powerful faith in the people of Texas . . . in their good intentions and their good will; their integrity and their courage.

Having resolved to do my best to deserve their confidence, I close now as the writers of the Texas Declaration of Independence closed—by "fearlessly and confidently committing the issue to the Supreme Arbiter of the destinies of nations."

Second Inaugural Address *

January 19, 1971

CHIEF JUSTICE CALVERT, LIEUTENANT
GOVERNOR BARNES, SPEAKER MUTSCHER,
MEMBERS OF THE TEXAS HOUSE AND
SENATE, OTHER DISTINGUISHED PUBLIC
OFFICIALS, MEMBERS OF THE CLERGY,
MY FELLOW TEXANS, HONORED GUESTS:

Two years ago, I stood before the people of Texas on these Capitol steps and said that the Governor of Texas must rely upon the people for his strength and for his inspiration.

Two years ago, I said that I had a powerful faith in the people of Texas—in their good intentions, in their good will, in their integrity and in their courage. Standing before you today with as much humility and dedication as at any moment in my life, I say to you, that the people of Texas have not disappointed me.

My faith is renewed and my hopes are enlarged. My pledge and my prayer that I have not failed, and will not fail, the people of Texas continues unabated. As we embark together on another term—the first in a decade which may yet prove to be the period in which our nation turns again onto the path toward greatness, with peace—I offer you the wisdom and the pledge of Abraham Lincoln as my own. He said:

"I shall try to correct the errors where shown to be errors, and I shall adopt new views as fast as they appear to be true views."

There is a vague awareness abroad in our land today—faint, yet clearly discernable—that Americans are changing step. It is almost the first few waking moments after a terrible nightmare—a restless sleep, one rent with the horrors of rioting, looting, assassination, hate, fear

Journal of the House of Representatives of the Sixty-second Legislature of the State of Texas (1971), pp. 58–60.

429

and distrust. We are stunned by the memory of that dreadful sleep. Yet, with our eyes now fully open, we see the winds of contention beginning to calm.

The turbulent seas we sailed throughout the 1960's are quieting. The 1970's once again hold promise, not bewilderment and despair, for the peoples of the greatest nation on earth. This does not mean that we are sailing into safe harbors of the past. The past is closed forever. But, the future opens wide before us.

To say simply that the nation is returning to its senses is futile, unless we recognize that those "senses" have new meaning. We cannot look back and judge by our old values or by outmoded standards. Those values and those standards have changed. They are changing, and they will continue to change. We cannot stop dreaming, yet we cannot be content merely to continue dreaming the American Dream, and hoping that it will miraculously be realized.

If we are to keep step with the distant drummer of the future, we must never lose sight of the fact that new times demand new and fresh ideas, leadership, courage and action.

While we dream of and labor for that tomorrow, which has been always our common desire as a nation and as a people, we must live in the midst of yesterday's mistakes. If we have turned the corner on violence and dissention, the turning has brought us face to face with new meaningful problems, as well as an abundance of unsolved ones from our past. The challenges before us are many, but they are capable of solution. When we speak of challenges, we must think of the continuing need for quality education for all at every level.

We must think of the continuing grave need for immediate action if we are to solve the problems of the environment and the supplying of life-giving water. We must think of the need for understanding among our people. We must think of insuring equal opportunities for all our citizens regardless of age, color, or religion. We must be sure that they have an opportunity to earn their daily bread, to have decent shelter, and to have a comfortable place in our society. We must remember that we are a state and a nation built of diversity. And we must think of finally dealing humanly and positively with the plight of those in our society who are less fortunate.

Those who endure the indignities of poverty do not do so by choice. Those who are compelled by circumstance or tradition to be poor, deserve the opportunity to better their lives in this, the wealthiest nation on earth. Those compelled to live in the physical slums of our cities or the mental slums of our society, deserve the same atmosphere and opportunity afforded the majority of our citizens. Their children deserve an environment in which they may enjoy natural childhood fantasies and in which they may learn to become full, productive members of our society.

Those who are fortunate enough not to be poor, fortunate enough not to be relegated to slums, should strive to end the blight and the dangers that poverty has come to represent in many minds.

The poor, indeed, deserve the chance not to be poor. And we must commit ourselves to insuring that the chance is theirs. The thing most wrong with America is the attitude of some that it cannot be made better. The man who says America is perfect, is blind to reality. The man who says that Americans must sacrifice their liberties to preserve America, does not love freedom. The man who says America must be destroyed to be saved, is mistaken. The ideals that are America, can be lost as easily by those who take this country for granted as by those who seek to destroy it. I, for one, reject the concept that America is not worth saving or changing. But the saving and the changing can only come with genuine desire, hard work, dedication, and a strong abiding faith in our fellowmen.

If we are, indeed, entering a new era, it must be a time in which we are totally honest with ourselves. It must be a time in which we are totally honest with the young people for whom the mantle of leadership is waiting. The concept that all growth is automatic progress should be cast out.

Sheer numbers of people and gigantic paychecks, allowing two or more cars per family and color televisions in every room, will not make this nation greater. Materialism must be rejected in favor of human compassion and dignity. The responsibilities to our state in keeping its air clean, its rivers and lakes clear, and its people healthy, must be accepted.

In our haste to right the wrongs and correct the errors, we must not trample business, professional, industrial or personal enterprise. The indiscretions against nature and man did not occur overnight, and they cannot be cured instantly. Yet, we must insure that the healing comes as quickly as human energy permits. Americans are not a people who can walk too long in the valley of the shadow, and it is my firm belief that we are emerging from that valley.

In the first half of the 1960's we looked at extremism on the right and it was rejected and in the last half of the 1960's we looked at extremism on the left, and its rejection is becoming more evident daily. Order rather than disorder, provides more surely guarantee for equal justice for all. I shall never tolerate lawbreaking and strident disorder, for whatever purpose, so long as it is my privilege to serve with the people as Governor of Texas. Texas has been a very fortunate state, because of the character of its citizens. We have not been treated to the sorry spectacle of campus riots, burning buildings, and bombings on any broad scale.

For this, we are grateful. For this, we must continue to strive and work. To achieve this, we must put an end to injustice wherever it is found. The future belongs to us and we must strive to be worthy of it.

Again, quoting Abraham Lincoln: "Trusting in God who can go with me, and remains with you, and be everywhere for good, let us confidently hope that all will yet be well . . ."

XXXVI

Dolph

BRISCOE

1973–1979

Courtesy of Archives Division, Texas State Library

DOLPH BRISCOE (*April 23, 1923–*   ) was born in Uvalde, Texas. He earned a bachelor of arts degree from the University of Texas. He served in the United States Army from 1942 until 1946.

In 1948 Briscoe won a seat in the Texas House of Representatives and served four terms, ending his service in 1957. A millionaire rancher and banker, Briscoe entered the Democratic gubernatorial primary in 1972. He campaigned in his private plane. Opposing him in the primary was a more liberal, female state legislator. Briscoe won the Democratic nomination in a primary runoff. Opposing him in the general election was an ultraconservative Republican. Briscoe won the election by a 3 percent margin and took office on January 16, 1973.

Briscoe, a conservative Democrat whose views on substantive issues were closer to traditional Republicanism, sought a second term in 1974. He easily won the Democratic nomination in the primary and won a second term in the fall general elections by capturing 63 percent of the vote. His second term began on January 21, 1975.

Beginning with the election of 1974, Texas governors would now serve four year terms. Briscoe stood for reelection in 1978 but was defeated in a bitterly fought Democratic primary.

Inaugural Address*

January 16, 1973

On this day of new beginnings, I ask God's blessings on the task we undertake together to magnify the greatness of our state, and the well-being of it's people.

In the thirteen decades of Texas statehood 38 other men and a distinguished lady have taken this oath of office.

They were people of different backgrounds, different temperament, different approaches to the responsibilities thrust upon them. But we must know that they shared at least one ideal, an abiding love for Texas and a determination to serve it's cause.

As your fortieth Governor, I share that love for my native state. With God's help I shall do my best to serve you to the utmost of my ability.

An inaugural ceremony is symbolic of the continuity of history. Because all that went before is vital to the decisions of today. It is symbolic to the continuity of government which is the very essence of the preservation of our political system.

It is also a time of starting again, a time for new hands and fresh ideas. It is a time for government to renew it's role as the one mechanism through which all of the people can exert influence over their society.

In a very real sense, few things in life have so much impact on our lives as that government which we create for ourselves. On the state level, the laws we live by, the policies which govern our businesses, the programs which determine the quality of our surroundings, are largely determined by the kind of state government that we have.

Now that the campaigns are over, all Texans must unite to face the future together. We face the struggle for a better government. We face the task of taking the machinery of government, repairing it where it is broken, discarding it where it is worn beyond repair, and adding new parts where they are needed.

**Journal of the House of Representatives of the Sixty-third Legislature of the State of Texas (1973)*, pp. 113–16.

437

Many years ago Vice-President John Nance Garner summed up his philosophy of government when he said,

> "There are just two things to this government as I see it. The first is to safeguard the lives and the property of our people. The second is to insure that each of us has a chance to work out his destiny according to his talents."

Tomorrow, I will deliver my first message to the Legislature on some of our specific goals for the coming two years. These goals we will seek to achieve within certain basic principles of performance. And it is to these principles that I speak on this Inaugural Day.

First, I believe that it is the responsibility of leadership to generate a spirit of trust and cooperation throughout our state, and that is a responsibility I humbly accept today. To meet this responsibility I will work with the Legislature to see that Texas develops and enforces a strong, clear Code of Ethics for those who hold public office. The people demand, and the people deserve the highest standards of ethics and morality in the conduct of the people's business.

Politics is the science of governing ourselves. We must restore politics to a high level of respect instead of being thought of as a dirty business. And this can be done only by restoring the confidence of the people in our state government. This is the challenge of each of us who now serve the people of this state.

The second principle of my administration will be to make our streets and our homes safe once again. We must carry out that first function of government—protection of the life and the property of each individual citizen. And towards that end I will make numerous crime deterrent proposals.

A third principle of my administration will be that the public is entitled to a dollars worth of goods and services for every tax dollar spent. Every tax dollar the state government acquires and spends has been earned by the hard work of the citizens of this state. And these are not easy dollars, to be spent on untested programs. The plain truth is that the average bread winner today must labor one third of his working day to the support of local, state and federal government. So these are precious dollars to be allocated wisely under a system of priorities.

I shall ask the Legislature and the people to make changes in our budgetary system, and to seek stronger controls on state spending after appropriations are made.

It is my firm belief that our present tax resources are sufficient to operate an effective, efficient government that meets its responsibilities without choking the initiative out of the working people and the businesses of Texas by constantly demanding more and more taxes. Our goal must be no new taxes in 1973.

My fourth basic objective will be to create an environment in which every person has the opportunity to rise to the maximum of his or her potential.

We will work to develop opportunities for blending new jobs, for the urgent need for a cleaner environment.

Opportunities for safe and rapid transportation in our metropolitan areas.

Opportunities for stronger consumer protection.

Opportunities for more effectiveness in education.

A greater emphasis on career-oriented education.

An adequate bilingual educational program.

Opportunities for supporting modern methods of health care and in the rehabilitation of men and women who want and can be productive citizens rather than exist on welfare.

We live in a time of great change. My administration will examine and reexamine the functions of government in view of these changes. Priorities must be reviewed. I am completely committed to a new wave of economy, efficiency, and effectiveness in state government. Poor management, inadequate performance cannot be tolerated.

But in no way should this be interpreted as a retreat from the responsibilities of state government. State government has an obligation to guide Texas in the only direction it can ever go, and that direction is forward.

My fifth principle which this administration will address itself concerns unity. We have a spirit in Texas unlike any spirit which pervades any other state. It is a bold and generous spirit. Historically, Texas has been a confluence of races and cultures. From the Rio Grande to the Red River, freedom loving people of many origins and languages gathered during our early days, hoping only to live in peace and reap the benefits of God-given abundance of this beautiful land. In modern times, many more have come here from other places attracted by our way of life, job opportunities, and the relative stability of our political system. So this is the social and cultural climate of Texas. We Texans are not all alike. And we have found that our diversity is an asset, not a liability.

When the cause is a just one Texans have always been able to put aside differences and work together for the common good. This is the type of unity that we must achieve.

It is unreasonable to expect our citizens to act in unity unless those in public offices are also capable of pulling together to solve the major problems facing our state.

This is one of those rare times when the state has an entirely new team, Governor, Lieutenant Governor, Speaker of the House, Attorney General, Chief Justice. Each earned his position of public trust. And each has his own views on carrying out his duty. I intend to cooperate to the fullest with my fellow public officials. We face two of the most important undertakings of this century: The drafting of a new Texas Constitution, and the reform of our Judicial System.

I will consult at all times with presiding officers of both Houses, and with the Members, on legislative matters. Our ideas and our priorities may differ from time to time but I pledge to give their program the same serious and sympathetic understanding that I know they will give mine. The same spirit of trust and cooperation which carved a bold and dynamic Texas out of the rugged frontier is necessary today.

Working at cross purposes we can only sow the seeds of confusion and inefficiency. Working together with mutual respect we can all do a better job for the people, and that is the reason, the only reason that we were elected to positions that we hold today.

I will not only commit my administration to a spirit of cooperation with all other branches of government. I will commit it to cooperation with the people of this state.

A man cannot enter this Office of Governor and see the heavy responsibilities thrust upon him, without feeling both humility and exhilaration. I shall be eternally grateful for the opportunity the people of Texas have given me to serve. And I commit myself to the task of building an administration in which you can take pride. Working to build a better Texas, a better way of life for each Texan. The future is in our hands. The kind of Texas, the way of life, that we pass from our hands to our children's in not too many years depends upon what you and I do in the immediate future. This is our challenge. This is our opportunity.

*Second Inaugural Address**

January 21, 1975

REVEREND CLERGY, LIEUTENANT
GOVERNOR HOBBY, MR. SPEAKER,
MR. CHIEF JUSTICE, MEMBERS OF THE
64TH LEGISLATURE AND OTHER STATE
OFFICIALS PAST AND PRESENT, FELLOW
CITIZENS OF TEXAS:

Upon this second inauguration as upon the first, I ask the blessings of Almighty God on all we seek to do at this challenging time in history. For me, the first person to embark upon a four-year term as Governor of Texas in more than a century, this is the renewal of a responsibility and an opportunity that I accept gladly and with great anticipation.

Tomorrow I will carry out my duty under Article IV of the Texas Constitution to recommend to the legislature such measures as I deem needed. It will be a substantial program, designed to carry out the platform upon which I was elected. If enacted by the legislature, it will touch the lives of all Texans. It will face up to the pressing problems of our times. It will help to set our priorities for years to come.

Without doubt, the work of the 64th Legislature will improve the basic services which the state government must provide to the citizens of Texas. But I shall ask for a commitment which goes further, a commitment to protect and enhance the fundamental rights and privileges to which all of us are entitled.

In this state we live under a Texas Bill of Rights no less compelling than the Bill of Rights of the United States Constitution. Under these great doctrines we are a free and equal people retaining all political

*Journal of the House of Representatives of the Sixty-fourth Legislature of the State of Texas (1975), pp. 165–67.

power in our hands within a system of local self-government, protected from oppression by those in authority. But there are other rights we hold to be important to our way of life, and it is ten of these rights to which I will address myself tomorrow. These rights must be both protected and perfected by the legislature of Texas.

Each Texan has a right to economical, efficient, and responsive state government which spends his hard-earned tax dollars wisely and frugally. Each Texan has a right to honest and open government, with full access to both its services and its decision-making processes. Each Texan has a right to fair elections and the opportunity for full participation in those elections. Each Texan has a right to quality education for his children, regardless of where he lives, or the economic condition of his family or his community. Each Texan has a right to safe streets and neighborhoods without fear of crime being committed on his person or property.

Each Texan has a right to privacy, free from unjustified harassment or intrusion by government officials or anyone else. Each Texan has a right to health care which is effective, readily available and affordable in all parts of the state, urban and rural. Each Texan has a right to a clean and fruitful environment, including adequate supplies of water for every area of the state, and an adequate supply of energy for the essential needs of our society. Each Texan has a right to mobility, the ways and means to transport himself and his goods from one place to another by highway, rail, water or air. Each Texan has a right to decent treatment when he is young, dignity when he is old, and opportunity throughout his life, regardless of his race or sex. It is to these rights that I pledge myself and my efforts during the next four years.

A Governor, as I see it, has a dual role to perform if he is to live up to the responsibility of his office. One is his role as chief executive, to uphold the laws of the state and to operate the machinery of government efficiently, effectively, wisely and compassionately. The other is his role as a leader, to lift the sights of the people he serves, uniting them and appealing to the best that is in them, and with their support and understanding, to chart the future course of the state.

I am mindful that no recommendation by a Governor and no act of a legislature can accomplish everything that is desirable. We must work steadily for progress, achieving that which is possible, but always reaching out in search of the new and innovative, never satisfied that we have found the ultimate solution to every problem.

History will judge us on how we respond to the immense challenges of this generation. I believe that we Texans will respond well. I believe we have the character and the wisdom to move this state forward as other generations before us moved it forward. I believe we have the judgement to establish priorities for both our efforts and our money, to focus on those needs which are vital and set aside those which are not. I believe we have the common sense to spend our energies on worthwhile goals, rather than on narrow partisanship and selfish considerations.

During this administration I have done my best to help create an atmosphere in state government that is conducive to unity among our people, firm in the conviction that an overriding philosophy of cooperation for progress speeds durable solutions to serious public problems. I am grateful for the cooperation I have received in return, from an overwhelming majority of the men and women who share governmental responsibility in this capital.

To our distinguished Lieutenant Governor, to the newly elected Speaker of the House, to all of the members of the 64th Legislature, and all other state officials, I extend my congratulations on the opportunity you share with me to serve the 12 million people of Texas. And to each of you, I pledge today a renewal and redoubling of my efforts to maintain the type of unity and cooperation which is essential to the proper fulfillment of our duties.

When we work at cross purposes, we only sow the seeds of confusion and inefficiency. When we work together with mutual respect, compromising our views with honor and candor, and avoiding strident partisanship as much as possible, not only are we more effective, but we also increase public confidence in the ability of government to function as it should.

We are mindful that we will soon enter the bicentennial year of the founding of the American Republic. How much longer we are allowed the privilege of survival as the greatest democracy in history is a matter of conjecture. There have been dire predictions that the greatest industrial and consumer nation on the face of the earth may soon sputter to a standstill, strangled by lack of energy resources and our own wasteful habits. We are told that a nation founded on the work ethic will die as a hopeless welfare state. We are warned that immorality and permissiveness will bring us down as surely as the Roman Empire fell to the barbarians.

I do not agree with these pessimistic views on the future of our country. The death knell of America has not been sounded. Yet we know full well that freedom and success are fragile commodities, that the greatness of this land could crumble into dust if we fail in our determination to manage our affairs wisely and honorably. If we are not willing to preserve and conserve what we have, then we do not deserve what we have.

This is a stormy world in which we live, but it always has been. The leadership of Texas does have within its power a way to create greater opportunity and better jobs for Texans, better schools for our children, greater safety and security for our families, and a better way of life for every citizen.

This is the responsibility we have been assigned, and it is a very heavy responsibility, demanding our full and undivided attention. There is much work to do, and the days are short. Our work must begin now, and not a moment should be wasted. We who are the stewards of the people's government must prove ourselves worthy of that stewardship, and the mark we leave on the pages of history must be the mark of success and honor and integrity.

The opportunity is ours and I believe we will seize it. During the time we have been allotted to serve the people, let it be said that we did our duty to state and nation to the very best of our ability. I pray God to direct our path, to bless us with wisdom, strength, and compassion for the work ahead.

XXXVII

William P.
CLEMENTS, JR.

1979–1983

Courtesy of Archives Division, Texas State Library

WILLIAM P. CLEMENTS, JR., (*April 13, 1917–*   ) was born in Dallas, Texas. After attending Southern Methodist University he was a "rough-neck" in the oil fields and a driller of oil rigs from 1937 to 1947. He founded Sedco Inc., in 1947, a manufacturing firm of oil-drilling equipment and which made him a multi-millionaire.

Clements was Deputy Secretary in the Defense Department from 1973 to 1977. With only this public service experience, Clements, a conservative Republican, entered the gubernatorial primary race in 1978. He defeated his opponent by garnering 73 percent of the votes.

Clements' Democratic opponent in the general election was Attorney General John Hill, a liberal Democrat. Despite Clements' heavy campaign spending, he won by only a narrow margin, a percentage point.

William P. Clements became the state's first Republican governor since Reconstruction. He took office on January 16, 1979.

In 1982, Clements ran for a second term. He successfully defeated his Republican challenger in the primary but lost to Democrat Mark White in the general election which was marked by acrimony.

447

Inaugural Address *

January 16, 1979

LIEUTENANT GOVERNOR HOBBY, MR. SPEAKER, MEMBERS OF THE SIXTY-SIXTH TEXAS LEGISLATURE, DISTINGUISHED OFFICIALS AND GUESTS, MY FELLOW TEXANS:

An inauguration traditionally marks the beginning of a new adminis-tration, and any beginning requires an awareness and an understanding of the past.

So, an inauguration is a time when we must pause to reflect on our past before embarking on the future.

An inauguration also is a time to offer thanks and I would like to begin by thanking our Divine Leader who is the fountainhead of our very existence.

The first Governor of the State of Texas, the Honorable J. Pinckney Henderson, said in his inaugural address of 1846:

"Who can look back upon our history, and not be fully and deeply impressed with the consideration that the arm of Deity has shielded our nation, and His justice and wisdom guided us in our path? It is there-fore our duty, in deep humility, to make our acknowledgements for His many favors."

As your public servant, I want to thank you for the trust you have placed in me and for the opportunity you have given me to represent you.

This being the first time I have ever taken the oath of public office as an elected official, I take it with extreme seriousness and with a keen awareness of its meaning and obligations.

Journal of the House of Representatives of the Sixty-sixth Legislature of the State of Texas (1979), pp. 121–25.

To take this oath is an honor because to be your Governor is to be the leader of the most exceptional state in the union, a state made great by its people.

This inauguration would be incomplete if we do not stop to publicly thank our outgoing elected leaders for their contributions to this state.

As a citizen, I want to thank Governor Dolph Briscoe for his six years of distinguished and unselfish service to this state.

He will be remembered as the Governor who successfully fought the creation of any new state taxes.

And, he will be remembered as the Governor who took the first steps toward returning the tax-generated surplus in our State Treasury back to its rightful owners.

This is Governor Briscoe's legacy to Texas, and it's one he can be proud of and one this state will always appreciate.

As your Governor, I, too, have goals for Texas and I am committed to making our state government accountable to the taxpayers.

I want to conduct government in a businesslike manner, with elected officials and government leaders responsible to the taxpayers just as a board of directors and company officials are responsible to the stockholders.

You will hear voices during my administration expressing doubts about some of my proposals. But, I will persist; we will prevail.

I will persist because I believe that you, the people, have made clear your desire for better government and for less government.

I will persist with my plans to return to you, the taxpayers, one billion dollars of the state's surplus. I will persist with my plans to give you long-term, constitutional safeguards—including the right of initiative and referendum—to protect against excessive taxation and wasteful government spending.

I will persist with my plans to reduce the size of our state bureaucracy.

And, I will persist with my plans to improve the quality of our education system so that we can give our children the basic building blocks they need to develop meaningful careers.

I will persist with these and many other priorities because I believe you have clearly stated that we must persist, together.

I believe we will be successful because these are issues and concerns that cut across partisan lines. These are not just Republican issues or Democratic issues. These are Texas issues and the people of Texas are the ultimate beneficiaries.

I believe we will be successful because Texans have elected a unique leadership team to address these issues and concerns.

This inauguration, where a Republican Governor takes office with a Democratic Lieutenant Governor, stands as living proof of the independent thinking of the people of this state.

I am uplifted and encouraged by that kind of spirit, and in that expression from the people of Texas, I see the clear message that I must be a Governor who puts quality, excellence, achievement, and the best interests of this state, above partisan loyalties.

We have a healthy blend of leaders, who like myself, are assuming the responsibilities and challenges of elective office for the first time; and, we have leaders like Lieutenant Governor Bill Hobby and House Speaker Bill Clayton who have dedicated many years of their lives to public service.

This leadership team is one of enthusiasm and experience, but foremost, it is one of dedication and unity of purpose.

As public servants, we all were elected by the people of Texas and we must be responsive to the needs and concerns of the same electorate.

The challenge to government is to help people deal with their needs and concerns. I believe our founding fathers provided us with the framework for doing this.

I believe this framework is often overlooked and that we often forget the words upon which our state and our nation were founded.

These are not the words of demagogues for demagogues are quickly forgotten. History has proven the value and meaning of these words and they bear repeating.

For Texans, these words are found in the first three sections of Article I, the Bill of Rights, in the state constitution.

The first section states: "Texas is a free and independent state, subject only to the Constitution of the United States, and the maintenance of our free institutions and the perpetuity of the union depends upon the preservation of the right of local self-government, unimpaired to all the states."

This Bill of Rights is saying that while we must work with other states and with the federal government for the betterment of the entire nation, we must be vigilant and protect our independence as a sovereign state.

For when the federal government weakens the power and independence of the states, the union itself is weakened.

In recent years, we have seen a disturbing trend toward the creation of a new branch of the federal government, the regulatory branch, a branch that doesn't include you and me among its constituency.

It is not elected by anyone and, in fact, is accountable to no one.

By an excessive and improper transfer of authority to these regulatory agencies, the Congress and the President have further removed government from the reach of the people and further weakened the power of the states.

This must not be condoned by Texans. We must assert our rights and our spirit at every opportunity.

And, at the same time, we must take steps to ensure that our state government does not usurp the rights of individuals or of local governments within our boundaries.

The best government is that government which is closest to the people. The second section of the Bill of Rights in our state constitution speaks to that relationship between the people and their government.

It states, "All political power is inherent in the people and all free governments are founded on their authority, and instituted for their benefit, the faith of the people of Texas stands pledged to the preservation of a Republican form of government, and, subject to this limitation only. They have at all times the unalienable right to alter, reform or abolish their government in such manner as they may think expedient."

Those are potent words and they create a straightforward message. That message is this: power in this state and in this nation rests not with political parties, not with governmental institutions, not with elected leaders, but with the people.

Like many other citizens, I have seen the governmental bureaucracy and some politicians trying to infringe on our rights as individuals.

We have seen the consequences of such infringement by government in other parts of the United States. When excessive intrusion by government into the lives of individuals is permitted, government becomes an economic master and the people become its slaves.

Texas, though, has had the benefit of more enlightened leaders through the years. We are still in the position of being able to control our state government, but warning signs are present and we must be aware of them.

Now is the time for us to set firm limits on our government. Now is the time for us to emphatically state that we want our government to serve us, not to dominate us.

In controlling government, in making it our servant, we must proceed without diminishing the rights of any citizen.

Section 3 of the Bill of Rights in our state constitution says: "All free men, when they form a social compact, have equal rights, and no man, or set of men, is entitled to exclusive separate emoluments, or privileges, but in consideration of public services."

That same section also says: "Equality under the law shall not be denied or abridged because of sex, race, color, creed, or national origin."

The greatest strength of Texas long has been the vitality and diversity of its people. They came to this land as Indians, as Spaniards, as Frenchmen, as Englishmen, as Germans, as blacks, as browns, as whites, as people from many different backgrounds. And they are still coming.

Yet when they arrive, they become Texans, people bound together by a common quest for a better life for themselves and for their children and grandchildren.

We must respect the rights of all Texans. Regardless of their cultural background. And we must continually work to safeguard those rights. We must see that equal opportunity is a reality for all of our citizens.

People came here because this was the land of opportunity. It still is today.

Texas was a frontier then and it is today. It is a frontier in the sense of unparalleled economic opportunity. It is a place where people can realize their dreams and aspirations—and a place where free enterprise can flourish—without laboring under the yoke of a burdensome government.

It's not difficult to explain these vast opportunities, but it is becoming increasingly difficult to protect them and extend them to all Texans.

By being ever mindful of these three sections in the Bill of Rights— by stepping back to that firm foundation of government outlined in our state constitution—our steps forward in the future will be steadier and longer.

These three sections in our state constitution help form what will be a guiding philosophy of my administration.

Condensed to its most basic form, my philosophy is this: the proper function of government is not to guarantee prosperity for its citizens; rather, it is to guarantee them the opportunity to achieve prosperity.

Putting our government into its proper perspective is a job too large for me or Lieutenant Governor Hobby, or Speaker Clayton, or the members of the legislature, or for any public official, without the direct involvement of the citizens of Texas.

You, too, have a responsibility to help achieve good government, and that responsibility goes beyond voting on election day.

When we as individuals, and as a state, are silent—when we let others make decisions for us without stating our beliefs—we forfeit some of our freedom.

When we stand up and speak out, when we express our desires and concerns, then and only then, will we have effective government.

I am confident we can achieve that kind of effective government because the people of Texas are the state's most outstanding natural resource.

I am confident, too, that we can achieve the abundant potential with what our state has been endowed.

Now is the time for us to begin. I ask all of you to join with me, to put the best interests of Texas at the forefront of your thoughts.

We must be diligent, we must be bold, we must be energetic.

All of us, all Texans, must lock arms and work together. We must shape a new alliance of greatness, an alliance that will perpetuate and enhance the blessings our Almighty God has bestowed on our state.

XXXVIII

Mark

WHITE

1983–1987

Courtesy of Archives Division, Texas State Library

MARK WHITE (*March 17, 1940–*   ) was born in Henderson, Texas. He earned a bachelor of business administration degree from Baylor University in 1962. In 1965 he won his doctor of jurisprudence degree from Baylor.

From 1966 to 1969 White was assistant attorney general in the Insurance, Banking and Securities Division. Also during this time he was fulfilling his military obligation as a member of the Texas National Guard.

In 1972 White, a Democrat, was elected secretary of state, a position he held until 1978 when he was elected as attorney general. It was from this position that he sought and won the governorship in 1982. He took office on January 18, 1983.

White sought a second term in 1986. He won his party's nomination but was defeated in the general election by former Republican Governor William P. Clements, Jr.

Inaugural Address *

January 18, 1983

My FELLOW TEXANS:

In the long history of this state, only 41 men and one woman have preceeded me as governor.

I am mindful of the great honor that has come to me.

And I want you to know that this is the proudest moment of my life.

I am mindful, too, of the great responsibilities that I have taken upon my shoulders.

I accept those responsibilities.

I welcome them—gladly—in the sure knowledge that government *can* make a difference for the betterment of all the people if it is wise and prudent and visionary and determined.

Finally, I am mindful that I did not come to this office alone.

The list of friends and supporters who believed in me and sacrificed for me is a roll of honor that I will always cherish.

That roll is headed by my wife, Linda Gale, whose love and devotion and counsel and untiring efforts were the inspiration of my campaign.

That roll also contains the names of men and women who never lost faith in me—or my candidacy—no matter how bleak things appeared to be—no matter how many others had conceded my defeat.

I owe a great debt of gratitude to many individuals and I pray I will be worthy of their support.

But let there be no doubt about this: I owe nothing to any group or to any special interest.

The only interest I recognize is the peoples' interest.

The peoples' interest will have a fresh start in my administration.

There will be new faces and new ideas as a new generation of Texans prepares to take over the reins of government

Journal of the House of Representatives of the Sixty-eighth Legislature of the State of Texas (1983), pp. 138–41.

It is a generation that was educated after World War II—

That grew up in the shadow of nuclear terror—

That lived through our transition from a rural to an urban state—

That watched towering buildings rise from the ground—

That saw the first signs of progress choking our cities and despoiling our environment.

It is a generation whose time has come.

It is a generation whose hopes and visions and policies and actions will lead this state into the 21st Century.

That is our destiny.

It is an exciting destiny for all of us.

Texas is the State of the Future.

As great and as vibrant as this state is now, it has only begun to achieve its full potential.

There is no doubt in my mind that Texas will one day become the industrial and financial leader of the United States.

But such leadership will not be without its challenges.

The question we must ask ourselves today is whether we are prepared to accept that role of leadership; whether we are wise enough to avoid the pitfalls that go with it.

Other states have gone before us—and we should learn their lessons well.

Other states have stood where we now stand—on the very edge of greatness.

And yet today, in many of those states, the residue of progress is more tangible than the blessings of progress:

decaying, congested crime-ridden cities—

men and women permanently out of work—

mounting budget deficits—

foul air and filthy water—

and a ravaged, ugly landscape almost everywhere you turn.

For a generation growing up in such an environment today, yesterday's progress has become a bitter heritage.

Are we doomed to repeat their mistakes—or will we learn from them?

Can we be the masters of our destiny—or will we be its victims?

As we stand at history's door, it is time to ask ourselves what kind of state we will be passing on to our children.

Can we be a modern, industrial state and still be a clean and beautiful state?

Can we maintain the quality of life that *we* knew and our parents knew as children?

Can we build great cities without slums and pollution and crime and congestion?

Can we preserve what is special about the Texas character—what is good and strong and honest about our people?

I believe we can.

As we prepare to move into the future, we still have a firm grip on our past.

Our frontier heritage and our spirit of optimism and determination are still with us.

So are our open spaces and beautiful countryside.

The sights and sounds that quickened the hearts of our ancestors are still here for us to respond to and enjoy as well.

But time is quickly running out on us.

Change is coming with an irresistible force—and if we are unable to control it and guide it, it will soon threaten much that is precious to us.

We have only a fleeting moment in history to decide how our future is to be shaped.

We had better use that moment wisely.

We can be the greatest state this republic has ever known.

Or we can enjoy our brief moment in the sun and go the way that states have gone before us.

The choice is ours.

I believe it is the *challenge* and the *responsibility* of this generation to lay the foundations for greatness.

The first foundation for greatness is education.

Our goal must be to build the best system of education that the mind of man can devise—from first grade through graduate school—and make that system responsive to the needs of every boy and girl in Texas.

To reach that goal, we must pay the kind of salaries that will attract bright, dedicated teachers and faculty members—and keep them as well.

To reach that goal we must demonstrate to our teachers that they occupy an honored place in our society.

Second-class citizens will not turn out first-class minds.

Education is not a luxury; it is a necessity.

We are living through a technological revolution.

Tomorrow's economy will have no place for the unskilled and the semi-skilled.

It will demand a constant supply of well-educated men and women. And it will require the best research that our universities can produce. The second foundation for greatness is people.

Throughout our history, we have been blessed with many resources, but our *human* resource is the greatest by far.

And yet we have *wasted* much of that resource.

Blacks and Mexican-Americans and women have not been given the opportunity to participate fully in our society—and we are a poorer society as a result.

The State of the Future cannot afford such artificial barriers—or the loss of such talent and brainpower.

Our human resources must be developed to their fullest—and used to the maximum.

We will never be so rich that we can squander the talents of a single human being.

The third foundation for greatness is prudence.

No civilization has ever been able to afford everything it wanted.

We are no exception.

We must learn to live within our means.

We must learn to order our priorities.

We must decide what is important—and then do the important things well.

Failure to recognize this basic economic fact of life in other states has resulted in ineffective government and massive public debt for future generations to bear.

The fourth foundation for greatness is the protection of our environment.

Nearly 20 years ago, President Lyndon B. Johnson warned us that, "If future generations are to remember us more with gratitude than with sorrow, we must achieve more than just the miracles of technology.

"We must also leave them a glimpse of the world as God really made it, not just as it looked when we got through with it."

The *Texas* that God made is a land of open, rolling hills, dense piney woods, warm, white sandy beaches, clear rivers and streams, and rich, fertile prairies.

In inhabiting such a land, we must never forget that we are God's caretakers.

If we are indifferent to that responsibility, our negligence will be a scar across this state for centuries to come.

The fifth foundation for greatness is a modern, efficient transportation system that will meet the needs of a burgeoning population and a vibrant commerce far into the future.

Thirty years ago, we built the finest highway system in the nation.

It has served Texas well.

If we modernize it and maintain it, it will *continue* to serve us well.

But the State of the Future will require more than the nation's finest highway system.

It will also require new and innovative mass transit systems within our major cities.

We have 13 million motor vehicles in Texas today.

By the end of the decade, that number will have grown to 17 million.

Unless we begin now to provide some realistic alternatives, we will be heading straight into a massive traffic jam.

And the lives of millions of Texans who drive to and from work every day will become a waking nightmare.

The sixth foundation for greatness is equity for all of our citizens.

That means schools that are equal.

That means taxes that are reasonable.

That means interest rates, insurance rates, and utility rates that are fair and justified.

I am firmly dedicated to the belief that the *burdens* of government must be borne equally by all of our citizens—and the *services* of government must be *shared* equally as well.

Texas has never known a privileged class—and I hope it never will.

The seventh foundation for greatness is a renewed spirit of cooperation among all the diverse elements of our state—particularly among business, labor, and government.

If we are to achieve our full potential, we are going to have to achieve it together.

The world is far too competitive for us to waste our energies pursuing narrow interests and harboring old grudges.

We will always have points of disagreement, but they must never divert us from our common goals.

We must all recognize that a healthy business climate forms the basis of full employment, just as a prosperous labor force makes up the best consumer that business will ever know.

The eighth foundation for greatness is a society that has recaptured its streets and neighborhoods from the grip of crime.

Unless our citizens can live and work in an environment that is free of fear, achieving all our other goals will be an empty victory.

These, then, are the foundations upon which we must build the state of the future: education; human resources; prudence; protecting our environment; transportation; equity; cooperation; and freedom from the fear of crime.

I hope and I pray that all of you—and Texans everywhere—will join us in our effort to lay those foundations.

They are not partisan foundations.

They are not dedicated to narrow self-interests.

They are foundations upon which we can *all* build our futures.

Under my administration, *every*one will share in this government.

It will be a government for *all* Texans.

My philosophy of government is basic and uncomplicated. It asks two questions before any others:

Is it right?

Is it fair?

Unless a decision can pass *those* tests, there will *be* no decision.

And finally, when I leave this office, I hope it will be said that we *did* make a difference.

I hope it will be said that state government was more open, more responsive, and more just than ever before.

I hope it will be said that we helped to guide Texas through a critical period of traumatic change, and at the same time preserved our heritage for generations to come.

With your help—and God's help—those goals can become our destiny.

Thank you.

XXXIX

William P.
CLEMENTS, JR.

1987–1991

Courtesy of Archives Division, Texas State Library

WILLIAM P. CLEMENTS, JR. (*April 13, 1917–*), defeated in his efforts to win a second consecutive term as governor in 1982, regained the position in 1986, thus returning the governorship to the Republican party. Clements became only the second governor to serve two nonconsecutive terms. He took office on January 20, 1987.

Inaugural Address *

January 20, 1987

LIEUTENANT GOVERNOR HOBBY; CHIEF
JUSTICE HILL AND MEMBERS OF THE
JUDICIARY; SPEAKER LEWIS; GOVERNORS
DANIEL, CONNALLY, SMITH AND BRISCOE;
MEMBERS OF THE TEXAS LEGISLATURE;
CONGRESSMEN; DIGNITARIES AND FELLOW
TEXANS:

There is no greater honor a Texan in public service can have than to be selected governor of this state. It is in this spirit of gratitude and appreciation and humility that I approach the opportunity and the responsibility you have given me.

My message today is the status quo is no longer acceptable. Texans are demanding change.

They want their state government to stop "business as usual" and to, instead, consider solutions that in the past were considered impossible. Without question, Texans are ready for new and bold initiatives that will move our state forward into a bright and prosperous future. Our only standard of performance must be to do what is right for Texas.

Certainly all of us realize that in Texas today we are going through a transition period that is, for many of our state's people, the worst of times. Too many people are out of work and worried about their families' health and well-being. The fundamental building blocks of our Texas economy are in trouble.

However, the suffering of our people can and will be cured if we muster the courage and discipline to seize the opportunity at hand and

Journal of the House of Representatives of the Seventieth Legislature of the State of Texas (1987), pp. 123–25.

move forward. This is a time of testing. It's the testing of the ingenuity, courage, and resourcefulness of our people. We, as Texans, can respond and be successful.

As Ecclesiastes tells us, "To everything there is a season, and a time to every purpose under heaven."

Now is the season and time for us in Texas to take advantage of our opportunity and create a new Texas. We must move on to a higher plateau. We must improve the quality of life for all Texans. We must make certain that our young people have the opportunities that we had. We must re-open our lines of communication with the federal government in Washington and with Mexico: both are vital to the future of Texas.

We must ensure quality education, attract and encourage the best teachers we can for our schools and universities, restructure the criminal justice system, protect Texans from crime, set our fiscal house in order and create a proper economic climate to attract business and provide jobs.

The next four years in Texas can be literally a historical time, but only if we believe the status quo is not good enough. Abraham Lincoln put it well: "As our case is new, so must we think and act anew."

We can have more jobs and a new economic base. We can establish new frontiers in research and development at our universities that are vital to attracting jobs and creating the new technologies for Texas' future. We can reach pinnacles of excellence in education that will provide our state a skilled work force. We can dream the impossible dream and make it come true. We can, if we act now and if we work for a future of new solutions, new answers.

And to those in need and in despair, I promise we will leave no one behind as we move Texas forward. Our efforts will always be guided by a strong sense of compassion.

Many of these tough issues will be addressed in the coming legislative session. Several will be tagged as emergency items for quick handling in the next few weeks. For example, I will immediately propose to the legislature reforms in our prisons so we can keep the prison doors open without a policy of early releases.

There is, indeed, an urgency that we get on with this job and so many more. Our situation cries for action.

Our problems are not insurmountable. Our salvation doesn't depend on some magic cure. It depends on us.

On what your leaders in state government do.

On what the men and women who run Texas businesses and farms and ranches do.

On the quality, spirit, and determination of our working people.

In short, our success depends on each and every Texan rolling up their sleeves and going to work together to get our state on the move again.

Churchill said that war was far too important to leave to generals. To paraphrase, our problems are far too severe to leave them to state government alone. This is the real world, and every single citizen has the responsibility to play a role in making this transition to a new Texas.

Some Texans have already, in a spirit of patriotism and selfless service to our state, joined me in working for this transition. Texans from every part of the state and from every strata of its society are serving on some blue ribbon task forces that are tackling these tough problems.

Today is not the time to unveil their detailed programs and recommendations. These will be discussed in my State of the State Address in a few weeks and at other appropriate times in the future.

But some of these task forces have been hard at work on how to create more jobs in Texas, how to make our criminal justice system more just and more certain, and how to solve the tough budget problem that faces our state.

I'll be forming other citizen groups to give me and all Texans the benefit of the wisdom and leadership of the men and women who will serve on these committees. We'll be looking at tort reform, higher education, the illegal drug traffic, the accountability and reform of our state government, the protection of traditional family values, and of the separation of church and state.

I am certain the legislature and all Texas will be receptive to the ideas and suggestions of these blue-ribbon task forces.

Another group which we will mobilize in our effort to help Texas are our state employees. They are a terrific resource. They are in the frontlines, so to speak, of providing the services of state government. In a spirit not of confrontation, but of cooperation, I will work closely with them to make our state government leaner, more efficient, and more effective and I know they can help show us the way.

Texas has reached maturity. We have grown into an integral part of the national economy, and, yes, even the international economy, and we must think in those global terms. Not just national terms, but global terms.

We are an integral part of the national and international community not because we have failed but because we have succeeded and have grown.

It is forecast that Texas will be the second in population among the states and our gross economy is now over $300 billion a year. If Texas was still an independent sovereign republic, our Texas economy would be number 13 in the world.

It is a part of this maturity that we must live, work, and compete in a very tough world.

These issues we face today are Texas issues. They don't wear the cloak of either the Republican or Democratic Party. It is our obligation to do what is right for Texas. For all Texans.

I will always listen and be responsive. I will always respect differing viewpoints. My door will be open. My actions will be straightforward, my word good, and our programs and proposals offered in a full spirit of cooperation and enthusiasm.

The people of Texas elected all of us to address these critical issues. They are depending upon us to use good judgment and reach the right decisions. The people of Texas want us to succeed. For them, the status quo is not good enough. They want action and results.

These are, indeed, the best of times and the worst of times. If we seize this moment of opportunity, we can move in a different direction, set new goals and achieve new heights of prosperity.

It can be done.

By relying on the work ethic.

By encouraging the spirit of entrepreneurship.

By unleashing the creative energy of our people, which can overcome any obstacle.

It can be done and it must be done. We must act today so that future generations of Texans look back at us and say, "They met the challenge."

Theodore Roosevelt described our responsibility: "We are face to face with our destiny and we must meet it with a high and resolute courage. For us is the life of action, of strenuous performance of duty. . . ."

T. R. Fehrenbach writes: "There are many who will always scoff at new frontiers and there are some who will seek them." The greatness of Texas is that we are a people who always seek the new frontier. Once again, we must seek a new frontier. We must move ahead in a determined fashion, to make our dreams come true. With God's blessing and grace, we will succeed!

XXXX

Ann Willis
RICHARDS

1991–

Courtesy of the Governor's Press Office

ANN WILLIS RICHARDS (*September 3, 1933–*   ) was born in Lakeview, Texas, the daughter of a pharmaceutical salesman. Governor Richards attended elementary school in Lakeview and graduated from high school in Waco where she was a debater and participated in the American Legion's Girls State and Girls Nation.

She graduated from Baylor University in 1954 with a degree in speech and a minor in political science. She later attended the University of Texas where she earned her teaching certificate. She had a brief career as a junior-high-school social studies teacher.

Governor Richards married at the end of her junior year in college and moved to Austin where her husband David attended Law School. When he completed Law School, the couple moved to Dallas. In 1969, they moved to Austin.

She was campaign manager for state representative Sarah Weddington in 1972. Weddington then appointed Richards to be her administrative aide. In 1976 Richards was elected as a Travis County commissioner and won reelection in 1980.

She resigned from the county commissioner position in 1982 to campaign for the position of state treasurer on the Democratic ticket. Richards was successful in her effort and was reelected in 1986. The Richards separated in 1982 and were divorced in 1984. She gained national attention as the keynote speaker at the 1988 Democratic National Convention for the line, "Poor George [Vice-President Bush], he was born with a silver foot in his mouth."

Her successful tenure as state treasurer led her to declare her candidacy for governor. In the March 1990 Democratic primary, Richards was opposed by Attorney General James Mattox and former Governor Mark White. None of the candidates won a majority of the votes. In the April run-off election, Richards was declared winner over Mattox.

In the fall 1990 general election she opposed political newcomer and multi-millionaire Republican candidate Clayton Williams. The campaign was a hard-fought one filled with personal vilification and rancor.

Ann Richards emerged as the voter's choice and became the second woman in Texas history to become governor. She was inaugurated on January 15, 1991.

475

Welcome to the first day of the new Texas!

And welcome to the official representatives of thirty-five countries and the governors of the four Mexican border states who have joined us today.

I want to thank all of you for being with us. I hope we will see you often in the capitol. We look forward to working cooperatively with your governments and to excellent relationships with your people.

Bienvenidos, mis amigos!

Eighteen months ago, I stood with many of you a few hundred yards from this platform and announced my candidacy for governor.

If you were there—in fact or in spirit—on that hot June day . . . if you gave your time and your energy to our campaign . . . if you held your ground and continued to believe when the odds seemed long and the outcome uncertain . . . my gratitude to you is profound.

Today is a day of celebration.

Today, we marched up Congress Avenue and said that we were reclaiming the Capitol for the people of Texas.

We say proudly that the people of Texas are back.

That statement will be given meaning by our actions during the next four years.

Today, the historians will record that a new administration, different from any in the past, began.

Twenty, fifty, one hundred years from now, school children will open their textbooks—or perhaps, switch on their video texts—and they will see a picture.

They will see us standing proudly on this bright winter noon. And looking through the eyes of a child will seem as distant and ancient as portraits of our ancestors seem to us.

Those children will read that on January 15th, 1991, a woman

*Advance copy of speech text provided by Governor Richards.

477

named Ann W. Richards took the oath of office as the 45th Governor of Texas.

That much is certain.

Today, the headline has been written . . . but the pages that follow are blank.

Tomorrow, we begin filling in the pages . . . writing line by line the story that will be told long after the joy of this day is forgotten.

Like the Reverend Martin Luther King, Jr., who was born on this day, we have come this far on the strength of a dream.

Our challenge is to transform that dream into reality . . . to fill the pages of history with the story of Texans who came into office envisioning a new era of greatness . . . and breathed life into that vision.

Today, we have a vision of a Texas where opportunity knows no race or color or gender—a glimpse of the possibilities that can be when the barriers fall and the doors of government swing open.

Tomorrow, we must build that Texas.

Today, we have a vision of a Texas with clean air and land and water . . . a Texas where a strong economy lives in harmony with a safe environment.

Tomorrow, we must build that Texas.

Today, we have a vision of a Texas where *every* child receives an education that allows them to claim the full promise of their lives.

Tomorrow, we must build that Texas.

Today, we have a vision of a Texas where the government treats every citizen with respect and dignity and honesty . . . where consumers are protected . . . where business is nurtured and valued . . . where good jobs are plentiful . . . where those in need find compassion and help . . . where every decision is measured against a high standard of ethics and true commitment to the public trust.

Tomorrow, we must build that Texas.

The people of Texas are back . . . and they are waiting and watching, anxious to see if their government can rise above personal interest, rancor and division . . . and get on with the business of building a Texas where the people come first.

Years ago, John Kennedy said that, "Life isn't fair."

Life is not fair . . . but government must be.

And if tomorrow, we begin with the understanding that government must stop telling people what they want . . . and start listening to the people and hearing what the people need, we will make government mean something good in people's lives.

Nothing is more fundamentally important to me than the understanding that this administration exists to *serve* the taxpayers.

Because service to the people is government's bottom line, we are creating a new position in the governor's office: a citizen's advocate who will cut red tape and bureaucratic stonewalling . . . who will report to me those agencies who fail to meet the test of the highest quality of service, efficiency and financial management.

The oath I have taken today is mine . . . but the responsibility, the trust we have sought and been given belongs to all of us.

And I hope that as we invoke the blessing of God on this adventure, we will all ask, in the words of the old gospel song, that the Lord lift us to higher ground . . . and that we will be wise enough and strong enough to do what we have set out to do.

Because when my time in office is finished, I want us to be able to look back together and say we—not he, not she, not me but WE came to this moment with a vision worthy of a great heritage . . . and WE realized that vision in a way that was worthy of a great future.

And as we turn the corner on a new millennium, I want us to be able to look forward . . . to see a small child with a textbook . . . thumbing through the pages . . . coming upon a picture of a group of people standing on the capitol steps . . . looking out at that child across years and changes that we cannot even begin to imagine.

I want us to be able to read words beneath that picture that say that on this date in the year of our Lord nineteen hundred and ninety-one a new era began in Texas.

And I want us to know that what we started here will reach out across time to that child . . . and do us honor.